Indian Cricket

Faces That Changed It

Attention Authors

Manas Publications is fighting a war to tell the world that India can win the battle not only by the bullet but also by the pen. We are converting fighters into writers as there is no dearth of intellectuals in our country but their knowledge is confined to them only. No sincere effort has been made by any other publisher to give right direction to their knowledge and the talent of every intellectual is lying hidden. An author always gives the raw material in the shape of a manuscript and it depends on a publisher how to make it a finished product. We have been motivating the intellectuals and publishing their manuscripts for more than two decades and would like to publish your manuscript too. If you or your colleagues have any manuscript or are working on it, please don't hesitate to contact us with detailed synopsis and contents, for its publication. We take utmost care in production and give wide publicity to the book and its author. We can also suggest you the title related to your subject for writing, as publishers we believe more in quality than in quantity.

Indian Cricket

Faces That Changed It

Shyamal Bhattacharjee

Manas Publications
New Delhi-110002 (INDIA)

Manas Publications
(Publishers, Distributors, Importers & Exporters)
4402/5A, Main Ansari Road,
(Opp. HDFC Bank), Darya Ganj,
New Delhi - 110 002 (INDIA)
Ph.: 23260783, 23265523:, 23842660 (R)
Fax: 011-23272766
E-mail: manaspublications@vsnl.com

ISBN 978-81-7049-344-0
Rs. 795

Typeset at
Manas Publications

Printed in India at
Jaico Printers, Delhi
and Published by Mrs Suman Lata for
Manas Publications, 4402/5A, Main Ansari Road,
(Opp. HDFC Bank), Darya Ganj,
New Delhi - 110 002 (INDIA)

Dedicated To

Colonel C.K. Nayudu
The First Ever Indian Test Captain from Vidharbha (C.P. & Berar)

Anil Deshpande
3000 Plus Runs, 86 Wickets for Vidharbha

Rakesh Tandon
First Vidharbha Cricketer to represent India in 1975

Ashok Bhagwat
The first Vidharbha Ranji Cricketer with a "Double"

Vijay Telang
The Inventor of Pyrotechnic shot in Indian Cricket

Imran Ali
Vice Captain, Indian National School Team, 1965

FOR
Their Contributions to Cricket in Vidharbha

FOREWORD

I have been asked by Shri Shyamal Bhattacharjee, a close friend of mine, to write a few lines in terms of Foreword for his book "INDIAN CRICKET : FACES THAT CHANGED IT."

On accepting the request, the first thing I did was to run through the manuscript of the book. I found that the writings were unique and bizarre.

Unique it is, because the time when Indian cricket's phase had changed, and the players who were responsible for bringing about that change of phase, have been covered by the author, in a style which befits the garb.

Bizarre it is, because he has taken the characteristics, and certain anecdotes of the game, and the events that had taken place during the changing phases, that the faces which changed them, enchanting and lively. "Undoubtedly the author has spared no effort to make this book a master-piece for the lovers and the readers of the game".

On going through the manuscript, I was highly impressed at the first "glance" of his compilations, which were eminent. I also consider this piece a unique work, in the sense that in the literary field of cricket, for the first time the author has used the "mother-tongue" influence, coupling it with certain songs and certain abbreviation of the Hindi movies, applying it on the cricketers, which bridges the gap by bringing out a biographical sketches of those faces which have captivated the imagination for the lovers of cricket.

I again add that the comparison, the examples laid by him and the statistics, Oh! What a jewels that they are. The language depicted is lucid, and attractive, and it brings forth, a vivid picture of the accredited players in their full capacity to give an impetus to the amateurs and the would-be players.

The "Tit–Bits" are exemplary, and fantastic.

I wish the author a mountain of success, for bringing out this most valuable book to serve the need of the person interested in the game of cricket and thereby be able to create inspiration for the future generation to be able in the footstep of the sportsmen as described in the book.

I sincerely hope, and I wish the author comes out with another masterpiece excelling the present work in the near future, and I wish him all the best for his future.

Thanks,

Surinder Khanna

PREFACE

THIS book "INDIAN CRICKET : FACES THAT CHANGED IT" is my first attempt, as an author to come out with a book on cricket.

My first "real" involvement with cricket dates back to 1969 when I was listening the running commentary on the Australia-India match played at the Brabourne Stadium in which Mansur Ali Khan Pataudi had hammered 95 runs for India. I was awe–inspired by Pataudi and cricket.

I have followed cricket very sincerely since then and it was only in 2000 that I felt that I should come up with a book on cricket. Actually the MATCH FIXING episode had turned me on. From 1969, when I first heard the cricket commentary, to 2000 when I first saw the cricketers going to explain their stand to the justice about match fixing on the TV, I had felt that cricket had changed, and so have the cricketers too.

It strucked me then, to come out with a book, which would cover every aspect of those incidents, and those cricketers, who have been responsible to bring about a change in the face of Indian cricket.

A lot of books have been written on Indian cricket, but nobody has written a single book on Indian cricket, describing exactly, what have been the incidents that had changed the Indian cricket, and who were the cricketers behind it.

Well, it was not a joke to spot those 17 glorious incidents, which have been described in this book, converting each incident, as a chapter. 75 years of cricket administration and 72 years of the test matches, it indeed was very difficult to choose those incidents.

My three years of extensive research from 2000 to 2003 helped me to filterate those 17 chapters, which have been the "faces" which had changed the course of the game of cricket in India.

Human memory being short and the written accounts being prone to aggregations and under-statement, I decided to present the history which had changed and transformed the Indian cricket, in stories, words and figures. Care has been taken to make this book as accurate as possible. Any improvement or suggestions will be gratefully received by the author.

It took me three years to do the studies and the research, beside 6 months to write, to finish this book.

At the outset I would thank Shri Surinder Khanna, a former Indian cricketer, and the MAN OF THE SERIES, ASIA CUP-1984, WICKETKEEPER and the SPORTS CASTER, for his forewords. Panditji, as he is fondly known, is a GREAT HUMAN BEING and is still a master of HUMANISM.

Then again my wife Rita who really inspired me all through the bad times. Despite her job as professor of Inorganic Chemistry, she took all the pains of household chores and kept me away from all worries, to go ahead full stream with my project.

I shall never forget the inspiration, the mental courage and the help provided to me by C.E.O., Shri Jagadish N. who gave me the necessary break, from my office to go ahead with the project, and also to my brother-in-law, Shri Sudip Bhowmik for all the necessary help at the time of desk editing this book, which had helped me tremendously to add so many text, fast and edit them accurately.

No words of praise will be too high, to express my sincerity and humbleness to Shri Ayaz Menon, *Times of India* and Mr. Rajan Bala, Consultant Editor, *Asian Age*, who kept on pouring their inspiration, bucking me always not to give the project up. Mr. Bala has been an inspiration, which helped me to keep the writing and the process going.

In my own way, I have tried to bring forward, to the present generation, about the story of those cricketers, whom they have not seen on the T.V. Sets. At places I have been critical, but I assure that these criticisms at all are very constructive, and if adhered properly, things can only improve, and that's what is the need of the hour.

And to the Oldies, I have tried to review their memories, of the good olden days of cricket as – Old is Gold.

Thanks,

Shyamal Bhattacharjee

CONTENTS

1

1962: CONTRACTOR OUT PATAUDI BATS

I was only 3 years of age then, and who would by that age, know that cricket is a game played between two equal team comprising of 11 players on each side. It was not until 1967 when I was eight years of age that I first heard of Gary Sobers while playing a cricket match with a tennis ball. The ball should have had the name Rod Laver inscribed on it, but it had the name of Gary Sobers.

Later, when I asked a few nuns, whom we called as "sisters" in Carmel Convent School at Bishrampur, Chattisgarh about Sobers, they only told me that it meant being cool and calm. Well that was the general standard of the nuns who used to teach us in the school and that is what our standard were in the school. We like our "sisters" who were cool and calm.

Later in the evening, I went to Mr. John Mathai, an engineer who was residing two houses away from the house where I lived along with my parents at Bishrampur, and enquired about Sobers, he told me who Gary was and what was West Indies in cricket.

But he turned my attention towards a poster which was placed in his drawing room. It was a black and white poster taken out from a Sports Magazine, "Sports and Pastime" and hanged on the wall.

I could make it out that it was a very old poster and it contained the photographs of Nari Contractor and Nawab of Pataudi. Why that poster, I asked. "Because Nari was the Iron Man of Indian cricket and Pataudi brought the green revolution to Indian cricket" was his answer.

This conversation drew my interest in Indian cricket. I could understand one thing from the poster that since Mathai uncle, as we called him, was the captain of Bishrampur Colliery cricket team, he had put up the poster, depicting the two great cricketers, on the wall. Now back to cricket please.

However, in between 1967 and 1971, India had played 5 different test series against West Indies, England, New Zealand and Australia, only to win the series 3-1 against New Zealand at their home ground. This was the first overseas series won by India, and the skipper was Pataudi then. Coming back to Nari Contractor, he was from Mumbai, called as Bombay then, a left handed batsman, very fluent on both the sides of wicket to execute his shot, and had a rock like defence. He would score at his will in the first class games, but his performance in the test matches was restricted and limited

However, he could play some memorable innings for India in the test match, and one such was an innings of 81 against England at Lords. A ball from Statham hit his hand and had fractured his arm, but he went on to play with a bandaged arm to score 81 which Alex Bannister had described as an innings of inspiration which would inspire the future generation to play like him during the times, when the chips were down.

He had an uncanny habit of reading the weakness of the batsman and would read the strength of the bowler very quickly and then would use the strength of the bowler to rattle the batsman further and make him very weak to concede himself to the bowlers.

Nari gave immense weightage to the all-rounders, as he was the one, first, to believe that it would be the all-rounders who would hold the sway of the game.

Captaining India for the first time in 1960-1961 against the arch rivals Pakistan, the series which was played in India, Nari had packed the Indian team with the likes of Chandu Borde, Polly Umrigar, R.G. Nadkarni, Rusi Surti and M.L. Jaisimha, everybody was an all-rounder in his own rights.

Though the series ended resultless, it was the belligerence of the Indian all-rounders who helped India to finish the series on the even keel. Moreover, Nari believed in positive attacking cricket and twice in the series, having full faith in Ramakant Desai, Chandu Borde and Polly Umrigar, went in for a calculated risk of declaring the innings to force result, but the Pakistanis would not respond. They preferred to play safe and the series ended without result.

Nari had laid a message to the all-rounders of Indian cricket stating that if they were only half as effective as they were while playing the domestic cricket, India had a chance to win a series. This had propelled cricketers like Rusi Surti, Salim Durrani and Bapu Nadkarni to pull up their socks and perform better.

He also stressed on the fact that cricket had to be played in an attacking manner, if possible, at a breath taking pace. He relied on the brilliance of Chandu Borde, Salim Durrani, Polly Umrigar and M.L. Jaisimha and of course himself, for the same.

His belief in his teammates, and over himself proved correct when the M.C.C. team led by Ted Dexter in 1961-62 was annihilated 2-0 with the two all-rounders, Salim Durrani and C. Borde claiming 23 and 16 wickets in the series beside scoring 199 and 312 runs respectively. Durrani was at his magnificent best at Calcutta where he had claimed 8 wickets in the match, and at Madras where he claimed 6 for 105 and 4 for 72, to squeeze England for India's first ever series win against England.

India since then has won so many series and even had notched a few creditable victories from the jaws of defeat, but it was Nari Contractar, under whose captaincy, India had won the first ever series in cricket against a team which was outside this subcontinent.

This series against England at home, brought a new Indian cricketer, who the country came to know as the Nawab of Pataudi. Making his debut at the age of 21 at Feroze Shah Kotla, New Delhi, the Nawab, in a Nawab like manner, clouted two huge sixes, to score 13, but the next two tests at Calcutta and Madras saw him scoring 64, 32, 103 and 10 in the respective innings.

The innings of 103 which he played at Madras was something which only the Nawab could afford to play, may be risking at times for paying a huge price for it. But Pataudi played like a real tiger crawling for his prey. Aristocratic drives, authentic pulls, aesthetic sweep of the spinners and those towering lofty shot, on the rise of quickies, every thing had a Nawab like charisma of its own.

Not only that, the Nawab, unlike the Nawab of those days, would run like a tiger to catch the ball, pick it, and use his shoulder and the arm, to throw it flat from about 65 to 90 yards, straight into the safe hands of wicket keeper. No balls would pass him easily if he fielded in the covers, cover point and the extra cover region. That was his general and overall standard of fielding.

If Nari's attitude towards batting had brought in a revolution in the batting of Indian cricket, the Nawab's attitude had brought in a revolution in Indian fielding. Nari stressed on allround quality of cricket, the Nawab was all for fielding. "A run saved is a run scored" was his slogan, more than the runs scored, the Nawab would save as many runs as possible by his fielding.

It was the tour of West Indies to be followed immediately after. Nari was incharge of the squad and the Nawab was his deputy. The team had the likes and the guiles of Umrigar, Manjrekar, Sardesai, Borde, Durrani, Nadkarni, Surti, Jaisimha, Prasanna and Engineer to name a few. All of them were the jacks of Indian cricket, but then there was one Nawab, not any king by the side.

This was the team which was to take on the King's of the world cricket, the mighty West Indies, which had Worrel, Kanhai, Sobers, Hall, Gilchrist, Boutcher, Stollymeyer Hunte, Griffith and not to forget the real king, "Lester King".

The series as expected was won by West Indies by 5-0. Nari was on the losing side for the first two test matches and in a game against Barbados, he was strucked very badly on his forehead by a bumper from Griffith. Contractor by then had scored 1611 test runs for his country and Griffith had taken 92 wickets for West Indies. Contractor, till that incident was considered to be a real "Purush" and not a "Nari" of Indian Cricket, and Griffith was considered to be the fastest bowler that the world had ever produced, till then.

The knock brought about a premature end of Nari's cricketing career, and the bouncer bounced Griffith out, with his career "over" in cricket. Nari had a longing desire to score 2000 runs, and become the first opener of India to score more than 2000 test runs, and Gilchrist wanted to become the first fast bowler from Barbados, West Indies, to claim 100 test wickets. None of the dreams and the individual wishes proved or came true.

Let me describe about the incident. It was a match which was played between the Barbados XI and the Indian team. Rusi Surti was batting along with Contractor. Before the match, both the teams were introduced to each other, and then the Indian team got to know that the Barbados team had a bowler who hurls the deliveries at a speed of about 180 kms per hour, and he goes for the blood, not only the scalps always.

When the game started, the Indians who opened through Sardesai and Contractor, saw Sardesai losing his stump broken into four pieces by one of the deliveries from Griffith. The next batsman, Vijay Mehra, who passed away recently at Delhi, was hurt in his cheek, by a rising delivery from Griffith, and was rushed to a local hospital for treatment. Came Rusi Surti, he faced two deliveries, and he fenced at them. After some time Nari Contractor was to face Griffith.

The first delivery to Contractor went past, flowing over his head and it beat the wicket keeper for a boundary. SKIPPER HE IS CHUCKING, yelled Surti from the other end. The second delivery too was the same, and this time Surti could not control his feeling, HEY SKIPPER, THIS IS FOUL, HE IS CHUCKING, COME ON LET'S GO TO THE UMPIRE FOR A COMPLAINT. Surti was on the top of his voice.

Contractor knew Surti-as a temperamental and also as a HOT COKE. He gently came to Surti and said LET THE OVER BE COMPLETED, WE WILL TALK TO THE UMPIRE. "YES BY THEN YOU WOULD BE KILLED," SHOUTED SURTI, "AND WE WOULD RECEIVE THE SAME FATE TOO," HE SCREAMED.

By that time the window of the hostel at one point which was in the line of the batsman taking strike got opened, some hostelier had opened it. This match was played on the ground of a University College at Barbados, and the hostel faced the ground. No sooner that the window was opened, the sunray fell onto it, and the reflection fell on the eyes of Contractor. This was another hindrance to the game which was played over there. The Indian team, which governed cricket then, continued with the play as Contractor waited for the over to be completed to take up the matter with the umpire.

By then the inevitable, which Surti could smell, had happened. In one of the delivery of the next over, the ball was bounced to Contractor's chest. He wanted to duck it.

The reflected light from the window pane which was falling on his eyes by chance fell directly on his eye once again, right at the time when Griffith hurled that one to his chest. Contractor lost the vision of the ball. He moved a bit lateral and then sideway to his left, and ducked. Because of the light falling on his eye, he could not sight the ball, and the ball straight hit his forehead, hard, true and perfectly fast. It was like Floyd Paterson, or might be Sony Liston landing a sucker punch to their opponent. Contractor in a flash fell down like a dead cut tree, the Barbadian fielders rushed and picked him up.

The sight was pathetic. Stream of pure fresh red blood was oozing down, and he was in a pool of blood. His condition was not very good, and he was gasping for breath. He was rushed to a local hospital, where an emergency national declaration was made to donate blood to save him. Sir Frank Worrel, who was playing in this match, gave his blood, and donated it to no limit, to see that he survived.

He was rushed to London for operation and was operated upon successfully with a steel plate inserted on his forehead. The doctors had asserted that his life was saved, but he would not be able to play cricket anymore. This was a deadly blow to Indian cricket

Man proposes and God disposes. As it would be, both Contractor and Griffith could never play cricket again. The doctors at London, who operated Nari advised him not to play cricket again as that would damage his brain, and Griffith was termed as "chucker" by the West Indies Board, and he was sentenced to cricketing death by the West Indies Board.

Nari for the record was hit three times very badly on his head before this incident. The first was against Larwood when a rising one hit him-thud on his forehead, but he survived, the second one of course was by Brian Statham, the third was against Mehmood Hussein of Pakistan in the 1960-61 series, the ball had hit his face at Calcutta, and the last one was Grifith which is once again described.

It was here that Nawab of Pataudi was made the captain of the Indian team at the age of 21 years and 77 days. It was here that the new ideas and new thinking got into the game of Indian cricket.

Pataudi took over a team which was in a state of shock and disbelief in themselves, after the Nari's episode. He did not disturb the team. He let everybody play accordingly, as they were following a set pattern of the game played till then.

He watched each and every cricketer and their approach. He found Surti being temperamental, Durrani being par excellent but very casual, Umrigar on the other side of the age but very best even at that age, Engineer, flamboyant and Kunderan very debonair, Prasanna was wily, foxy and full of guile. Dilip Sardesai had the talent and was superb in butchering the spin, but was raw in handling the express pace of the bowlers like Griffith, Hall, and Lester King. His technique was compact and without any fault but his settling down on the wicket very quickly contained a bit of limitation and certainly, some question marks.

All said and done, he noticed that the fielding was a bane of Indian cricket. If a catch had come to an Indian fielder, then he would open his hands like a Rajkamal, and make an attempt to catch it, thus spilling the beans. Running was something which resembled an old man going out for a walk in the park. So slow and casual were the "runners" of Indian cricket.

The quickies were good as Desai and Ranjane were accurate in length and direction, but were not venomous at all the time. However the spinners, Durrani, Nadkarni and Prasanna were world class.

This insight made the Nawab to think and feel that if Indian cricket has to move, it has to tighten its grip on the fielding and the general fitness of the players. If India had to be effective by playing spinners to win the test matches, then the close-in field has to be sharp, quick and agile, as without it, he had felt the tiger would be the king of jungle but without claw to kill its prey. As said a tiger without a claw is as good or as bad as a rabbit. This Nawab, whom the world called him and knew him as Tiger was not a rabbit in the making.

He also noticed that a professional approach has to be inducted to the game, for players like Durrani, Kunderan who just played the game for the heck of it, not seriously. He wanted the players to be very serious with the game. Cricket means business, is what he told to his colleagues and there cannot be a callous attitude for anything in the game, was his explanation.

He had noticed that the Indian cricketers were shy and would put them behind the curtain whenever a reception was accorded to the team. Language was a barrier and there was a lack of communication amongst the members of the team. Guys likė Ranjane, Vijay Mehra, who had the moffussil background behind them would shie away from the sort of things that came to them because they felt like they were not fit to handle the occasion; and also for them the language or the communication was a barrier.

The Nawab inculcated the sense of being important, and communicative for everything. He was the one who told his boys that whatever you do, do it with your head held very high. He made everybody to feel that everyone is important in the team and they are the best cricketers that the country could afford. If at all they wished to drink, let them drink the purest and the finest of wine, and not the country made liquor.

Let me again explain why this wine etc... at all has been described over here. The Indian team had a few players, and I would not like to cite or mention their names for some reasons. They after a very hard day on the field, would like to wear down their tiredness by gulping two or three pegs of wine. Money was a hindrance, and sometimes the tiredness and the pain evolved after a hard day in the field would keep them awake for the night.

The players, to ward off this pain, took the wine, but as said earlier that the money was a hindrance, to quench their "thirst", and to kill the pain, they resorted to the country made liquor which was cheap and easy to purchase. The players did it openely till the Tiger took over the rein of the Indian cricket team. Once the Tiger was incharge of the team, for his charismatic personality, and the gravity that he carried, the players continued to take this tonic, but in a hidden place.

Everybody knew that it was a crime they were resorting to, but they had no choice. The problem was where to store it. The best place would be the cistern tank. This was the place where the "nector" was hidden. Pataudi did notice that, more often than not the players at the time of sitting in the pavilion were moving towards the bathroom, and even in the hotels he observed that very frequently the players would go to their respective bathroom, whenever the team meeting was held.

He became suspicious of this act, and one day he sincerely followed a reputed batsman of the Indian team who, during the course of the team meeting, asked his permission to go to the toilet. Pataudi went to the same toilet, after that player came back finishing his act, he searched the entire toilet. First he found nothing. "OH, WHY DO THEY AGAIN AND AGAIN GO TO THE TOILET, THEN, HE ASKED HIMSELF".

He acted in a different manner this time, and Lo! he found his answer. Just it hit his head and he lifted the cover of the cistern tank. He found that the tank had as many as seven bottles of country made liquor.

He brought all of them, to the room where the meeting was held, and explained them about to drink or eat qualitative and good stuff rather than these kinds of country made items, which could be deteriorating factor to health. However his eyes had opened, and he placed his points very clearly to the Board, after the team landed at India, after the West Indies sojourn ended in 1962. Simply, he told the BCCI then... "Rupees Two-Hundred and Fifty per test as payment, and Laundry expenses for the players on per day basis to be borne by the Board."

The Board bargained over it, as they felt the Rs 250=00 per test was a big amount, and they settled it for Rs 150=00 per test, with lunch and tea to be served by the association where the matches would be played, and the amount for the dinner to be reimbursed to the players if they did not attend any parties during the night. Thus it was he, who first brought the system of payments for the players.

He was open to all and he gave a patient hearing to every cricketer, about their problem, both on and off the field. He in a way became a communication transmitting instrument for all cricketers who played with him and under him. It may be recalled here that the Tiger was a footballer of a good quality for his college team at Oxford, and he played a lot of University football matches for them. He was a speedy player in the flank, and was not a good, but an exceptional scorer. While during his studies at London, if at all he got a chance to watch football, he would never miss that, George Best was his all time favourite and the best footballer

He was the one who took the cricketers for round of jogs before and after the game, he was the one who introduced the free hand exercise and made all the cricketers to do it, before and after the game. He inculcated the concept of fitness amongst the cricketers playing the game. He introduced the concept of youth in the game. He made the corporate to take cricket seriously and recruit the cricketers on the rolls of the company.

Organisations like Jeep Flashlight, Caltex, Tata Iron and Steel, State Bank of India and the Associated Cement Company just to name a few came forward and recruited a host of cricketers. This brought about a security and a sense of pride to the cricketers.

The Nawab was the one who made cricket and cricketers, either to feel like a king or to be one like a king. In 1967, the late Prime Minister, Mrs. Indira Gandhi spoke about green revolution and it was the Nawab who brought a “Green Revolution” to Indian Cricket in 1962, much before than the Indian politicians could think and talk about it.

There was a great change, both in the performance and in the attitude of Indian cricketers. India, till then was considered an easy meat for their rivals, held Australia, led by Ritchie Benand to a 1-1 draw in 1964, beat New Zealand 1-0, at India in 1965 and 3-1 at New Zealand in 1968, and the nucleus of the side, which he formed in 1969 against Australia series in which India had lost by 1-3, the same team went on to beat West Indies by 1-0, and beat England twice by 1-0 and 2-1 to become one of the cricketing giant.

The changing face of Indian cricket was due to the Nawab who changed it first, and very rightly he is considered to be the best captain that India has ever had in cricket. In fact to be true to oneself, and to be true to this game which is worshipped in India, it was Pataudi who had laid the platform for the Indian cricket team between 1962 and 1969, and the result was witnessed and seen by everybody between 1971 and 1983.

In 1964 he was the captain of a World team which had Worrel, Sobers, Hanif Mohammed, Graeme Pollock, Eddie Barlow, Mike Procter, Farokh Engineer, Graeme McKenzie, Rohan Kanhai and some of the great cricketers of world cricket of that time. Surprising is it not, even when Frank Worrel was there in that squad, the Tiger was chosen as the skipper of that team, this only proved to what an extent he was ahead in his way, to lead the team. He was all brain and intelligent when he led the team, whether it was the U-Foam XI in the Moin-ud Dowlah trophy, or the J.K. XI in the Buchi Babu Memorial Trophy, or the Delhi/ Hyderabad team in the Ranji Trophy, or the South Zone team in the Duleep Trophy.

However if there was a mistake which the Nawab did during his tenure as captain, was that he left out Salim Durrani, after the first test against West Indies, in 1966-67 after the Brabourne Stadium test till 1971, when the Indian team toured West Indies.

If only Pataudi had used Salim Durrani then, when he was in the pink of the health and form, perhaps Salim Durrani could have won at least four of the 17 tests which he had missed during those period, for India, and the Nawab could have extended his kingdom of victories to the territory of "unlucky thirteen".

> *The greatest revolution which Pataudi had brought was the "Unity" and "Understanding" amongst the team mates. It was he who introduced the idea of sharing the prize money for the man of the match award amongst the players equally immediately after Ajit Wadekar had received a cash prize, after the Indo-Aussie test match at Delhi in 1969.*

The award in kind would belong to the player who would win it, but the cash would be shared equally amongst the players. As I write about Pataudi in praise, I shall be effectively doing a great injustice if I also do not mention some of his illogical character.

The first is his lop sided love-hate relationship with Salim Durrani. Many believe that it was Pataudi's nonchallant decision which killed Durrani's career, but there are many who feel that if it was not Pataudi, Durrani's career might have not blossomed at all.

The second such incident was the third test match at the Eden Gardens at Calcutta in 1974. He was hit by a rising delivery from Andy Roberts and was taken to the pavilion with blood oozing out of his eye lid. Anshuman Gaekwad was coming in to bat at his place. When Gaekwad was crossing him, he just uttered the words–hard luck skipper–Pataudi was not to answer anything.

Later when Gaekwad asked him about the same, Pataudi replied that the seniority in the team and the place that one earns comes by hard work and not by wishing goodluck, hardluck or badluck. Gaekwad was speechless when he further heard that seniority is for the keep, and not to throw it away. Anyway this was a lesson for Gaekwad to learn, but as he scored a fighting 36 in that innings, he from thereon, went to play 40 test matches scoring 2001 runs for India. Gaekwad has a highest score of 201 in the test.

Anshuman Gaekwad came into the prominence after hitting that magnificient 104 for the University against the Clive Lloyd led West Indies at Indore in 1975-76 series, and the man who helped him to get that ton, partnering him from the other end was Ravi Tuli, who had scored 33 in the first innings, and an unbeaten 14 in the second knock. In fact Tuli was even better than Gaekwad in terms of the techniques and the application that he showed while amassing those runs for the university, but thereafter he chose his studies over cricket, and was never to be heard of.

The administrators who are running the game, my question to them is "Have you ever heard of Ravi Tuli"? The West Indies captain Clive Lloyd was full of praise for him. Gosh; has he receievd even a single penny from the Board, what the others are getting for having played in the Ranji Trophy. Don't you all feel that Ravi Tuli should be paid this amount. Playing against a visiting team, and scoring 33 against the fiery of Andy Roberts, is no joke.

The reason is that the chairs of the B.C.C.I. are packed with the chums who do not know any thing about cricketers and the game. They are there to fulfil certain aspiration.That is why the cricketers who have served the richest sports body of the world are paupers and beggars. There is nobody to correct the Board as most of the people who can do the same, fear that they would loose their seat if they go to brush their shoulders with the jokers sitting at the helm. Moreover, the Board is not prepared to listen to those who know more about cricket and its history as compared to the Navratnas that surmounts the Board. All bullshit is what is going on in the Board.

Over and above is the media, who has helped doing nothing more. They are busy fulfilling their horrendous objectives. They run after these so called Brand Ambassadors, and are always busy keeping them happy, highlighting their activities for no real cause. Maybe by this, they are fulfilling their individual objectives. The sportscasters of almost all the media are hardly aware about anything, that relates to the history or the geography, of the games in India, but they are simply enjoying their time, in the process, wasting the time that could be constructively devoted to the sports.

Some of the media channels, which have hired some of the experts, are horrendous and pathethic to be heard off. The ladies seated with these experts, to anchor the programmes, are a pack of ignorant individuals, who are totally misdirected, and misguided about the fact that whatever they do will be appreciated by the viewers. It is really a haemorrage to the brain to hear them forcefully appreciating some experts who come for anchoring a project, labelling them as very great to force the words coming out of their cobs, as the gospel of the truth. The words that comes out of the mouth of some of the experts it seems they believe is the AMAR VANI OF LORD SHIVA, but in reality those are all nonsense.

Most of the experts airing their views now-a-days in the media and on TV channels are top class failures in international cricket. Look into their test records, most of them have not even played 5 test matches and say twenty one-dayers. But the way they speak on the game defies all logic. One of the experts along with a media anchor for a famous sports channel, was once discussing about Sachin Tendulkar's technique, and the flaws into it. My God, what a great species of Albert Einstein of sports we have in these anchors and the super flops international cricketers, to point a fault in Tendulkar's technique.

They keep on muttering those very things, after the game, which the viewers have watched on the screen, and are in a better position to know it, and analyse the same for themselves rather than these experts commenting on them, and explaining it. What do these sportscasters think. Is it that the viewers watching the game on the TV do not know what cricket is all about, or is it that the *muhavaras* and the *dohas* that they use to explain the deed of the cricketers, are something out of this world, which the others do not know about it. The language 'specially the Hindi language' that they use, and the pronunciation that we hear from their mouth, might make the dead body of the Great Rajendra Prasad, alive, with surprise.

No doubt Chandu Borde in a programme, staring at a lady anchor very clearly mentioned that MUJHE TO KOI KHAREED HI NAHIN SAKTA, and in one of the programme that he was invited to speak upon as a chief guest, Salim Durrani also, more often than not in a programme, had purposely kept his mouth shut, rather than speaking all illogical nuisance.

These young anchors feel that by putting the money into the pocket of the experts or the chief guest, courtesy the channels, they can speak anything on or in favour of certain cricketers, but ultimately the truth comes out when the performances in the matches are reflected.

In this regard, I fully salute Mahendra Singh Dhoni, the way he had handled the team at Australia, defying the press, the electronic media, and the scribes. Everybody was for his head for having dropped seniors like Sourav, Rahul and Laxman, but he led the team in the manner, in which Pataudi had led during his days, and inculcated a fighting spirit, which culminated into the best of the performance coming out of the young coots, for the mighty Aussies were tamed in their own den.

That is what is the captainship all about, and I'm very happy to see Mahendra following the footstep of Pataudi. I fully support the young captain of India for his tough stand, and this is the way to move forward with the young guns. If the Board supports Mahendra Singh Dhoni, and Mohammed Kaif, I can assure the entire countrymen that India will have a tremendous future in the days to come in cricket.

The media will keep on howling, and that is their cause, I agree, but as a lover and good enthusiast of the game, we will have to stand behind the skipper, and encourage him to take positive steps to take Indian cricket upwards, and forwards. The seniors have to be respected, but they also would have to understand that they too would have to leave, honourably. The howls and cry of the media for them should not rattle anybody, as change of the old guard at the appropriate time is the need of the moment.

Pataudi was a different character when he was on the field with the players. He was for each and everybody during the course of the play, but at times after the game got over for the day, he had his own people to mingle and mix with.

It happened at Calcutta in 1974 when India were playing with West Indies. There were three guys in the side, Madanlal who till then had played two tests and both Gaekwad and Karsan Ghavri were debuting in this match. After the day's play would get over, the entire team, specially the seniors would pass their time in each others' company led by Pataudi. Left stranded were the three juniors whose name I have mentioned above. There was nobody to accompany them and they would be left to their mercy. Only Gundappa Vishvanath would hang around with them for some time, before making his way out.

Yet Pataudi has many instances when he would fool around and crack jokes with the guys. Yes he would do it, but he had a world of his own to choose from, and do it. The educated got some respite and some of the seniors whom he liked were the beneficiaries of his jovial joke cracking mood. The others had to find their way out to pass their time.

However in spite of being a bit different, there is nobody in the world of cricket, with whom he had not played, and nobody did speak a bad word against him. He was revered in the world of cricket, and some like Prasanna, Bedi, Vishvanath, Engineer, Chandrashekar, and to some extent some of the English cricketers too, worshipped him.

He definitely was the best captain that India has ever produced. Do not mug over the records of some other captains, especially the modern ones, who would have to show more number of test victories as compared to Pataudi. The way that Pataudi had played with so many deficiencies that crept into the game, and the side he led which always had unimaginable limitations, but with that kind of limitations, and with no money at the coffers of the Board to support the players, he won those nine test matches, and ran very close to win the other two against Australia at Brisbane in 1968, and against the West-Indies at Madras in 1966-67, were an abject lesson for anybody to believe and learn about–HOW TO WIN WITHOUT ADEQUATE RESOURCES.

He never really bothered about what the media were to write and report about him. His overall track record as a leader has always shut the mouth of his adversaries as well as the contemporaries. That was the real Tiger on the prowl, and that is what Mahendra Singh Dhoni is doing now, GREAT.

Birds of the same feather, Mahendra has started flocking like Tiger.

2

WADEKAR WADI : LUCK IN AND OUT

OURS is a country which is peninsular. This is what I had first learned at the school. It means that it is surrounded by water from the three side and mountain form the fourth. I was told that because of this, the outside threats are warded off, and nobody dares to attack us freely and the mountain helps to ward off any ill threat to the country especially from China and Russia.

If I apply the same logic to our cricket, we find that between the period 1969 and 1973, we had notched up three victories. The first one was an incredible 1-0 win over West Indies in 1971, the second one was against England by the same margin, at England in 1971 and then the last one was a 2-1 win against MCC (Marylebourne Cricket Club) at India. Unfortunately the mountain of victory was not built thereafter till 1976 when the Kiwis led by Glenn Turner were beaten by 2-0 at home ground under the captainship of Bishen Singh Bedi.

Well, who was the captain of the Indian team then, who had helped India to carve out this three mighty oceans of win. It was none other than Ajit Laxmanrao Wadekar. Born on fool's day 1st April 1940, Wadekar never played cricket seriously, until he was in Ruia college where he was a student of Science with Mathematics as his favourite subject. As a student, Wadekar had passed his B.Sc degree in first class, scoring 79 percent in Maths.

One really cannot explain why it took so hard and so long for him to earn a test cap at the age of 27, and one really finds it so hard how within four years of playing his first test, he was catapulted on being leading India from the front, and three years from then, one hardly gets to understand, why was he thrown out from the cricketing scene for good.

With Wadekar, everything was fast, so fast and then the end the very end. Immediately after his epoch triumph in West Indies in 1971 he wrote a book "My cricketing years" which was a tremendous hit and it sold like a hot bun on the Bond street and the Ruskin Street at London, and twenty months later these cricketing years were done with, it had gone with the wind.

Wadekar's ouster really caused a lot of heartbreak and the mind always boggled thinking why and how do the selectors behave so abruptly, but then that is the way the Indian selectors behave, when they have to behave. But then Wadekar's career too has been a case of contradiction and an expectation, full of twills, twist and turns.

As said earlier, he had to score mountain of runs in the Vizzy trophy and the Rohinton Baria trophy, playing for the West Zone Universities and the Bombay College team. Then when he was included in the Bombay Ranji team, he had to score tonnes and tonnes of runs to retain his place in his side. No other Indian cricketer had to score these kinds of runs then to push their stake for a claim in the test squad.

Take for example, when he played the first time for India there were a few, who were born a year or two ahead of him. But they did not have to score runs in the Rohinton, Vizzy, Ranji or the Duleep Trophy like Wadekar to cement their place in the side.

When Ajit wore his first test cap, there were several, who were born a year or two ahead of him, playing for India. To cite an example, there was Dilip Sardesai (born 1940) with one overseas tour and 13 tests expertise. Jaisimha with two overseas tour and 23 tests, Budhi Kunderan [b 1939] with one tour and 13 tests behind him, Venkataraghvan [b 1945] with 4 tests, Chandrashekar [b 1945] with 8 tests, and the Prince Charming of Indian Cricket Salim Durrani [b 1934] with almost 24 tests behind him. This was Wadekar's bad luck that he had to score mountains of runs which went unnoticed to gain his first test cap, whereas the other mentioned over here just made it to the test team with little or less effort.

Just to cite an example, when the Pakistan team under the captaincy of the Late Fazal Mehmood toured India in 1960-61, Wadekar and Dilip Sardesai played for the Indian Combined University in a match against the Pakistan. Sardesai scored a blitzkrieg 89 in that match in the first knock, and Ajit Wadekar had scored a brilliant and enterprising 79 in the second. Dilip Sardesai was to book his ticket for the West Indies sojourn in 1962 immediately next, whereas Wadekar had to wait till 1967 to baptize himself into the highest level of cricket at Madras against the West Indies, and that too after he had played a superlative knock of 67 against them for Board President XI in a upcountry match.

Of course, destiny had its own way to set the things right for Wadekar. As it would have happened, he was chosen to lead this pack of cricketers, platformed by Pataudi in 1969 which had lost to Australia by 1-3, in West Indies and England in 1971 to a historic win. There were many in that squad like Jaisimha, Prasanna and Sardesai, who could have been given the mantle of the leadership, as they possessed a tremendous cricketing brain but Ajit it was he who drew blood to draw a line. What I meant to say is that there were other cubs and colts who had been blessed with test cap long before they were twenty five, Ajit by twenty seven could have regarded himself as a tired and an old man by the time his turn had come.

Now let us talk about his batting. From 1967 to 1974, he batted with grace and aplomb, only to score a ton, a knock of 143 against New Zealand, and that was the only three figure mark that he had to show, whereas his team mates from Mumbai, Farukh Engineer and Dilip Sardesai had two and five. Wadekar had three knocks of unbeaten nineties, and some over eighties. All those could have been catapulted into a test ton, as century making was no unfamiliar experience to him, yet somehow he fizzled out by making as many test hundreds as he ought to have.

Anyway, he had his luck turning on and turning off to him. It was after the series of 1969-70 against Australia that an Indian team was chosen to tour West Indies in 1971. The skipper of the Indian team Nawab of Pataudi had declined to tour and preferred to "skip" the tour due to his indulgence in and for a Lok Sabha election from Gurgaon, Haryana to be precise, which he lost. Wadekar had won a casting vote, courtesy Vijay Merchant, to lead India and the rest was a history.

If Pataudi emphasised on two aspects, the fast bowling and the sharp fielding, Wadekar emphasized on the spin bowling. Pataudi always preferred Erapalli Prasanna and used him in such a telling manner that Prasanna was soon termed as the best offspinner that the world of cricket had ever produced, Wadekar made Venkatraghavan as the competitor to Erapalli Prasanna for the post of the off-spinners then. Chandra and Bedi remained "static and constant" to Wadekar as per his mathematics and its theory, but Venkat was his "arm" under the sleeves.

Now when he was not scoring runs, he was taking catches and grappling it swiftly, high or low in the neighbourhood of the batsman to clutch 44 altogether, in the slip region, wherein ability to sight the ball quickly was an invaluable asset. His movement sometimes were restricted to batting, but his electricity-like movement at the slip fielding were invaluable asset to Indian cricket. People do forget about good things done to others, that is the human tendency, but those present at the Eden Gardens, Calcutta, on the last day of the test against England on January 4th during 1973, would not forget the catch he took of Bedi to get rid of Derek Underwood and bring India nearer to victory, would not be easily forgotten by the pundits of the game.

Let me describe about the catch. At the slip Wadekar had swayed to his right as Underwood had edged, before he saw the ball going the other way, he had hurled himself in the reverse direction and as he landed himself on the left knee and right palm, was still able to clutch the catch one handed. This was an example set by him as a brilliant slip fielder, and this infected the team that he led from 1971 to 1974, and along with the finest close-in fielder like Gavaskar in the slip, Solkar in the forward short leg, Venkatraghvan in the gully, Abid Ali in the backward short leg, provided the finest support to the Indian spinners they had ever received from the field.

In his tenure as a player, and later as a captain India drew eleven and won nine. In the seven out of these nine, Wadekar's bat contributed in a little, and at times a large measure to victory.

The large measure was in the third test against New Zealand in 1968 when his six hour long 143 out of 327 in the first innings gave India a huge lead to enforce an eight wicket win. That was in 1968 against New Zealand. In the opening match of this series too at Dunedin, his brace of 80 (out of 359) and 71 (out of 200 for 5 wickets) paid into winning the test. Among the little measures were his innings of 49 and 40 against New Zealand at Bombay in 1969, 48 and 45 at the Oval against England, in 1971, an unbeaten 91 at Delhi against Australia, with Gundappa Vishvanath (44*) keeping him the company with an unbroken fourth wicket stand which saw India home. The stand had produced 120 runs and the partnership was unbroken.

Wadekar, for whatever reason, is and will be considered as the best left handed batsman that India has ever produced. He was miles ahead of the present day left handed batsmen like Sourav Ganguly, both in terms of technique, fielding and fitness. He will also be considered to be the best first slip fielder that the country has ever seen, and perhaps the luckiest captain, after that trick of wins in the test series against West Indies and England.

He would also be remembered for harbouring the spinners with Venkat as his trump card, at the expense of Erapalli Prasanna, though Chandra with his magical spell of 6 for 36 at the Oval, brought him the maiden series win for India at the English soil, the Arjuna Award and the Padma Shri title beside a promotion at the State Bank of India immediately then. Also Wadekar will always be remembered for being the captain of the Indian team which was bowled out for 42 at the Lords during the summer of '74.

Actually the three wins carved under his captaincy gave a new dimension, a new brand value to Indian cricket, and though the nucleus of the side was platformed by the Nawab himself between 1964 and 1969, Wadekar walked away with these three wins and all the credit associated with these wins. Had the Nawab continued to play and not politicize himself, he would have been credited for these brilliant series win, but the lady luck smiled on Wadekar, and that's why he is considered to be the luckiest captain that India has ever produced. Yes some lucky ones and the great ones are born on the Fool's day.

Indian cricket started looking upward after these three consecutive series wins under Wadekar. Wadekar was lucky to get the captaincy and was unlucky about the manner he was thrown out of the team in 1974 after the series against England. No doubt, somebody has once remarked that lucky are those who are born on the Fool's day.

Also Wadekar, it was, first who had won a TV set in 1969, for his valuable contribution with the bat, to bag the man-of-the-match award in the Delhi test match against Australia.

> *It was for the first time that a cricketer was awarded in kind as the man-of-the-match, in a test match. The scooters, bikes and the cars were to follow later.*

This is for the readers to know, as I feel that they have a right to know it, if they do not know it. The entire world believes that Wadekar was elevated to the point of being the captain of India by none other than Vijay Merchant through the casting vote. Well, nobody will doubt that. But the man who really made Wadekar to get that plum post of the Indian cricket was none other than Hanumant Singh.

After leading Rajasthan to the Ranji finals in 1966-67, where he had scored a 107 in the first and an unbeaten 207 in the second, and after the Irani Cup tie in which Hanumant Singh led Rest of India had defeated Bombay on the basis of the first innings lead, the A.I State Bank of India XI had named Hanumant Singh to lead their side for all the invitational tourney that the State Bank was to participate then.

The State Bank of India during those day was a virtual India XI team. Just look at the players, Venkat Sundaram, Vinay Lamba, Maheshwar Prasad, P.K. Beliappa, Ajit Wadekar, Gundappa Vishvanath, Ambar Roy, Hanumant Singh, V.V. Kumar, Abid Ali, B.S. Bedi, Rajinder Goel, Rajinder Pal, Suresh Luthra, Gopal Bose, Subroto Guha....et al.

During those days it was concluded that a person who would lead the State Bank team would be the captain of the Indian team. Leading the State Bank team would have been the reason that Hanumant Singh has taken his seat to the Indian team. But Hanumant Singh was a man of different character altogether. This school socalled the Daly College, Indore and the Mayo College, Ajmer and their education had instilled "values" in this lad, he was very different when it boiled down to education.

With Pataudi reluctant to tour and play outside the country due to his politics and his association with it, Hanumant Singh felt that if he relinquishes the post of the captainship and make way for Wadekar, Indian cricket will be benefited.

Hanumant had a reason to believe. In spite of scoring so heavily in the domestic season, he was never taken into confidence by the selectors. In retrospect, Ajit's place in the side especially in the number third position was for granted. This made Hanumant to feel that if Ajit is given the skippership of the Bank, then Indian cricket will at least move ahead. Hence he relinquished the captainship.

Hanumant Singh from 1957-58 to 1979-80 in the Ranji Championship had scored not only the most number of runs, but also the most number of centuries. The most number of runs record was later broken by Ashok Malhotra in 1993, and the most number of tons was broken by Arun Lal, in the year 1994.

Ajit Wadekar led the State Bank team to victory in the Moin-ud-Dowlah Cup, the Buchhi Babu memorial tournament, The Times of India shield, the Jeep Flashlight invitational tournament and the Rusi Modi invitational tournament for two consecutive years.

This made the selectors feel that Ajit Wadekar had all the stuff in him to be a good leader, and his captainship record in this tourney went a long way to establish himself as the skipper of the Indian team. Had it not been Hanumant Singh to sacrifice for his own benefit, Ajit Wadekar would never have been that fast to be considered for the post.

Hanumant Singh, it is said, right from his boarding days at the Daly Public College in Indore, to the last he breathed, never looked at himself. He always placed the other's problems and their benefits above himself. That was the value of the education for this Prince of Banswara.

Today these so-called modern cricketers keep on complaining that too much of cricket is killing them physically, and a lot of modern cricketers of India have come up with a statement that during the earlier days, cricket and its calenders were not so tight. My dear, the Souravs, the Dravids and the Sachins of this era, and the likes of them, during that period, there used to be at least seven invitational tournaments, besides the Ranji, the Duleep and the Irani Trophy, and the international calender in which a cricketer had to play.

The office cricket was a must for everybody who had enrolled themselves in a company purely on the sports quota. The promotion, the increments, and the seniority were very minutely witnessed by the companies where the cricketers were employed. Moreover the tournaments like the Rusi Modi Invitational, played at Jamadoba, the Sheesh Mahal tourney at Lucknow, and at times the Jeep Flashlight tourney at Allahabad were played from the midst of April to the midst of May where the temperature would be about 44 degree centigrade. Those who played would know where the shoes were pinching them. There was no chance for anybody to skip the tourney if their offices would participate in those tourneys.

How many cricketers of today would turn up to play these kinds of tourney without being paid separately if their office asked them to. That's how the game was played then. Do not count down the cricketers of the former years by playing them down by saying that their batting average is not even thirty plus. They never had the thigh guards, the back guards, the hip guards, the stomach guards, the anklets, the calf muscles guards, the chest guards, the wrist guards, the middle fingers guards and above all the "helmet" etc to protect them when they would face Hall, Griffith, McKenzie, Trueman, Bedser, Taylor or even Fazal Mehmood to cite a few. Yet they faced them bravely and scored, rather than complaining about the green and a hostile wicket being laid for the match, and ...., hope that readers understand them.

There has been a test cricketer of the present generation who in a swash, tucked me saying that none of these former players who talk so much about cricket, have an average over thirty. My dear friend, the modern day cricketer, it was your luck that you were not born in the thirties and the fourties. Lucky have been you to have been born at the mid-seventies. For if you had been born then, never would have you ever been picked, if you had played cricket. Cricket atmosphere was not that rosy and easy as you see it today.

Ajit Wadekar hit the headlines in the late fifties, 1959 to be exact, but it took ten years for him since then to cement his place in the side. Things were not easy then as it is now. Moreover, the overall standard of this game really had started sinking since 1994.

During those days it was in-and–out, during these days it is try him, try, try and try again and keep on trying him. Virendra Sehwag, Ajit Agarkar and Gautam Gambhir, Mohammed Kaif, and Yuvraj Singh are the classic examples of these systems. This system has not helped the Indian cricket in a big way.

3

SUMMER OF 42

IT all started with Erapalli Prasanna and Gundappa Vishwanath. In 1968, Karnataka then known as "Mysore" were beaten by Bombay in the Ranji Trophy semifinal match, but two musketeers of that team, Gundappa Vishwanath who had scored a magnificent breathtaking 109, and Brijesh Patel, known as "Tabbu" to his friends then had scored a scintillating 107 had the nation thinking that something worst was in store for the Bombay's team in the days to come. Both the tons came in the second essay in that match in which Karnataka finished on the losing side.

Bombay due to a magnificent 323 from Ajit Wadekar then, aided with a tortoise crawling 111 from Dilip Sardesai, had surpassed Mysore's total and later had lifted the Ranji Trophy. However, though Mysore under V. Subbramanyam has lost, it had formed the nucleus of a team, which was to bulldoze their opponent for the next 17 years then in domestic cricket specially in the Ranji Trophy.

Vishwanath (18), Brijesh Patel (15), Jayprakash (17), Vijayakrishna (17), Syed Kirmani (15), Vijaykumar (18), all in their teens, were to shake the Indian cricket then. These hexagon went on to play cricket, with such an authentic manner that for the next one and a half decade, many a great cricket pillars collapsed and wilted under their pressure.

Gundappa Vishwanath (93), Syed Kirmani (88), Brijesh Patel (21), played for India, while A. V. Jayaprakash, Sudhakar Rao, A. V. Vijaykrishna just missed playing for India. They were distantly unlucky. The Karnataka Ranji team was guided and handled very well by Earapalli Prasanna (49 tests - 189 wickets) and B. S. Chandrashekar (58 tests - 242 wickets). That is the primitives story of Karnataka cricket.

Well, coming back to the subject, let me focus on the Ranji Trophy. Bombay had been winning this Trophy continuously from 1957-58 and for 15 years at a stretch they kept on winning it. Jokingly, after the 1968 match against Bombay Erapalli Prasanna had asked Sardesai, how many times more would Bombay win it consecutively; Sardesai smiled and replied "till I continue to play" as he was a regular member of the Bombay Ranji side since '57.

It was in 1974 when Dilip Sardesai did not represent Bombay in the Ranji Trophy. And Mysore, that had become "Karnataka" by then, was to meet Bombay in the semis. Bombay did not have Dilip Sardesai in the side. Yet it had a team which was very strong on the paper. Gavaskar, Parkar, Sudhir Naik, Ajit Wadekar, Karsan Ghavri, Ashok Mankad, Abdul Ismail, Padmakar Shivalkar...so many of the stars in the side, so why Sardesai would play who was 34 years of age by then and was considered to be too slow to move on the field.

All these years when Ajit Wadekar was leading, either India, or Bombay, Sardesai stood like a rock behind Wadekar, Tactical moves, on the spot advises, and technicality of the game and situations, were something, which Dilip Sardesai was very brilliant at. Besides his batting was a magic. No cricketer, after late Vijay Manjrekar, looked so solid against the spin of Prasanna and Chandrashekar, the exceptions were Salim Durrani and Dilip Sardesai. The two 'Ds' were class and exceptions, but during that season, the Bombay selectors chose to drop Dilip Sardesai for the game. That ended Dilip Sardesai's career from all form of cricket.

Well, the semis were played at the Chinnaswamy Stadium, and Bombay had never thought that without Dilip Sardesai in its rank, would be crucified by Karnataka.

As it happened, Erapalli Prasanna had "tossed" out Ajit Wadekar on the morning, and elected to bat first. Abdul Ismail got the early breakthrough and Bombay were under the impression that they were on the right track. But within an hour after that, the history of cricket in India was to take a drastic change.

Paddy Srivalkar got one through the defence of the other opener Vijaykumar and that was that. In came Gundappa Vishwanath and after some time when in strode Brijesh Patel it was the repeat of the 1967 semi-finals where Vishy and Tabbu were to kill Bombay, like a Panther killing a gazelle for its prey.

The only hitch was a confident appeal for catch behind which Vishwanath survived against Shivalkar. No sooner did the umpire Satyajit Rao ruled it otherwise, Karnataka were to swallow Bombay like the patient swallowing the anacin pills to get rid of the headache.

Vishwanath before this season, was advised by Nawab of Pataudi to do certain 'dumball' exercise to make his wrist more stronger and supple. This was the only exercise that Vishwanath had done for a year between 1973 and 1974, and also during his entire cricketing career, seriously.

That the wrist had become steel and if used, the bullet like shots would come out of it, was evidently testimonied and testified in the game. The kind of wristy stroke that followed from this "little" master's blade were beyond description and words. On the other hand Brijesh had a liking for the Bombay's bowler. Whenever Brijesh played either for South Zone, Mafatlal XI or Karnataka, he would see to it that he minced-meat of the Bombay bowlers.

Well, that afternoon, it was a bamboozling Vishwanath and a rampaging "Tabbu" all the way. Bat in hands, and their feet on the sand of Chinnaswamy Stadium, they, by the end of the day's play, put Bombay and Ajit Wadekar in no man's land. Brijesh was out for 109, but Vishwanath was still there with 124 by the end of the play.

This partnership raised a vision of Karnataka scripting a new chapter in the annals of Indian cricket, and the next morning when Prasanna requested Vishwanath to score and add another fifty runs to help Karnataka to swell the total, youngsters like Sudhakar Rao, Vijaykrishna and Syed Kirmani, "promised" to help Vishwanath to get past 400 runs in the first innings.

Karnataka did not score 400, they were four short of it by the end of their first innings, neither did Vishwanath add another fifty, to his overnight score of 124, he fell 5 short of it, but Bombay by then had felt short of Dilip Sardesai to overhaul this total, as they fell short by 40 runs while chasing the Karnataka's total in the first innings. Even at that age, Dilip Sardesai would score 40 runs and made everybody feel that he was as young in age as Jeetendra who during those days would advise others to use a "fourty plus" ayurvedic pills to remain young in an ad campaign.

As it would have happened, the two spinners of Karnataka, spun a web around the Bombay batsmen and got them back into the pavilion with Prasanna accounting for 4 and Chandra netting 6. Karnataka had brought a windfall of summer in 1974 for Ajit Wadekar and Bombay.

From there onwards "Prasanna's" army marched to Jaipur at the Sawai Man Singh Stadium to lock their horns with the warriors of Rajputs. The legacy of Tipu Sultan were to wrestle with the legacy of Bhilwara and

Banswada. The only fear which hovered was whether the "Prince" Salim Durrani was playing or not in the finals for Rajastan.

It was not, for both the teams were vying for their first Ranji title and Salim Durrani was the balancing factor. He while playing for Ranji matches, the quarter finals against the Indian Railways, on a matting wicket, got strucked by an "awkward" rising delivery, on the bridge of the nose, by Gunawant Desai and was "out" of the match. But before that he made the road, in for Rajasthan by strucking a breezy 96 (unbeaten) against Indian Railways, in the quarters before that delivery from Gunwant Desai did him in and dug him in forever, forced him out of the Indian team. Salim was never to play for India again after that "knockout" delivery. This knock closed all his doors for a comeback, if any to the Indian team though his knock of an unbeaten 96 in that match knocked the stuff out of the Indian Railways in that Ranji match.

Salim missed the semis against Hyderabad then, but it was expected that he would be fit for the finals. He was not, as his vision was a bit suspect after that blow and the doctors advised him not to play in the finals. This was the first Ranji finals that Salim might had to miss, for every finals that Rajasthan had figured till then, Salim would either score a century, or take 6 to 7 wickets in an innings and without Salim, Rajasthan were a "tiger without its–claw", and the pink city would sometimes, look redless, as if no paintings was done on the walls of the buildings of Jaipur. Rajasthan without Salim Durrani used to be a meaningless team then.

However despite all the odds, Salim chose to play, and Hanumant Singh knowing fully well that his vision were not in order, made him to play. For Hanumant Singh, and for Rajasthan, a Ranji team of Rajasthan, without Salim Durrani was like the town of Paris without its Eiffel Tower.

As it happened, Rajasthan on both the innings applied tremendous pressure, but the handicap of Salim's vision came in, and it came in both the innings. If it were A. V. Jayaprakash, V. S. Vijaykumar, and A. V. Vijaykrishna in the first innings, it were A. V. Jayprakash and Syed Kirmani in the second. The former three scored 65 plus in the first with Vijaykrishna hammering 71 to lay a solid foundation for Karnataka, and the latter two were involved in a very crucial 130 runs partnership in the second, when everything appeared lost for Karnataka. Vishwanath and Patel were the abject failure in the match.

Though Hanumant Singh scored a fighting 86 in the first and Parthasarthy Sharma a solid 56 in the second, it was Erapalli Prasanna all the way. He claimed 12 in both innings, distributing his claims equally and won the match and the maiden title of Ranji Trophy for Karnataka. How bad did Rajasthan missed Salim's "vision" could be gauged by the fact that, except Shaktawat, Rajasthan did not have an effective bowler to check the Karnataka batsmen. Moreover, the kind of "sweeping" innings that Hanumant Singh played to compile 86, if Salim's contribution had been there, believe me my readers, Rajasthan would have swept Karnataka for a first innings lead. Except for Hanumant and Parthasarthy, Rajasthan did not have an experienced batsman, who could counter the guile of Prasanna and Chandra. What was needed was Salim, and his contribution was not there. His myopic vision killed Rajasthan, and that was the last Ranji finals that Rajasthan and Durrani have ever played together.

Well, Hanumant had scored a valiant 86 and had staked a claim to tour England with the Indian team, but the selectors had thought otherwise. Durrani very badly wanted to "tour" England with the Indian squad, but the Almighty had thought otherwise.

Karnataka on their way to the title had dethroned Bombay for the first time as the "King of Indian Cricket" in 1974. What was to follow four months later was a Alfred Hitchcock thriller. Wadekar was to be dethroned as the Indian skipper.

Immediately after this, the Indian squad for the English tour was announced. There were a few surprises in the squad. Sudhir Naik, Gopal Bose, Madanlal and Brijesh Patel were in. Karsan Ghavri, Pandurang Salgaocar and A. V. Jayaprakash were left out. In my opinion, there was no need to pick Ashok Mankad. A. V. Jayaprakash, by his display, both in the batting, and the bowling should have been an automatic choice as an all rounder.

Wadekar had strongly claimed the need of Mansur Ali Khan Pataudi, who declined to tour. Wadekar went to the extent of making a statement in the press that if Pataudi was to tour England, then he would hand over the captainship to him, but Pataudi did not pay heed to this national outcry. While Pataudi not being there, it would have been a wisest of the thing to select Salim Durrani, who at the age of 39, still was "head and shoulder" above any cricketer like Gopal Bose, Madanlal, Brijesh Patel, Ashok Mankad and Sudhir Naik, who were the other members of the team.

This was the second occasion that Ajit Wadekar was leading a side for the tour of England. And as we all know, the English season is divided into two summer. The first half of summer sees the "swallow" for which the English would say that "one swallow does not make a summer." It is a bird which is seen only during the first half of the summer at England.

Whether the Indian had "swallowed" this bird, is something I do not know as they had swallowed the "mountain chicken" in the Caribbean Island in 1971. That brought them the series win. Perhaps the Indian did not swallow this bird. But what was to follow in due course of the time was something unbelievable. The English lion led by Mike Denness, in all fairness was to swallow the Indian lion and without much ado.

As one should know, the Indian team was touring England in the first half of the English summer. Cold, chill, wind as one might call, or like to call the English condition during that period of summer is unbearable. Over and above it, the overcast conditions and the chill of wind associated with it, makes it hard, very very hard for the bowlers to grip the ball properly.

The visiting teams from abroad find it very hard to acclimatise with the condition, but the home team is sound and fair playing in these types of conditions. The ball swings appreciably and the pitch because of the overcast conditions, has "juices" always to give it to the bowlers. One of these reasons that the quickies of West Indies like Roberts, Holding, Marshall, and Garner of West Indies, Richard Hadley of New Zealand, Sarfaraz Nawaz and Imran Khan of Pakistan have excelled in the English condition is because of the conditions that helped them to derive the swing in these conditions.

India can never afford to have a Marshall or a Garner, or an Imran Khan, hence, India should have always encouraged likes of Ghavri or Salgaocar, but "neigh" India has never learned to respect the "quickies". We do not have them, and even if we have them, we kick them out or kill them.

Had Salgaocar toured, this tour would have been an "A plus", that is a terrific asset on the balance sheet of the Indian team, beside Ghavri should have been there. There was no need to have a plethora and a "mix" of opener in Ashok Mankad, Gopal Bose, and Sudhir Naik beside the make-shift opener in Farokh Engineer and Eknath Solkar, who were the certainties to play for India in the test. What was the use of having five openers in a team. Was India going to play as "Opening XI" because Sunil Gavaskar was a permanent opener in the side.

It was here that the likes of Salgaokar and Karsan Ghavri should have been representing India. They were young. Both Salgaocar and Ghavri were "22", the ugly duckling as they were the pacers, and with Madanlal who was another "22", could have shared the cherry and learned a lot from this tour. From this tour would have emerged the "trio" of pacers, but that was not to be.

It has been India's misfortune, and Wadekar's fortune that he always had the spin quartet and he always made use of the spin trio win the matches for India. Had the selectors chosen Pandurang Salgaocar, or A.V. Jayprakash and Karsan Ghavri for Ashok Mankad, Indian Cricket, for the days to come, would have been on a "profit-plus" on the profit and loss account. The credits would have been more, and the debit less, for the selectors, but then if the selectors do everything right, why should someone miss out calling them "a pack of Jokers"

For Salgaocar was lost in wilderness after this tour, and Madanlal was "in-and-out" for and of the favours of selectors. It was not until Kapil Dev Nikhanj appeared on the scene in 1978, but by then his partner Karsan Ghavri was burnt out though he continued to bowl with zeal, zest and fire.

This summer, actually, had dried the thinking of the Indian selectors, and had killed the Indian cricket by their untoward and awkward selection. It is this what I'm going to narrate.

The tour of England followed and everything was going right till the first test match. But just on the eve of the first test, the problem started surfacing. And Ajit Wadekar was amongst the picture of all that one could see and behold ! He started the tour well with the score of 9 versus D. H. Robbins XI, 25 and 20 against Somerset, 17 and 0 versus Hampshire, 138 and 8 versus Leicestershire, 1 and 47 versus Yorkshire, 82 versus Lancashire, 61 versus M. C. C. at Lord; 103 and 1 versus Northamtonshire; 57 and 58 not out versus Essex and 47 versus Surrey — a tally of 674 runs from 16 innings for an average of 44.93.

But at this point came a finger injury on the eve of the test, and he did not want to "skip" the test, instead wanted to remain outside. Who would lead India them, Venky!, and there started the revolt.

The other seniors in the side were not too much happy to learn that Venkie was the right member to lead the side.

There were seniors, especially Farokh Engineer who strongly believed that he was the fittest element then who could lead the team, and not to forget Erapalli Prasanna who had helped Karnataka to win the Ranji Trophy, that also by flooring down Bombay. Prasanna's captainship was acclaimed by one and all, then.

Wadekar sensing the heat preferred to lead the team. If he had wished to dilute this matter, another one had surfaced during the dinner reception ceremony at the residence of the Indian High Commissioner at London.

At that party, thrown by the Indian High Commissioner, a discussion took place about what was the condition of the Indian cricketers in terms of money, and how was their financial position. Wadekar spoke on the positive terms just to be an able ambassador of his country, during that moment. But no sooner that he spelled his opinion, Bedi, Prasanna, and a senior cricketer who had played for India and was settled at England, spoke very harshly and in a negative tone on this matter.

This agitated Ajit, and he tried to pacify the players, but to no avail. The seniors of the team started saying that this matter could have been handled better with the Board if Pataudi was the member of the side, and if he spoke to the Board about the players and their monetary aspect, in which Ajit was a silent spectator.

This infuriated Ajit, and so called an "berg-ice" Ajit screamed that enough was enough, and he would not tolerate any further nonsense. "YOU ARE ALL PATAUDI'S MEN" he screamed, and later added that he would give up captainship once he landed in India. It was a shock for the juniors of the team then to witness such a wobbling show.

This revolt was no laughing matter; but the "Jokers" manning the administrative affairs of Indian cricket made it look and appear so. The manner in which it conducted the probe after the tour and closed it once for all, made our cricket and its administration, a laughing stock. The world laughed at it. The world once again laughed at us when we had won the World Cup in 1983, but that was differently...in a different way.

Instead of bringing the rebels into the book and taking a corrective stand, it cleared the whole team and then arbitrarily reopened the case against Bedi, whereas in reality Bedi was not to be crucified for his action. To be frank, it should have been Prasanna too, who should also have been interrogated before fixing Bedi.

There was another episode also during that tour. No sooner that this episode breathed its last, the "Socks Stealing" episode was the last nail which killed the Indian cricket. The Indian team was out for a shopping and while shopping, somebody put a pair of socks in the bag which Sudhir Naik was carrying. This was caught by the close circuit camera.

While billing the item this sock raised all the bluffs about how did the socks came into the packet of Naik. There was no answer that Naik could provide, and the matter became serious and this was to be handed to the bobbies by the owner of the shop-keeper. So that the matter does not blow out of propotion, Colonel Hemu Adhikari asked Sudhir to accept that he by mistake had put the socks for which he forget to book during the time of payment.

Poor Sudhir Naik. To keep the moral and the respect of the team intact, he took the blame on himself. This was not accepted in toto by one quarter of the team which felt that Naik was unnecessarily crucified, and there were a lot who castigated him for his action and the acceptance of the same. Poor Naik, he had to digest the shock and absorb it, because he was directed by the Colonel of the team to do so for the interest of the team. This had crushed the spirit of the tour.

With Wadekar not playing, it should have been Farokh Engineer to lead the side as he was the senior most in the side. But Engineer never had to show that he was the captain of the Bombay Ranji team, or the West zone side, to have won the Ranji or the Duleep Trophy. Also, at the age of 35 his fitness was in doubt. The next man was Prasanna, but he was not a permanent figure in the side, because Ajit Wadekar always preferred Venkat to play and nobody wanted Venkat to be incharge of the team then.

Prasanna always had a feeling that his cricket was destroyed to a large extent by Wadekar, as Wadekar always preferred Venkat, whereas in reality, Wadekar always rated Prasanna an inch above Venkat, but he chose Venkat because of his fielding which was better than Prasanna on any day matches, beside Venkat was a handy bat, whose highest score in the test match has been 51 against the West Indies.

Moreover, Venkat was the Deputy to Wadekar, and during those days, a Deputy in Indian cricket was something and someone whose place was granted. So this would have crippled India, if the Vice Captain was dropped, and taking this into notice Wadekar preferred to play with Venkat always as compared to Prasanna. Venkat was also in the side, because beside he being the Vice Captain, suppose if during the course of the play, had Wadekar been off the field, at least the Vice Captain would have kept the "team" intact. So the team management chose to leave out Prasanna.

There were already groups in the team, as there was when Wadekar came to the Indian team in 1967. During those days, it is believed and said that either a cricketer playing for India, belonged to the "Nawab's group" or the "Borde Group", which I personally do not agree – "Bore-Kar- diaya" would be the result, then at the end of the day. Of it during '74, in the midst of the tour Wadekar had again staked a claim for including Salgaokar, but the Board refused.

There was a different feeling amongst the cricketers playing for the team and each went on his own way. The captain himself miserably failed with the bat scoring 6 and 14 at Manchester, 18 and 3 at the Lords and 36 and 5 at Edgbaston. Moreover, in a test match at Lords during that series, Wadekar had set a field for Bedi, and has asked him to bowl according to the field set, but Bedi refused. On being reminded again to follow the captain's instruction, he threw the ball back to Wadekar telling him that his fingers were too stiff to even hold a ball in those English condition. Some players who were very close to Wadekar, and were playing the match even had confessed that Bedi had told Wadekar not to teach him spin bowling and how to bowl them. This was the state of affairs of the team then.

The runs on that tour came from Sunil Gavaskar who had scored 217 runs, Gundappa Vishwanath who had scored 200 runs and Farokh Engineer who had scored 195 runs, though he was physically considered unfit by the standard of Mr. Hemu Adhikari, who was the Manager of the side. Fringes in terms of benefits, came in from Eknath Solkar, Syed Abid Ali and Sudhir Naik, but that was not enough for India, to be butchered 3-0 by the Englishmen.

Before this series, England had played 18 test matches against its opponent in the first half of summer, winning 14 and squaring the rest of them. The ball, cuts like a knife, and swings like a banana. England had Christopher "topper" Old, Mike Hendricks, Bob Willis and Geoff Arnold to "swing" India out of favour in the series, whereas the Indian think-tank was grossly involved to think, either to play 4 spinners or leave out Prasanna from the squad.

In 1971, at England when Wadekar won the series 1-0 there were two occasions, when the "Lord Indra", had visited him to "shower" his blessings on him. It was during the closing stages of the first test, and again in the second test at Manchester. Here, the lady Indira was riding a wave of success and euphoria after tumbling Pakistan in an encounter at Bangladesh. Ever since that, for most of the times she was very busy reshuffling her cabinet then, and as she could not visit Lords or the Edgbaston then, may be she could have ordered "Inderkumar" Gujral, who in turn might have acted as "lord Indra" to visit Indian team at England. Nobody visited England then to save India

But came Emergency thereafter, and even before the emergency of sunlight could turned dim, dim, it maybe, hit the Indian team then, for in any case, the "Lord Inder", or "Indra", was not into visiting the "lords" of English cricket. The entire team was bundled out for 42 and this is the lowest total of a completed innings by any Indian Cricket team. Compare it with the English effort. They hit 629. A year before, the West Indies hit the English for 652 on the same wicket with Gary Sobers, aged 34 then, Rohan Kanhai aged 36 and Clive Lloyd scoring tons. Kalicharan missed it by a whisker.

Records of three kinds were set then. This 629 was the highest by England against any visiting team, and the 42 was the lowest at Lords, by any visiting team, and the lowest ever by India. It only showed that our cricket, under Ajit Wadekar had came to a full circle and now it added up to a big zero. We were out-batted, out-bowled and out-fielded by England — a team, against whom our two victories before, made us feel and think that the English cricket squad was a second rated stinging side. Eknath Solkar, who had scored a fighting 43 in the first innings, top scored with an unbeaten 18 in the second, which was the highest individual score, whereas the next highest was 5 made by Gundappa Vishwanath, Erapalli Prasanna, and Sunil Gavaskar.

Here again, the captain Ajit Wadekar, was made our punching bag. He had failed to inspire the team and he did not deploy his resources too imaginatively. Some, like Crawford White came to his rescue stating that the earlier series win was something which was unique to history of Indian cricket, but Indian cricket has never learned from history.

He led India, after the series was over, for the one-dayers. That was for the first time that India were playing the one-dayers at England and at Lords. It was 1974 and 9 years later in 1983, India was to win the World Cup at Lords, but in 1974 that match saw India posing a huge total of 284, with Wadekar scoring 67 and Brijesh Patel 88 to lose the match to England. Nine years later in the World

Cup finals, India scored 181, to whip West Indies out for 140 to win their only World Cup.

In 1974, Wadekar in that series, from the Edgbaston test, where he slowly started getting into his own groove, started getting runs. A steady 36 at Edgbaston, a 67 against England in the first one-dayer and a 36 in the second brought some confidence in his batting. But the selectors had lost the confidence in him.

West Indies were to tour India in September 1974 and Ajit had expected to be in the Indian squad, if not as a captain but at least as a player. He was regularly seen at the SBI's net at Bombay, batting, bowling and fielding seriously. He was full of hope that he would be leading the West Zone squad at least. But, in the evening, when the West Zone squad for the Duleep Trophy was to be announced, he went to the office of CCI to enquire "what is my side". Pat came the answer "you are nobody in the side".

Bruised by England, battered by selectors, feeling humiliated and insulted, he ran to his office at the State Bank of India, to pull a type writer and type a letter that "he is resigning and retiring from all form of cricket. It took him 15 minutes to type the letter and another 65 minutes to hand over the same to selectors. Eighty priceless minutes to do away with cricket, as against the 82 runs he had scored in series against England then.

Well, if the summer has come, then would the spring be far away? After the series against West Indies, thereafter, the Indian team had lost to the WI by 2-3, the Bush XI, the sponsors of the match, played two one-dayers against West Indies. Bush India Limited was the team and they were also the sponsor. The two one-dayers were the "Wadekar Benefit" matches and Wadekar had played in both of them. India had won the two one-day's match series, against the West Indies by 2-0. Fantastic—wasn't it?

Ajit Wadekar had scored a fluent 80 in the first, getting run out and in his very last innings for India, he again was run out for 17, had he continued playing on the basis of this two innings, he would have been at England to play in the First Prudential World Cup cricket. But he was not? Whether he ran himself out, or the selectors run him out, was the question of conjecture!!

Salim Durrani, who was 39 years of age then, had scored 37 runs in both the matches, was touted by Clive Lloyd, who was leading West Indies, then to have been included in the Indian squad for the World Cup. He was not, whereas Salim always had a desire to get back into the Indian squad. The other Indian batsman, who was touted by many pundits of the game then, to have made it to the World Cup squad, was Surinder Amarnath, but poor man, his fault was that he was the eldest of the three Lala's colt, who was playing then. He was chopped straight, hard and dire. Wadekar at 34, then felt that he had been insulted, humiliated and ashamed, to continue to play, be in the Indian squad, or the West zone squad, left the scene in a hurry.

Well, the annihilated summer for Wadekar which was started and originated by Prasanna in the Ranji Trophy, was completed at England and was over during the summer of 1975 when these two "Bush one dayers" were played in India, and summer had set in cricketing life of Ajit Wadekar for whom the spring was never to set in. The "Wadekar-Wadi" was built, never to be completed, and to stand for ever. From losing the Ranji Trophy in 1974, he lost everything in cricket thereafter.

Erapalli Prasanna was the first captain, in modern cricket, who licked Bombay like an ice-cream, to prove that Bombay cricket can be put to lick the mud. The player and the captain, to be toppled was Ajit Wadekar.

Erapalli Prasanna's floater flow like a butterfly, and the loops of his delivery which turned sharply after pitching, hitting the deck, stung like a bee. For all the cricket heads who were analysing to counter his loops, they would refer his loops as the eighth wonder of the world. The mastery that he had over his flight, and the control that he had over his loops were even one degree ahead of the control what Adolf Hitler might have had over Germany. His smile always, before and after the delivery, made some people like me think that he was "smiling assassinator", and he was the one to first assassinate Bombay in the annals of Indian cricket.

It was Chinnaswamy Stadium where Bombay after 15 consecutive years of reign in Ranji Trophy, lost out to Karnataka, thus bringing about a change in the face of Indian cricket. Earapalli Prasanna was the one who was instrumental in bringing about the change. This is another reason why he is considered a great.

Bombay and their cricketers were always under an impression that in India if someone and somebody knew what cricket were, and if somebody knew how to play cricket, it were they. There were so many incidents that the Bombay cricketers during the course of the match would make a mockery of their opponents by some scathing remarks.

At times the remarks would be provocating too, beside unbearbable to digest. At times the umpires were so awe of them. The reputation that they carried, nobody would dare to open their mouth against them. Prasanna changed the scenario and made Bombay to feel that they were as good and as ordinary as any of the other cricketers and at times bad or even worst if at all they were available, worst, too even think of.

Prasanna had changed the face of Indian cricket and it is for nothing that he is a LEGEND of Indian cricket. A little bit on Prasanna which would make an interesting reading.

Prasanna, M.E. in Engineering, best schoolboy, cricketer in 1958 at the school, best student at the NIE College, best offspinner of the world, best night watchman between

1967 and 1974, fastest 100 wickets taker in the test matches for India, best employee for the I. T. I, and the NGEF-General Manager at the NGEF-Arjuna Award-Padma Shri, and right now a freelance consultant for many software firms at Bangalore. Is there any field in which he has failed, I would like to know, and somebody who knows it may kindly tell me so.

I was questioned by some very young and enthusistic students when I was an Associate Professor in one of the famous and leading Management Institutes at Bangalore about Prasanna's name missing from the muster rolls as captain of the Indian cricket team. What could be the reason Sir, a student had asked me who was a Sachin enthusiast.

My answer was, if somebody had to write a book on the wisdom of the Indian selectors, and the BCCI, it would have put the entire cricketing fraternity into a SHAME, and this would have put in the book "PLUNDER INDIA" written by Nadir Shah, in Persian which if translated in English would put Plunder India into a great shame, as the story narrated in that book describes how he plundered India—and the reason of doing so.

If someone writes a book about the BCCI and the Indian selectors, it would not put the author, the BCCI and the selectors into a shame, because the deeds of BCCI and the selectors, that are known to everybody, but the book itself will find it into a state of shame - shame, because, the one reason that the readers will find in the book is: The BCCI and the selectors do everything WITHOUT ANY REASON AND AT ANY SEASON. Nadir Shah had a reason, and had selected a season to loot India. The Somnath Temple and the Peacock throne were the reasons, and the infighting of the foolish Indian Emperors during that period served him the season.

Hello the BCCI, its administration and the selectors, are you reading the book, are you. Gentlemen, if yes, mend your ways fast.

4

FILTRATION, DISTILLATION AND DECANTATION OF INDIAN CRICKET

THE period between 1971 and 1973 was a transitional revolution in Indian cricket. The Indian cricket got revolutionized during that period. For between the period 1955 and 1973, 18 long years, Bombay had held the sway in the domestic cricket. Ranji Trophy was their fathers' property. But the other trophies too, in cricket, preferred to stay either in the West, or may be with the players from Bombay.

Karnataka broke the stranglehold of Bombay's reign over the Ranji Trophy in 1974, but the one memorable day, if it is and if it could be written in the golden words, would be March 14th 1972. For this was the day when Hanumant Singh and Central Zone were the proud winners of the Duleep Trophy. Central owed its success in a very large manner, to a cricketer, who was named as SALIM ALTAF DURRANI and the Duleep Trophy in 1972 was christened as "DURRANI'S TROPHY".

Along with Salim Durrani, Hanumant Singh, Kailash Ghattani, Ashok Jagdale, Sanjay Jagdale, Mehboobullah, a very famous cricketer from Uttar Pradesh during those days, Anil Deshpande and Rakesh Tandon, had done every thing, in terms of performance for the Central Zone, to win the Duleep Trophy, but Salim's magnanimous and a giant like performance, awesome in deeds and gruesome in performance, separated his performance from others, and the performance of other cricketers mentioned here took a back seat.

The Duleep Trophy of 1972 from the first match where Central Zone had defeated North Zone by an innings at Nagpur, to the end of the finals was ONE MAN'S PROPERTY, and it was Durrani's. The selectors did not take a serious notice of it, and these worthy performers of the young gems of Central Zone then, went unnoticed. Salim Durrani stood out and the selectors kept him in mind. Especially the performance of Ashok Jagdale and Anil Deshpande got entirely covered under the Houdini act of Salim Durrani during that epoch, Duleep Trophy win.

But the next year saw a total change, a sweeping one in the scenario of cricket in India. As described earlier, Karnataka had dethroned Bombay to win its first Ranji Trophy title, ending Bombay's monopoly over this trophy. Then the Vizzy Trophy also went to North Zone for the first time. Delhi under the captaincy of Mohinder Amarnath had annexed the Rohinton Baria Trophy, establishing the supremacy of the cricket for University in India. Uttar Pradesh for the first time had won the national school cricket championship under the captaincy of Mohd Shahid and the Cooch Behar Trophy, the symbol of supremacy for the Zonal school's was won by East Zone under the captaincy of Pranab Roy, the son of late Mr. Pankaj Roy. The only consolation win for Bombay was their triumph over Rest of India in the Irani Trophy, but there also, Gundappa Vishwanath and Salim Durrani had almost won the trophy for the Rest, however, in the very next year, Rest of India led by Erapalli Prasanna, aided by

Gopal Bose (173), Gundappa Vishwanath (76) and Brijesh Patel (56), with Chandrashekar (6 for 106) had crucified Bombay to win the Irani Trophy. Bombay's supremacy over cricket had started taking a back seat and it was Prasanna, who as a captain on two different occasions, had hit the nail in the Bombay's coffin. Other's too consecutively, and on a very consistent basis to pin-and-prick Bombay, whenever they got a chance were Gundappa Vishwanath, Salim Durrani and B. S. Chandrashekar.

Yet, it did not go into the "nut" of the selectors, the sleeping giants, that cricket was changing and Bombay were no more the "Adolf Hitler" of Indian cricket. However, one victory really changed the entire scenario of domestic cricket in India, and it was the Duleep Trophy triumph of North Zone under the leadership of Bishen Singh Bedi. That was in 1973.

Bedi led a very raw, inexperienced but a bunch of young, energetic, exuberant and dedicated cricketers for their Duleep campaign in 1973. The North Zone team had players like Venkat Sundaram, Sarabjit Singh, Vinay Lamba, Mohinder and Surinder Amarnath, Yashpal Sharma and Madanlal as the youngsters. It also had experienced warhorses like Hyder Ali, Mohd Tarif (Railways), Gokul Inder Dev, R. K. Ohri and Dinoo Deshpande (Services) besides Rajinder Goel (Haryana).

Instead of relying on the old experienced warhorses, Bishen Paaji in a very unprecedented and a sudden move, dropped all the experienced hands, except Haider Ali, Dinoo Deshpande of the Services and Rajinder Goel and included the fresh pairs of leg for their Duleep Trophy campaign. The result was, North Zone had won the trophy, beating West Zone in the semi finals and Central Zone in the finals. Central once again fought tooth and nails in the finals, but no sooner did Anil Deshpande (44) and Salim Durrani (48) got out to Madanlal and Rajinder Goel, respectively, the match was virtually over and North Zone, for the first time in 1973 had emerged as the winner of the Duleep Trophy.

In 1971, it was East Zone, who made it to the finals of Duleep Trophy, losing to South Zone, in 1972, it was Central Zone, and now the North Zone. From 1971 to 1973, players like Ambar Roy, Gopal Bose, Barun Barman, Rusi Jeejeebhoy, Govindraj, Brijesh Patel, A. V. Jayaprakash, A. V. Vijaykrishna, Syed Kirmani, Surinder Amarnath, Madanlal, Yashpal Sharma, Vinay Lamba, Suresh Luthra, Mohinder Amarnath, Anil Deshpande, Rakesh Tandon, Vijay Telang, Ashok Jagdale, Parthasarathy Sharma, Mohd Ibrahim, and Imran Ali had emerged. Everybody mentioned here was a champion in his own right. Yet they were constantly ignored by the selectors for the reason best known to the selectors. The selectors still held the opinion that if a player did not represent Bombay or West Zone in cricket, was not a complete cricketer and did not fit in the bill to play for India.

It was here that sincerely, the media started attracting the notice of the players coming from the regions other than Bombay or West Zone, to the Board and it was M. M Jagdale, a selector of Central Zone, who raised a serious voice for inclusion of certain players, outside Bombay, in the Indian team.

The Indian national cricket team then was virtually a Bombay Ranji team. About seven to eight players of the Indian team would be from Bombay or West Zone. The remaining 3 or 4 places would be the players from Karnataka [either Prasanna, Chandrashekar] Hyderabad [Nawab of Pataudi], Delhi [Bishen Singh Bedi] and Rajasthan [Hanumant Singh or Salim Durrani].

It was the twin tour of New Zealand and West Indies in 1975 – 1976 that as many as 10 players represented India, out of a sixteen in the squad, who were never from Bombay and had nothing to do with Bombay's cricket, with Karnataka contributing as many as six players and Delhi, as many as 4, Erapalli Prasanna, B. S. Chandrashekar, Gundappa Vishwanath, Syed Kirmani, Brijesh Patel and Sudhakar Rao represented Karnataka, while Bishen Singh Bedi, Mohinder Amarnath, Surinder Amarnath and Madanlal Sharma were from Delhi. Only three, Dilip Vengsarkar, Sunil Gavaskar and Eknath Solkar were from Bombay. It was for the first time that more than one third players of the squad were from Karnataka.

Bombay's grip over cricket in India paved the way for "Quota" system in Indian cricket. It was seriously given a thought and consideration, that at least, on an rotational basis, players representing the other associations too, should be given a fair chance to represent India, if they were found to be good. This was the reason that some from Gujarat, Hyderabad and Punjab, got the favour of the selectors to play for India. Dhiraj Parsana, Narasimha Rao and Yashpal Sharma were the basic examples of this rotational policies who got the chance to don the national cap.

The induction of Yashpal Sharma gave a tremendous boost to cricket in Punjab, and within three years of representing India from Punjab, Yashpal took Punjab to Ranji Trophy quarter finals against Karnataka in 1982. From that batch, two players Rajinder Singh Ghai and Mahesh Inder Singh had arrived on the scene, of which Ghai had represented India. This was the real decantation of Indian cricket.

Players from other associations and zones too started making waves, and players from weaker associations like Assam, Orissa, Madhya Pradesh and even Andhra Pradesh started throwing players on the national front. Indian cricket had started coming out from the Bombay's stranglehold. Jugal Kishore Ghai of Andhra Pradesh just missed making it to the national team, while offspinner Ramnarayanan from Hyderabad could not make it because of Prasanna.

The process of distillation of Indian cricket had neither a funnel nor the filter paper, yet one hardly understood how was the filtration done, and what was the basis.

It all started in 1958, when Farokh Engineer was selected to represent India. He did a good job behind the wicket, but after that for no fault of his own, he did not find the favour from the selectors to play for India till 1964. From 1960 to 1964, Indian test team had as many as three wicket keepers, Nana Joshi, Inderjit Singh and B. K. Kunderan. The selectors kept changing one and bringing on the other, for the reason best known to them. Yet every time after the series, if a postmortem was conducted to review the performance of the wicket keepers, the selectors would pretend to come out with an "Engineering" solution. However and no sooner came the moment, the nuts which had formed those ideas for the solution would dry up with the idea by that time.

In between 1961-62, under Nari Contractor when India had won her first test "rubber" against England, Engineer was tried, tested and trusted by the Indian selectors, but once the series was over, the name of Engineer was once again rubbed off by the Indian selectors from their mind, or may be from the paper.

It was not before the 1965 series against New Zealand that Engineer, permanently cemented his place in the squad with a whirlwind knock of 90. From 1965 to 1974 -75, Engineer was a unanimous choice as wicket keeper number one for India. His tally of 46 tests, and 2674 runs with 82 dismissals, and two centuries, does not really reflects the kind of cricketing talent he had possessed. Between 1960 and 1964, he purposely was made to miss at least 15 tests.

If Engineer was not engined properly, Dilip Sardesai for a very long time might have found it that had his name, being spelled as "Sir-Desai", that would have been better, for the Indian selectors had turned their "sar" on this man, who was at his sparkling best between the period of 1959 and 1964.

He was not only castled by the selectors, but also by the so called Indian coaches then. Aggressive during the game, he would treat the Indian spinners with scant respect. And Sardesai was born and meant to demolish the spinners. At this point of time, the Bombay coach Vasu Paranjape advised him to change his batting grip, which he did. The result was disastrous and he did not get many runs between 1959 to the mid sixties.

He was so frustrated that he started trying too many acts to get runs, but was not successful. It was 1960 – 61 when Fazal Mehmood had brought a Pakistan team to tour India, and Dilip Sardesai had got a chance to "chance" his arm against Fazal Mehmood and his team. At this juncture came Vasant Amladi, who was the coach of Bombay University. He saw Dilip Sardesai at the nets and had noticed a flaw in the grip. He advised Dilip to go back to his "old" self, and not to worry about his failure. The result was evident in the match against Pakistan, playing for Combined Universities, Dilip Sardesai played such glorious innings of 87 against Pakistan, that it ended up the Pakistan captain Fazal Mehmood telling to Lala Amarnath that, if India can't let play Salim Durrani and Dilip Sardesai, let them be sent to Pakistan, so that Pakistan's cricket makes use of their talent.

Dilip Sardesai was eventually in the Indian squad for West Indies tour in 1962, only to be overlooked again by the selectors till 1965. Again in 1965, Sardesai took the series against New Zealand by breeze to hit a double century and a century in the series. Again from thereafter till 1968 he was a forgotten man, until he made a grand comeback for the tour of Australia, under Pataudi at the end of '68.

He was denied his chance in Australia, and he remained in wilderness till the Australians, under Bill Lawry landed here in India. The first test at Bombay saw India getting shunted out by 8 wickets, and from here till 1971, Sardesai was out of the Indian side.

1971 brought him back to the squad only after a high recommendation by Ajit Wadekar, to one of the highest regarded member of the BCCI then, though his performance was such that he would score a century in every second game that he would play for his team here at India. He ultimately made it to the team to play against West Indies and England in 1971. He was a "twin edge" hit with 642 runs in West Indies and 147 runs against England, eventually helping India to record a 1-0 victory in both the series.

However, he was to meet his Waterloo against England, here at home at New Delhi. His score of 12 and 10 were valuable to him as he had coasted to his 2000 runs in test cricket, but it wasn't of any help to India. India had lost the "test" and with it ended Dilip Sardesai's patience and its time of test.

He eventually gave up playing test cricket. 30 tests, 2000 runs and five centuries, including two double hundreds, does not exemplifies and glorifies the true treasure of Dilip Sardesai's cricketing talent. For he had the capacity of playing fifty test matches, scoring at least 5000 runs, and was one of the best brain who could have led India between the period 1971 and 1973.

If the yardstick of performance was to be applied to select the team, then one wonders, how a cricketing talent like Subroto Guha was ignored by the selectors, to tour Australia in 1967 – 68 under Pataudi, or on what reasons the two Rajasthani warriors, Salim Durrani and Hanumant Singh, were not selected to tour Australia, how a genius like Ramesh Saxena was totally ruined by the Indian Selectors, how a wrestler like Umesh Kulkarni was included in the side to tour Australia under Pataudi, how V. V. Kumar was excluded from the squad of Indian team, immediately after his spell of 5 for 85 against Pakistan in 1960-61. The seeming cocky, peppy and the funny part of the commentary is even when Chandrashekar was not in the side, V.V. Kumar was ignored constantly, may be because his teammate Venkatraghavan was to be pushed ahead. The criteria of hiring and firing the players was, and had been, the eighth wonder of the world in Indian cricket.

Between 1956 and 1959, there were "ONE MATCH WONDERS" but between 1960 and 1967, the selections and the dropping of the players from the Indian team remained the puzzle of the "Bermuda" triangle. One could have hardly understood on what basis were players like S.G. Shinde, who happens to be the father-in-law of the present Chief of BCCI, Mr Sharad Pawar, S. N. Sohani, V.N. Swamy, selected to play for India, and how come players like Kailash Ghattani, Ambar Roy and P. K. Bellippa were totally ignored, despite scoring so heavily in domestic cricket. Players like Ramesh Saxena, Rajender Pal were simply ignored and not considered good to play for India, whereas, if they could have been persisted with, India's cricket would have been benefited and richer. In this regard one really feels sorry for Ramesh Saxena, Rajinder Goel and Rajinder Pal, from whom Kapil was to learn the nuisance of seam bowling in the sultry, hot and the humid condition of Delhi, before he boarded the plane to England in 1979 for the World Cup and the English sojourn.

Let me talk a bit of the process of decantation that takes place in Indian cricket and the selectors are the "bunkums" of it. I just cannot forget two incidents which would remain lingering in my mind till I breath my last.

It was the year 1967 and the mighty West Indies were to tour India, to be led by Sir Garfield Sobers. Prior to the series, a conditioning camp was held at Madras and during the phase of the camp, it was decided to include an extra leg spinner for the camp.

The selectors then got to Mr. Rusy Mody, the chairman of the Tata Steel, to request him to "leave" the leg spinner of Tata XI from his job to assist the cricketer in the camp. Rusy Mody acted accordingly and allowed the leg spinner to rush to Madras to join the camp.

The leg spinner rushed to Kharagpur from Jamshedpur, got into the unreserved bogie and travelled all the way to

Madras and reported to the camp. The moment he reported, he was told to go back as the selectors had made a mistake to call him from the Tata Steel. In fact, they wanted Baloo Gupte as the best, at the nets to help out the Indian team for their preparation against the West Indies. When this leg spinner from Tata Steel told and reminded the selectors that Baloo Gupte had long hanged up his boots, did the selectors realize that they had really committed a grave mistake. Just imagine the knowledge, and the wisdom of the selectors then, who were "taught" and told by the players about the whereabout of the cricketers, having played for India. The spinner of the Tata Steel was none other than Anand Shukla, who was a very good leg spinner, beside a good batsman and at that time he played for Bihar along with his younger brother Rakesh, who later played for Delhi. And Baloo Gupte, the younger brother of Subhash Gupte, was working for Tata Electricals, and not .... . Tata Steel; and moreover it was more than 6 years by then that Baloo Gupte had announced retirement from all the norms and forms of cricket.

The second incident was in 1976-77, when M. C. C. under Tony Greig were visiting India and were to play a match against the Combined University and under-22 eleven at Nagpur. A team was selected from the bunch of cricketers, who were playing for their colleges or the universities, either as students or as Ranji Trophy players, for their association, but the criteria of selection was that the player had to be within the age of 22 years. A young lad Dharmaraj Jadeja was included to play in this match. He was an unheard element. A left arm spinner, he was neither a collegiate then nor a Ranji player for his association. How was he selected to play and who selected him still remains a mystery. He had scalped 5 wickets in the second innings in that match, and was a hit. But from there where did he go and where is he now, is anybody's guess. Which association did he belong, remains a question, which I think would be the "KBC" question to be asked by Shri Amitabh Bachchan, if the show is held once again?

That team had the guiles of Yograj Singh, Rajendra Jadeja, Rahul Mankad, Vijay Mohanraj, Roger Binny, Arshad Ayub, Faiz Baig, Vedraj and Kapil Dev besides Ashwini Minna. The team was led by Dilip Vengsarkar. After the game was over, I along with my friend Bharat Chandraker, made an attempt to meet these players and we chose the time after 7.30 p.m. to meet them at the Nagpur Railway Station hoping that we could meet them.

Yes, we were right. No sooner we landed at the platform we saw Gopal Sharma and Kapil Dev standing at one corner with a sullen face. It was obvious because both of them did not play in the game. Then there were Yograj Singh and Ashwini Minna, apeing Mike Brearley and Bob Woolmer and playing pranks. This was the habit of Yograj Singh then, as he was full of mischief and prank in his young days.

We went to platform number two and saw Roger Binny sitting on the platform and waiting for Kerala - Karnataka express to come in. We saw him puffing a "BIDI" then. He was asking the coolie to help him get into the unreserved compartment in broken Hindi. We came to his rescue requesting the coolie to help him in all the way. No sooner that the coolie learned that he was a cricket star in making, he helped him gladly.

Our next stop was again in the platform number three, to meet the Bombay stars who were to leave for Bombay. We could see Rajendra Jadeja, Vijay Mohan Raj and Rahul Mankad on the platform. When asked where was Dilip Vengsarkar, we were told that he was on his way to Madras to join the Indian team for the third test.

We could see that the Bombay cricketers were to travel by the first class coach. After sometimes, we saw Mr. N. K. P. Salve approaching the Bombay cricketers, along with a selector of Vidarbha Cricket Association. Also with him was Mr. Gopu Kelkar, the President of VCA. They first enquired about the well-being of the Bombay cricketers, and immediately they introduced Mr. Ravindra Jain, a noted music Director of those years and Hemlata, a renowned singer, and then directed Rajendra Jadeja and Rahul Mankad that, these two film personalities would accompany the cricketers for their journey towards Bombay. If needed so, let the cricketers bear certain problems during journey, but let the film stars be comfortable to travel with them for their journey.

Both Bharat and I looked dazed. First of all, we were wondering how come these film personalities were in Nagpur, when there was no news about their arrival, in the media. Secondly, why should they "accommodate" these film stars and cine personalities. Moreover, when I personally enquired to Rajinder Jadeja, about Dharmaraj Jadeja, he, and nobody else could give me a proper answer for it. Nobody knew where he had headed for.

Anyway, I and my friend Bharat left the station. We were happy that we could meet some of the stars of India, who, we felt would be going to places in the future to help India get all the glory of cricket in the days to come. But we also were surprised to see that the cricketers from other associations were neither taken care of, nor looked after properly for their journey towards their home, in retrospect the Bombay cricketers were arranged for a first class travel. What excited me more was the induction of those film personalities with the cricketers for their journey to home. However, we could not find any clue of Dharmaraj Jadeja.

While returning to Y. M. C. A. Nagpur where I stayed as a hostelier for my B.Sc studies, with Bharat Chandrakar as a room partner, we often asked a question to each other, why were the film personalities included in the Bombay squad to travel back home. Bharat got me the answer, "you cannot expect the googly to be read and understood fine, until you do not play high standard of cricket". Yes! the selectors are the real googlies of Indian cricket, and no sooner they combine well, with the administrator, running the game, they become a "faster one". For that is Indian cricket all about. Chandra's googly is and might be, is nothing compared to them nor might be Ghavri's "Chinaman".

Of late, a lot of former cricketers have become selectors, either on the national panel, or on the panels of their associations. What do they do now! They ask the players to give them the money for getting selected in the under-19, under-22 or even the under-17 teams. The sum charged is anything between Rs. 40,000/- and Rs. 1,00,000/- each depending upon the tournament that these players would play. We already had the Abhijit Kale incident, and the Ritesh Yadav's incident, and there is nothing more to write about. I'm right again, no sooner than the selectors mix up with the administrators, running the game, they become a faster one, for again, those are the selectors of Indian cricket. Well thereafter since 1976-77, I did not hear about Dharmaraj Jadeja at all though his performance in that match was FANTASTIC.

From that batch of the cricketers, who never played the game at all at Nagpur then, against the M. C. C., Kapil Dev Nikhanj went on to become the Indian millennium cricketer, and he was ignored and overlooked by the selectors for that game, for the reason best known to them. And this is how the talents are "used", "abused", "confused" and "diffused" by the Indian selectors.

Wonna! That's Indian cricket. Well that is the procedure of selection of the cricket players in India!

Before I end my note on this chapter I would wish to add a very interesting information which should make a very interesting reading. It was the summer of 1976 and a summer camp for about two months' duration was held at Bombay in which all the best players ranging from 18 years to 21 years attended as per the directives of BCCI then.

In one of the nights when the food was served, Kapil called on a waiter serving the food and asked him to serve a few chapatis more. The waiter refused and there started the argument. Mr Keki Tarapore who was asked to be the

Administration Manager for the camp was called in to handle the matter.

"What is your problem", asked Mr Tarapore. "I want a few chapatis extra", said Kapil. Why do you need it, said Mr Tarapore. Because I work more, I'm a fast bowler and I have to work hard, so I need to eat more, as I'm more hungrier than any other boys attending the camp, said Kapil.

Oh, fast bowler is it, dear chum, said Mr Tarapore, perhaps you are too young to understand it, but let me tell you, India never had produced a fast bowler after Independence, and will never have one. Your eating even a chapati more is not going to produce any fast bowler, eat whatever is laid for you.

Kapil gave it back and very fast. If India did not have it, look into my face and do not forget the same face. India will have a fast bowler very soon after the Independence and it will be this face. It can only be possible if he is nourished and fed more. Ask your waiter to give me some.

Yes, Kapil kept his words. Maybe not as a genuine fast bowler, but as a pacer who held a world record of 434 wickets, which was later broken by Courtney Walsh.

Whether those few extra chapatis were served to him or not, is for the BCCI to answer but there was and there will be no answer, except a name that can emerge out from all the answers, who was the captain of the Indian team when India won the World Cup in 1983.

Whether for a chapati, or for the I. C. L., Kapil it seems was born to take those "Chappads" of the B. C. C. I., for the World Cup that he gave it to this nation. My Gosh! what a destiny, and how cruel it can be if one has to compare it with that extra chapati that he asked the B. C. C. I to serve him.

Well the World Cup that Kapil gave it to the nation definitely was much more than those extra chapatis that he might have eaten at the camp in 1976.

There was a very famous song sung by the GREAT Hemantda, and the song was thus-:

HUM LAAYE HAIN TOOFAN SE

KASHTI NIKKAL KE

IS DESH KO RAKHNA

MERE BACHCHO SAMBHAL KE

Yes this is the message that Kapil Dev had given to this country after the World Cup win, but ALAS....... if only our administrators have the brain to....... . T...K

5

A DREAM COME TRUE: JIMMY, JIMMY, JIMMY, AAJA, AAJA, AAJA

HOW can one forget the year 1969. It was the MONTH of "Come September" for as many as 6 cricketers between the age of 17 and 20 years......However more about it later in this chapter.

It all started with the Indian team touring Pakistan in 1982-83. The team was led by Sunil Gavaskar and Mohinder Amarnath had staged a comeback to the national team then.

For Mohinder, the Lala's second colt, for the reason best known to the selectors was ignored according to the whims and fancies of selectors. Making his test baptism in 1969 under Nawab of Pataudi in Madras against Australia, Mohinder was instrumental in the decline that followed in the Madras test for Australia in the Aussies' second essay. He claimed the first two wickets to send Australia reeling for 14 for 2. From there Prasanna took on and sent Australia panting down for their life with the score board reaching 26 for 6. That was during the second innings.

How did this Lala's colt get the nod of the selectors. It was because of his tremendous performance at England in 1967 when he toured that country along with his Badpaji Surinder, being a member of the Indian school team.

His performance was so good that when the Australian team was playing against the North Zone at Burlton Park at Jullundhur in an upcountry match in 1969, he was selected to bat at the number fifth position against them.

For Australia has posed an imposing total, and when they came in to field, they had floored 5 North Zone wickets for just 59 runs on the board. It was Mohinder who stood tall between the defeat and Aussies on that day. He hooked, drove and thumped in style to score a priceless 69 in that innings. Hyder Ali with an unbeaten 58 gave him the necessary company and all the encouragement to play a gallant game. Vijay Merchant was the one who selected him for the Indian team for the series, along with his Badpaji Surinder.

It was late Vijay Merchant who gave a call to six youngsters between the age of 17 and 20 at Nagpur at the nets for choosing a few for the twin series that was to be played between India and New Zealand and later between India and Australia. Many, who had and who have been following Indian cricket very seriously call this as COME SEPTEMBER CALL.

The notice to them was served during the month of September 1969 to attend the nets at Nagpur prior to the India-New Zealand test match.

Making his debut he did not do anything of note in the first innings either with the bat or the ball, but in the second innings, he started the rot and the rout. He removed both the openers in the second essay of the Aussies, with the score reading at 14 for two. Prasanna was to take it over from him and the Australians score read 15 for three, sixteen for four, twenty for five, and then 26 for six. Prasanna had twilled and twisted the Aussies by then.

Wadekar was to miss Ian Redpath thereafter, with the score reading at 26/6 in the slips of Prasanna, and then the match, from there onwards was "advantage" to Australia. However Mohinder Amarnath had arrived in the national scene.

The tours of West Indies and England were to follow, and for both these tours, Mohinder was out of the Indian team. From 1969 to 1976 Mohinder was a forgotten man of Indian cricket. From 1976 to 1979-80, he was in and out of the Indian team. He had again and in-between got decayed, decanted and distilled particularly between the period of 1981 to 1983 before he booked his ticket for the Pakistan sojourn.

From here in 1983 to 1987, Mohinder was again an in-and-out figure of Indian cricket, till the ruler of Banswara, Mr. Rajsingh Dungarpur put a full stop on Mohinder's career in test cricket. No doubt, it was Mohinder who had referred the Indian selectors as "bunch of crackpot and jokers in the business".

However, in 1982-83, Mohinder after he had staged a remarkable comeback had scored 3 centuries at Pakistan, in the test series to book his seat for West Indies. There again, he scored another 598 runs to become the Vice Captain of the Indian cricket team for their campaign for the World Cup, 1983.

The World Cup cricket, the "Prudential Cup" in 1983, by any means, and by any standard would be remembered for two great histories which were created during the tournament.

This was for the first time in the annals of cricket, that during the tournament, every team participating in the tournament, had won at least a game against their opponent, to prove their mettle. It started with Zimbabwe under the leadership of Duncan Fletcher beating Australia and in the return encounter, Sri Lanka led by Duleep Mendis had overpowered New Zealand.

The second was the "Cannon" fodders India, as the British Press would call India, who dethroned the mighty

West India by 43 runs to win the World Cup for the first time. Kapil Dev Nikhanj, 24 years of age, was to kiss the Cup, on the balcony of "Lords", thus becoming the first Indian to do so. WHEN WILL WE HAVE ANOTHER ONE TO DO SO. Will M.S. Dhoni provide the answer?

What was to follow next was Mohinder Amarnath, going to claim the huge champagne bottle, and a cheque, to become the first Indian to be honoured with a Man of the Match award in a Would Cup finals. After receiving the award when Mohinder was strolling back to his place he, and we, the Indians, were noticing, how Kirti Azad was smiling, looking into the giant size champagne bottle which Mohinder was holding, ... as if passing a message to Mohinder, ... well! Well! tonight I will have my share.........

Well, it all started at the West Indies, a place named Berbice at Guyana, where the two greats of West Indies, Rohan Kanhai and Alvin Kalicharan were born. And this was the place where the Indian cricket was also born. I might start wondering, and one would call me a MAD.... . but I'm again to add that Indian cricket was in the mother's tummy till then, but it was Berbice in 1983 where the Indian cricket was born and the date was March 27th.

It all started with 3 one-day international which was to follow after the test matches then. Batterred 2-0 by the Windies, India were to take the "King" of cricket for the one-dayers, and with Joel Garner, Malcolm Marshall and Micheal Holding in their rank, nobody had given India a chance to do well in the one-dayers. It would be a 3-0 black wash, wrote a newspaper in the Island.

Yes, very soon it was 1-0 for the West Indies. Came Berbice and the Windies Bank got a cheque prepared for the captain Clive Lloyd to receive it at the end of the match hoping that Lloyd could finish the series then and there.

But the "Devil" had some other idea. Came the hour, he won the toss and elected to bat first. India had rattled 287 runs from the fifty overs with the "Devil" himself contributing a whirlwind 100 to be exact, while Mohinder's share was 87. When the Windies Indies came in to bat, Gordon Greenidge and Desmond Haynes got them through a good start with Larry Gomes, "King" Richard, Uncle Lloyd, Jeff Dujon and Faoud Bacchus to follow. One felt that 287 would be a small total to defend for the West Indies.

But what was to follow soon was a magic, in between the 15th over to the 23rd over, India were to script a story for their first win in the one-dayers at the West Indies. The Indian "Quick" attack of Balvinder Sandhu, Madanlal, Mohinder Amarnath and Kapil Dev were to break the backbone of the West Indies team, and with a very able support coming from Venkatraghavan whose tight offspin had checked the run flow of the Windies, Windies were hammered and nailed into the coffin box and buried into the grave at their own backyard.

This was the start, but the world considered it to be a fluke. India had lost the test series 0-2 and were later beaten in the one-dayers by 1-2. But the seed was sown and 3 months later on June 26, 1983 what we saw was a dream of every Indian, coming true. Unbelievable, if it was, it was "home they brought the World Cup, alive and alive". It was not a magic, but the "Devil" act of Kapil Dev and his boys being realistic. It started in Berbice with the West Indies, and it ended at the "Lords", by the grace of the Lord and of course the God, against the same Uncle called Clive Lloyd, and West Indies.

That summer between the month of March and April took the Indian selectors to pick a squad for the World Cup which included as many as eight all-rounders in Kapil Dev, Mohinder Amarnath, Roger Binny, Madanlal, Kirti Azad, Balwinder Singh Sandhu, Ravi Shastri and Sandip Patil, besides Yashpal Sharma, who not only could bat, but if needed so could turn his arm over and keep the wickets. There were as many as nine useful bowlers in the side, and everybody could chance his arm over. The team had Sunil Gavaskar, K. Srikanth, Dilip Vengsarkar and Syed Kirmani, purely as a batsman to compile runs.

In the tournament that followed, the "seven golden men" strucked vital blow after blow in all the matches that India played and lifted the Cup.

The start was not good. After the team had left for the sojourn at England, it was two first class fixtures played against two very ordinary teams and India had lost them pathetically. It then played a game against England, comprising of all those players who were overlooked by their countries, only to loose to them.

It was here that for the first time Kapil Dev, the Indian skipper spoke very harshly to each and every members of the team. He was very critical about the standard of the fielding of the team, and he made it very clear that the "passengers" of fielding would be packed, back to their homes.

The British Press, and its remarks had irked Kapil to a large extent. The British Press had hailed India as the "cannon fodders", and had surcasted the Indian team to go back rather than tarnishing their image. It gave no chance to the Indian squad.

Against this moral shattering background, just before the start of the tournament, India took on West Indies in their first encounter and with the help of Yashpal Sharma, who cracked 87 and Roger Binny who scored 28, India scored 262 runs and then, with Binny claiming 3 for 48, India bowled out West Indies for 216 runs, winning the match by 46 runs. This had set the tempo, and this was the first match that West Indies had lost to any team in the World Cup till then.

The World Cup at England during those days used to be a 60 overs affairs with a "make up" day next, if the game was disturbed or held at bay due to rain. Each bowler would bowl 12 overs. This was the tonic needed by India, and mind you over a period of time between 1975 and 1983, this win was the second victory registered in the World Cup by India. The previous win was way back in 1975 when India had beaten East Africa by 10 wickets with Farokh Engineer scoring a 60 plus and B. S. Bedi registering a figure of 12-8-5-1 which till this day is the best economical bowling figure by any bowler in the World Cup.

The World Cup 1983 was played on return encounter basis, where every team in its group, would play each other twice. India had beaten West Indies, but had lost to Australia in the phase one of the tourney. In the return encounter West Indies swallowed us after Dilip Vengsarkar was forced to retire hurt after he had hit them for a sparkling unbeaten 80, but we banged Australia to keep our hope alive. It was Roger Binny again as the quickie against the Aussies, who broke their backbone again with a spell of 4 for 48.

Came the moment against Zimbabwe, and came the Devil. For Zimbabwe put India in totters sending 6 wickets down for 17 runs. It was here that Kapil Dev played his heart out. He added over 60 runs, for the seventh wicket with Madanlal, another 60 plus came when Roger Binny helped Kapil, and Binny himself had 26 to score, but the crowning glory came when Syed Kirmani and Kapil added an unbeaten 126 runs for the ninth wicket. India ended with 266, and Kapil himself had scored 175 of those runs. He had blasted as many as seven sixes, all of them out of the stadium, in Turn Bridge Wells.

Unfortunately, on that day, the British Media and the British TVstations had been on a "catcall strike" and this magic of Kapil was not recorded on the camera. Till now, none of us have had the pleasure of watching this Devil act of Kapil, but Zimbabwe were done away with for 216 runs.

As said earlier, India then banged Australia, and then took on with England in the semis. In the series, the English Media, the English fans, and the world of cricket, took it for granted that it would be a repeat of the 1979 finals where England would have to rub their shoulders with the West Indies. Many of them had believed that

Clive Lloyd would be the first skipper to achieve a hat trick of World Cup wins.

But that was not to be. Winning the toss, and elected to field first, England were cruising at 60 without loss, when Roger Binny broke the stump of Chris Taware. He then claimed the next to bring in Allan Lamb and Ian Botham to the midfield act.

No sooner these two bulldozers had set their feet on the pitch, Kapil deployed a move, which still today is considered to be the best moves set by any captain in the World Cup. He brought in Kirti Azad and Mohinder Amarnath. Azad and Amarnath bowled 24 overs between them and conceded 48 runs, thus restricting the English batsmen to score at an average of two runs per over for the 24 overs that they bowled between them.

In between, Kirti had castled Ian Botham while he had shaped to play a square drive, and Allan Lamb was done in by a smart piece of work from Yashpal Sharma. The Indian ground fielding, for once had touched the sky and for men playing for the Indian team, fielding then, sky was not the limit. It was something more.

Once the "Badshahs" of Delhi had completed bowling 24 overs between them, Kapil came back and he roared like a lion. Bowling at a nagging length, and laying a heavy stress on the accuracy, beside being helped by extra ordinary fielding, he claimed 5 wickets thereafter, conceding 42 runs in total to leave England in a total disarray.

The Indian batsmen held it altogether. There were certain hiccups when the overs started running out, with Mohinder, finding it hard to pierce the field in spite of scoring 46 runs. Once he was run out, by a brilliant throw from Paul Allot, Yashpal was joined by Sandip Patil. Sandip struck the purple path. He dispatched Willis for four consecutive boundaries and from there Yashpal took it over. His six of Willis where he, lazily strolled to the offside and picked a delivery of Willies, to flick it on to the leg side, was a real treat to behold. He ended up scoring 61 before being out. Kapil then joined Sandeep and it was a scorching extra cover drive by Sandeep of Bob Willis that saw India to the finals. "Devil" paaji was unconquered scoring nine, but he had two boundaries to relish that score. History was made at England and the English media was slapped by the Indian bat. Mohinder Amarnath was the man of the moment, and the match. The cannon fodders had blown the English cannon.

What followed on June 26 of 1983 was neither a Cindrella's tale nor a fairy affair. The cannon fodders of Indian cricket, pulverized the mights and the knights of West Indies cricket, in one of the most low scoring finals, till then, to win the World Cup for the first time.

Batting first, after winning the toss, India were shot out for 183 with Srikkant and Mohinder Amarnath scoring 38 and 26 respectively. The other Indians, whenever they looked set for a big score, lost their wickets playing some injudicious and indiscreet shots. Gavaskar, Patil, Kapil, Kirti Azad and Roger Binny were the worst offenders. A little resistance had come from Yashpal Sharma and the Indian tail too had wagged with Madanlal scoring a gallant 17. Sandhu and Madanlal had helped the innings to swell a bit.

Well, 183 was not a big score and with the likes of Gorden Greenidge, Desmond Haynes, Viv Richards, Faoud Bacchus, Larry Gomes, Clive Lloyd, and Jeff Dujon, this perhaps was a total which the Windies felt "small and very little."

A very late inswinger from Sandhu did break the off stick of Greenidge then, and when king Richard was held by Kapil, running against the flight of the ball for about 20 yards before holding the catch off a pull shot of Madanlal, Windies still had nurtured the hope for a victory. In a total of about 48 runs, of which king Richard had scored 30, Windies had the batting left till Malcolm Marshall, to hope for a win.

But no sooner did Clive Lloyd exit at the score of 51, caught by Kapil in the short extra covers of Roger Binny, the writings were on the wall. The late batsmen of the Windies, in that game, starting from Jeff Dujan till Malcolm Marshall, put up a dogged resistance and a purposeful fight but were undone in their purpose by Mohinder Amarnath.

Every time a partnership flourished and every time when it appeared that West Indies would sail through, Mohinder put a break into their plan. Bowling slowly, but accurately, Mohinder would hit the deck with the seam hitting the pitch, and the ball from there would swing in like a banana, drawing a curve, or arching like a rainbow, and would catch the Windies on the wrong foot but plumb in front of the wicket. The umpire's finger would go up if there was an appeal and there were plenty in that match whenever Mohiner's ball would struck the Windies pad.

On three different occasions, the little finger of the umpire pointed upwards and when it pointed up for the last time, then Michael Holding was adjusted leg before to Mohinder, India had won the World Cup.

A sojourn of cricket for India, which began on June 26th, 1932 at the Lords, when India played her first test match against England, came to full circle on June 26th 1983, with India winning the world Cup. A Punjabi then, Lala Amar Singh was the bowling hero shattering Bert Suttcliffe and Jack Hobbs Timber then, and now another Panjabi Mohinder Amarnath had done the same to win the World Cup for India.

The team, when it reached home, was given a kind of a reception, which is very difficult to describe. In Kapil's own words: "I have lost the counts of the number of champagne bottles that I had to open after this win, whenever I had to be on the reception party", well the one he had opened with the late Smt. Indira Gandhi at Delhi was his twenty fifth, may be........... said a newspaper columnist then.

Smt. Indira Gandhi had announced a cash prize of Rupees one lakh each to the cricketers but the question was, where would the money come from. One lakh during those days was an extra astronomical figure. A house built on a plot measuring 80' x 50' then, would cost about a lakh of rupees if built in Nagpur during those days. Over and above it the Board did not have the money to pay the cricketers in lakhs. What could be done to save the face and the words of Indiraji and the Board.

In came Lata Mangeshkar. She at the request of Smt. Indira Gandhi, held a show at the Siri Fort Auditorium at New Delhi. The cricketers of the winning squad, and the elite of India would converge in the Auditorium on that day. Tickets were sold like a hot cake and the show pooled in about half a crore of rupees. Rajiv Gandhi presented all the cricketers a lakh of rupees each and Lata Mangeshkar did not charge any fee for her effort. The film world had saved the day.

It was only after Lataji's association with this show that I realized the importance of the film stars, and their association with our cricket administrators; and their after-effect on the game. Raj Singh Dungarpur whole heartedly has to be credited for arranging the show, and bringing in Madam Lata Mangeshkar to save the face of Indian cricket on that penniless day.

A lot of companies thereafter got involved with cricket, a lot of ads and commercial activities got the flood gate opened for them in cricket, money from all walk of life started entering the game and cricketers became, more or less a demi-gods after that. Cricket, since thereafter, became a "thing of glamour, and a joy forever". All that was possible due to a man called Mohinder Amarnath who was till then always the punching bag of the Indian selectors and the linen bag for the administrators.

From Pakistan in 1982-83 to West Indies, Mohinder had amassed over 1100 runs in eleven tests. And then the World Cup thereafter. No doubt, during those days, a movie named "DISCO DANCER" featuring Mithun Chakravorthy had a song in it, Jimmy, Jimmy, Jimmy,

Aaja, Aaja, Aaja. This song became a craze for the youth of those times, after Mohinder "Jimmy" Amarnath had hit the bull's eyes at the World Cup. For "Jimmy" Amarnath had arrived at the Indian cricket scene; once again, to be hired-and-fired by the selectors, at their will and fancies, till 1987 when he was finally told by the selectors "WE NO MORE NEED YOU", to which Mohinder had rechristened them as "BUNCH OF JOKERS NOT TO BE SEEN ON PLAYING CARD".

6

BLOW HOT, BLOW COLD: KOI CHABILI KOI AJNABI

I was sitting at my desk with Mr. P. V. Nayudu, my boss at the "Hitvada", Nagpur and we were chalking out the matters, which were of importance to be placed in the "SPORTS SPECIAL" of the "Hitvada", just on the eve of the Wills Trophy match which was to be played between Hyderabad XI and Bengal XI at the VCA stadium in 1981.

During our talks, I was talking about being highly impressed with the personality of Dilip Doshi then, who was leading Bengal. Dilip, even at that age was an impressive personality. Over it, the way he spoke and presented himself reflected the flavour of Xavierite's of Calcutta.

In fact, the late Subroto Guha and Raju Mukherjee, who were in the same squad, which was to play Hyderabad then, were also from Saint Xaviers. Calcutta University had won the Rohinton Baria Trophy in 1969 and these three Xavierites were instrumental in carving out the win for Calcutta 'varsity. That was the only occasion that Calcutta 'varsity had won this trophy.

We were so impressed with the personality of Dilip Doshi and Raju Mukherjee that we all got engrossed in our conversation that day and we found the other cobbers at the "Hitvada" office, Vijay Phansikar, Alok Tiwari, Subhash Deopujari, Sharad Rotkar were all got engrossed with us in the animated discussions and the soft discussions, about whom was the most handsome looking cricketer, had turned its wavelength to the romances that had taken the Indian cricket by storm.

As far as smartness was considered, the center of discussion revolved around Salim Durrani, Imran Khan, Mansur Ali Khan Pataudi, Abbas Ali Baig and M. L. Jaisimha. These few cricketers had an impressive personality and were handsome by every mean, by every standard. However, it was Vijay Phansikar, who turned the conversation to the "Romance of Indian cricket". Vijay had this habit of turning on the heat, the sensational but a sensual conversation.

No sooner did Vijay turned this topic, it was P. V. Nayudu who started the talks. He spoke about the Commonwealth XI touring India and playing a match at the VCA Stadium, way back in the late fifties. This team had a "thorough-bred" gentleman as a cricketer, and he had left a very lasting impression on the mindset of the people, wherever he played the game. Yes, I'm talking about Sir Frank Worrel. He was here at India, in Nagpur to play a "county" match against a selected team which was representing Commonwealth XI.

The Commonwealth team was lodged at the famous C.P. Cottage and on the eve of the match a dinner was hosted by the members of the club for both the teams. Nagpur during those days, used to be a quiet city with no hubbles – and – bubbles, but this party took the orange city by storm.

The party had just begun, and a lady named Sangeeta Jhangiani had stepped in to the party. She was a beauty queen of India at one point of a time and had settled in Nagpur temporarily, because of her job with Indian Airlines as a flight purser.

Actually, Sangeeta had met Sir Frank Worrel during the flight which brought him to Nagpur for that game, and during the course of the flight, within no time they had become friends. Sangeeta was bowled over by the magnanimous personality that "Sir" Worrel carried, and Worrel was trapped in by the beauty that Sangeeta possessed.

The party got along and started getting old with the time. Somebody had suggested to the guests to dance and Worrel had proposed Sangeeta to accompany him on the dance floor. The others joined them. It was not till the early hours of the morning that Sir Frank Worrel and Sangeeta kept on dancing on the floor.

The next day, when he arrived at VCA stadium for the match, he was fast asleep. He just told the Manager of the team to wake him up when his turn comes to bat. The Manager did the same. And when he came, Worrel had just washed his face, has put on his gears and batted in a manner which might have kept Nagpur awake for at least a week. He scored a fluent flowing 88 in the match. The romance on the floor just did not have any impact on his game. He danced again on the pitch and made the bowlers and the people watching the game dance to his batting prowess. However, along with his batting his association with Sangeeta Jhangiani on the dance floor made news in the world of Indian cricket.

Whether it was a plain friendship that had generated instantly, or whether it was the "Courtesy" extended by Sir Frank Worrel to the lady, for being so attentive to the "Sir" during the course of the flight, this was not the question. The moot answer was Indian cricket at Nagpur had changed the statics of cricket, and the gates were opened for "socializing" in cricket.

For Sir Frank Worrel did never visit India again, neither was Sangeeta to be seen at Nagpur again. A few weeks after this incidence, Sangeeta was to marry an Indian businessman settled at Kenya, and a few years later, Sir Frank Worrel had to leave for his heavenly abode.

However, this friendship and the dance that followed was to take a new turn and open out a new chapter in Indian cricket. It started in 1964 when Mike Smith had brought his team, M. C. C., to India and by that time Mansur Ali Khan and M. L. Jaisimha were the household names in Indian cricket. Both represented Hyderabad and the South Zone.

By this time, a lady by the name of Sharmila Tagore also had made a wave in the Indian Film Industry. Spotted by Mr. Satyajit Ray, at the bus stop at Esplanade, "Rinku", as Sharmila was named and called by her family member, was "hand picked and selected," on the spot by Mr. Satyajit Ray to play the lead role in "Apur Sansar". The film was an instant hit and it brought a wealth of awards for Mr. Satyajit Ray. Sharmila Tagore had come to stay in the films.

The next was Shakti Samant's venture called "An Evening in Paris", where Sharmila, for the first time wore a two-piece bikini, and the photograph of Sharmila donning the two-piece was published on the covers of "Star & Style", "Filmfare" and "Illustrated Weekly of India". The film was a mega hit and so was Sharmila.

In between "Apur Sansar" and "An Evening in Paris", there was "Kashmir Ki Kali", and it is better not to talk about the success of that film. With Mohd. Rafi lending his voice, Shammi Kapoor acting on the lyrics and the songs, and Sharmila lending her silken touch to her acting ability, "Kashmir Ki Kali" and Sharmila had taken the Indian film industry by storms.

It was just after the film was released and the fourth test between India and M. C. C. at Delhi was on the verge of being over, a party was arranged at Delhi. The Indian skipper Mansur Ali Khan Pataudi had made country go berseck by playing a knock of unbeaten 203, that he had, it seems stored for the test.

Well, in the party, Sharmila Tagore and Simi, the two leading Indian Silver screen romantic actresses were invited to be a part of the evening gathering. It was more of a social gathering. The entire Indian team, including M. L. Jaisimha, Salim Durrani, Pataudi, Engineer, B. K. Kundaran and Dilip Sardesai too, were present at the party.

Now the party was in full flow. The two Indian silver screen ladies at the party were present, physically, but not mentally. Simi was all the time gazing and glazing at the Nawab, while Sharmila could not take away her eyes of Jaisimha. Simi always had Pataudi in her heart, while Sharmila always would go ga-ga, gala-gala over Jaisimha. Came a moment thereafter and both Jaisimha and Sharmila were standing opposite to each other. Sharmila was star strucked by Jai's personality and she could not speak or utter even a single word.

To make her comfortable, Jai called in the Nawab and introduced him to Rinku. After that Jai made his way out, and left both the CEO of Indian cricket then, and the Kashmir Ki Kali to be in each other's company. This was the start of a new innings in the life of both the stars.

The conversation started with a general introduction of each other, and it got down to the serious talks of man management, general politics, and about everything except films and cricket. The Nawab was strucked by the knowledge that Sharmila possessed on various subjects. Moreover, unlike the Bengalis, Sharmila avoided talking much about politics and communism, whereas Pataudi was very good at politics. He had studied politics, and he knew a lot about it, but on that occasion it was not the politics. It never was at any other moment thereafter too. This was the first meeting and a round of talks–the first round of talks.

Thereafter, several rounds of meetings followed and the Pataudi-Sharmila friendship story became the center page news of every magazine published in India. And then, as I said earlier, when those photographs of Sharmila depicting the two-piece swim suit she had worn while picturising were published in the "FILMFARE," for October 1967 edition, all hell broke loose in India.

It was at this time that Sharmila really found the bearing, and the BARING, too hard to handle, and she was broken mentally. Right at this time came the Nawab to her rescue. He taught Sharmila how to handle the pressure. The moment had come and gone. This brought Sharmila more closer to the Nawab. In between after that, the Nawab was to present Rinkuji with a refrigerator, which then was considered to be an owner of status symbol commodity, and it washed the Nawab's wallet down by Rs. 3,000 then.

The Begum of Pataudi today can give any amount of a daring statement, after fourty years, that she was not scared or depressed of the fact that she wore that two-piece for that photo session, but the fact is she was heavily depressed after the public had raised their indignation on a national level, because of the magazine, the Filmfare hit the stand with the Kashmir Ki Kali exposing. The Nawab's role then and his support, proved to be the succour to the future Begum.

Immediately after the tour of England in 1967, where the Indian cricket team was whitewashed 3-0 by England, Pataudi went to Paris for a visit and Sharmila was shooting there for a movie. It was in the evening that both had gone to see the "Eiffel Tower" at Paris. There Pataudi proposed her, and Sharmila agreed for the marriage. In true sense, for them it was AN EVENING IN PARIS to remember.

They married, but not before, turning most of them OFF, as the Tagore had to face and put up a stiff resistance. The objection was that Nawab did not have a 9 to 5 job, and the future on the silver screen too is not permanent.

This was a question that came in the mind of the Tagore family. Moreover, Sharmila came from a family where her parents were dependent on the salary of a civil engineer, which her father was. Moreover, the caste and the tradition were different which was a bane then for the society to have digested this marriage. But God had scripted this marriage and the marriage had to take place.

Tagores agreed to everything as Sharmila was adamant, and went ahead with the marriage. Sharmila happens to be the grand-niece of the great Rabindranath Tagore, who had won the Nobel Prize for Literature and was the first Indian to win it. The Nawab was the 'Nawab of Pataudi'. This marriage was the sensation of the late sixties.

The story of the romances in Indian cricket just did not end there. There was more to be added to it. In 1967 when the West Indies were touring India, a dinner party was arranged at the Taj Hotel at Bombay, where West Indies were playing against India. Here a fairy tale was to begin and end.

In the party, a heroine named Anju Mahendru who had made some kind of wave for her roles in films like 'Jewel Thief ', beside her modelling assignment, and the publicity that she drew out of it, met Gary Sobers for the first time. What hit Gary was something not a sharply turning one from Prasanna, nor a deadly bite of a Chandra's delivery, but his shot at Anju Mahendru. One could not imagine, but by the end of the party, Gary had slipped in a diamond ring and his engagement with Anju Mahendru was over, even before the tour got over. So fast was never an over faced by Gary in the matches that he had played, but this one was a faster than the fastest one from Tommo's man. This again was a news that took the Indian cricket world by storm. Sir Gary was hooked.

However, the marriage did not come off. For after leaving India in 1967, Gary was to tour Australia in 1968 along with the West Indies team. There he came across an Australian beauty, whom he married after so many years of courtship, and Anju was left in the lurch. She later got associated with Rajesh Khanna, again to loose him to Dimple Kapadia.

By the middle of the seventies, the association of the film industry with the Indian cricket stars began strengthening, and whenever a foreign team would tour India, a lavish party would be thrown by the film stars, and the cricketers would be the showpiece, the center of attraction.

It was in 1977, just before the tour of Australia that four members of the Pakistan team, Mushtaq Mohammed, Imran Khan, Sarfaraz Nawaz and Sadiq Mohammed had been at Ahmedabad to play a match for the Chief Minister XI team of Gujarat to raise certain money for the flood affected people of Assam and the drought affected people of Gujarat.

In the course of the match, the Pakistan pacer Sarfaraz Nawaz met an Indian heroine, in fact a vamp on the screen, Sheetal and the romance ignited. However the marriage just did not take place although Sheetal had tried her best to marry Sarfaraz.

A Bengali film heroine Chitra would want to go all the places to see John Lever playing in India. The "Vaseline" hero John Lever, had scuffled India out by claiming eleven "wickets" at the Feroze Shah Kotla at New Delhi in 1976. He was to add another five, at the Eden Gardens in the very next test, and here it was that he met Chitra, who was a well known figure in the Tollywood film industry.

Thereafter both met occasionally during the tour, and even after it. John Lever's career did not last long after his tour of India, and so did Chitra's career in Tollywood. Both faded with the time. John Lever did not marry till 1986, but one did not know where Chitra had headed for.

Like John Lever, the Sarika-Sikander Bakht affair also made some headlines before it evaporated off the scene. Sarika was the Bollywood star in her own right and had met Sikander Bakht, the opening bowler of Pakistan when

Pakistan were touring India. Like in all the other cases, they met in a party and the liking...... took place. They were to be seen everywhere when the tour lasted. As soon as the tour was over, everything was over. However, this association drew the attention more for the fact that Sikander Bakht was the leading wicket taker during that series with 26 wickets.

But the one which shook the Indian film industry and the world of Pakistan cricket was the friendship and the association which took place between Imran Khan, one of the most handsome cricketers that had ever played cricket, and the "Satyam" beauty Zeenat Aman.

Zeenat had rocked the film world in 1978-79, by her bare bold scenes in a Raj Kapoor directed "Satyam Shivam Sundaram". And there was Imran, who had knocked the cricket world by the kind of magnanimous personality he possessed, besides knocking the timbers of the best batsmen of the world by his express deliveries. The Australian press had termed him as "God of Machoism" when he was playing in the Kerry Packer series.

This association raised a "hue and cry" in both the countries and there was a feeling that finally Zeenat would renounce the tinsel world by marrying Imran Khan. It never happened as Imran's family did not approve the relationship or the associationship. As it would be, the Pathans would never accept their "bahu" being a film heroine and the association ended then and there. Zeenat was married to Mazhar Khan and from this marriage they had two kids, but the marriage broke off. After sometimes, Zeenat also lost her husband Mazhar, who died an unnatural death.

However, in the eighties, Pakistan again toured India. This was just after the World Cup 1983. The Pakistan team was led by Zaheer Abbas. The team had an opening batsman named Mohsin Hassan Khan. He had met Reena Roy, who between 1975 and 1980, made a desperate attempt to marry Alvin Kalicharan but failed.

This time her efforts bore the fruit. Her meeting with Mohsin Khan culminated in marrying him. However, after this marriage, Mohsin later on lost his place in the Pakistan team. Then Reena brought him to India, and spared no effort to push him and promote him as hero in the Indian films.

Mohsin acted in a few films but could not make it big in the Indian film industry. The marriage also saw Reena delivering her first child "Jannat". But a few years after, Mohsin went back, taking away all the money that he had made in the films in which he had acted in India, as well as his "Jannat", to leave Reena high and dry. Reena to this date remains a lone soul at Bombay.

There were two more fairy tales after this and the first one featured the "Champion of Champions" Ravi Shastri and Amrita Singh. This was just after Ravi had won the Audi Car in Australia. He had met Amrita Singh, a heroine in her own right, during inauguration of a film shoot at Bombay. The association took off fast, only to be broken fast.

For Ravi had married a Punjabi girl Ritu, some years later Amrita was married to Saif Ali Khan, the son of famous Mansur Ali Khan and Sharmila Tagore. Some years after the marriage, 1992 to be precise, Ravi gave up playing cricket to become a commentator, and Amrita totally gave up acting.

The last of the partnership that the tinsel world had with the cricketing world, worth mentioning was the one between Mohd Azharuddin and Sangeeta Bijlani. Azhar was married to Noureen and had two sons from the marriage. Sangeeta to be frank, was a "flop star" and their partnership had to encounter many a storm, before Azhar had to divorce Noureen and marry Sangeeta.

There were so many, and in the days to come, there will be so many stories of the film stars getting associated with the cricket stars. However, the one which really made news was the Nawab-Sharmila episode, and the issues contained in it, it surpassed all expectations and today they are considered to be one of the happiest couple, an example of emulation.

One of the unluckiest episode was the one which surfaced when Sandeep Patil was shooting for "Kabhi Ajnabi thhey". The romance started when Debashree Roy first saw Sandeep on the screen. It blossomed and bloomed till the shoot would stay. Debashree was Sandip's lucky lady in the film.

Once the shooting was over, the association was also over as Sandeep went back to his business of cricket. He was not to be seen in the Indian team after this film as he had lost all his interest for cricket. Debashree Roy had made a serious attempt to keep the association flowing, but gave it up after Sandeep did not seem interested for marriage.

His first marriage had also broken, just before the World Cup 1983, and he did not want to take a calculated risk by getting involved in any kind of a hurry-burry marriage. He was not interested in marriage also then. This was the end of the Sandeep-Debashree Roy and their affair.

Though so many tales have been written on the film stars and their involvement with the cricketers, it was Nagpur, the scenario of the first ever "social associationship" of a beauty with a cricketer.

The "beauty-cricketers" liaison story had started from there and it was something which went ahead in a big way to bring about a change in the face of Indian cricket. The "Nawab-Sharmila" episode has survived, the others went into oblivion. In other words, the "Tiger's Tale" had no ending, the others did not get the kind of a start to persist with and keep the partnership going.

> *From my end, this piece of article in this book, in the chapter 06 is separately, my tribute to the late Mr. P. V. Nayudu and this chapter is dedicated to him. A magnificent journalist that he was! So sorry to state that he and his talent went unnoticed and unrewarded.*

7

SPIN VERSUS PACE: THE FIRE AND THE ICE AT LOGGERHEADS

WELL it all started in 1932 when the Indian cricket team, for the first time in the history of the game, toured England under the captainship of M. M. Natwarshingh of Porbander. He was a Prince of Porbander, Ghanshyamsinghji of Limbdi, another prince was his deputy.

Though the skipper and his deputy were from the family of the royal members, it was C. K. Nayudu who led the India from the front in their first test match against England. The team had late Amar Singh, Mohammed Nissar, Lall Singh, M. Jehangir Khan, the father of the "majestic" Majid Khan of Pakistan and P. Palia. Hello! the scribes covering the games now, it was P. Palia from Uttar Pradesh then, who was the first from that state to play for India, and not Gopal Sharma, for your information. Also Palia hailed from Bombay but played for U.P., as the Nawab of Lucknow was financing him. These were the pacers that India had in the squad. It was for the first time and perhaps the only occasion that India had as many as five pacers in their squad, out of which the duo, Mohd Nissar and Lala Amar Singh were "genuine" quickies.

The first test at Lords was played between June 25th 1932 and June 28th 1932 and the match was a four days affair. It ended with England beating India by 158 runs. The only fifty of the match, a blitzkreig 51, was scored by Lala Amar Singh, batting at number ten in the match for India in the second knock.

It was not for the fifty which Amar Singh had scored that the world started remembering India, and still remembers India. Yes from historic point of view, this was the first half century registered by any Indian in the test match, but it was the way, by which the Indian fast bowling duo of Mohd Nissar and Lala Amar Singh had bowled in that match.

England for all practical purposes had Sir Jack Hobbs and Bert Suttcliffe to open for them. These two Englishmen would any time score a century and putting 150 runs or more on the board were a child play for them. In their career of 15 partnership together they had amassed over 100 runs for the first wicket in the test match and on 7 different occasions, they had put over 150 runs on the board for the first wicket.

It was expected that this pair itself was enough for England to beat India, the other players were not necessary to bat to put India on the wrong foot. But what followed within a span of 5 overs, was a total catastrophe, that the English crowd would see and believe. The first 4 overs from Mohd Nissar and Amar Singh were maidens. But the fifth over saw Mohd Nissar bowling an express delivery which shattered the middle stick of Bert Suttcliffe. One over later, he again produced a lethal delivery which broke the off stick of Sir Jack Hobbs into three pieces and when the score was 19, Amar Singh produced a dream ball, which was pegged outside the off stump, which broke back by a yard and send the stick of Wally Hammand into cart wheeling, with England reeling at 19 for 3.

The world noticed the Indian quickies and the stuff they produced where England tottered hopelessly at 61 for 5 at lunch. As it happened the butter finger and the inexpertise of the Indians as compared to the Englishmen, Amar Singh had dropped a lolly catch of Douglas Jardine, from where the match slipped out of our hand, and finally it saw India caving meekly to England by 158 runs. Mohd Nissar had figure of 26-3-93-5 in the first and 18-5-42-1 in the second, whereas Amar Singh had a figure of 31.1-10-75-2 in the first and 41-13-84-2 in the second.

The last two players too batted in the team, Amar Singh and Nissar had signalled the entry of India in the Test era. If Amar Singh became the first cricketer of India to hit a 51 in the second knock, it was Mohd Nissar, who became the first bowler in the annals of test cricket of India to claim 5 wickets for 93 in a test match.

From 1932, after this test till 1946, just after the World War II, India had played three test series, all against England. The combination of Mohd Nissar and Amar Singh was to haunt England till 1936. Till then India had played 7 test matches and this duo of Nissar and Amar Singh had played together in six of them.

It was in 1946 when once again India took on England at England and for the first time the Indian squad was without the lethal combination of Nissar and Amar Singh. Amar Singh had played in all the seven tests for India till then and his international statistics read as under.

Batting:

M	I	No	Runs	MS	AVE	100/50	C
7	14	1	292	51	22. 55	-/1	3

Bowling:

Balls	Maidens	Runs	Wickets	Average	5wi/10wn
2182	95	858	28	30. 64	2/-

No less impressive was Mohd Nissar in test cricket, his statistics read as under.

Batting:

M	I	No	Runs	MS	Average	100/50	C
6	11	3	55	14	6. 87	-/-	2

Bowling:

Balls	Maidens	Runs	Wkts	Average	5wi/10wn
1211	34	707	25	28. 28	3/-

Well together, in bowling they had this statistics to show:

Name	Balls	Maidens	Runs	Wickets	Average	5wi/10wn
C. Amar Singh	2182	95	858	28	30.64	2/-
Mohd Nissar	1211	34	707	25	28.28	3/-
Total	3393	129	1565	53	29.43	5/-

Till the end of 1936, when these two pacers operated in tandem, Indian test bowlers had claimed 88 English wickets of which the pace duo of Amar Singh and Mohd Nissar had claimed 53 at an average of 29.43, the percentage of success being almost 64%.

It was for the first time in 1946 that India were without the services of these two great bowlers. Just after the World War, Amar Singh died a premature death at the age of 29, whereas Mohd Nissar had given up playing cricket. He settled in Pakistan where he breathed his last.

The 1946 test squad had a real genuine pacer in Shute Banerjee. But he had only Lala Amarnath to help him for bowling the quickies. There were others like Vinoo Mankad, Chandu Sarwate, Golam Mohammed, C. S. Nayudu and S. G. Shinde, the father-in-law of the present President of BCCI, Mr Sharad Pawar, were all spinners. The three test match series ended with a 2-0 win for England. The astonishing factor was that Shute Banerjee who was considered one of the fastest bowlers during that time, was never given a chance to play for India. From 1932 to 1946, till the beginning of this series, India was a pace dominated bowling attack, but this series saw the ultimate firn of spin domination and from here onwards pace was to die in Indian cricket.

It takes 9 months for a lady to deliver, it took 14 years for India to deliver the spinners, and it takes at least 50 years, on an average for a human being to die, it only took 10 years from 1936 to 1946, for the pace to die in the annals of Indian cricket then.

The man who brought in the transformation was none other than Vinoo Mulwantrai Himmatrai Mankad, whom the world came to know as Vinoo Mankad. He started it and Chandu Sarwate, Gulam Ahmed, Subas Gupte, Salim Durrani, C. G. Borde, Erapalli Prasanna, V. V. Kumar, Srinivasan Venkatraghwan, Dilip Doshi, B. S. Bedi, B. S. Chandrashekar, Narendra Hirwani, Arshad Ayub, Ravi Shastri and of late Anil Kumble and Harbhajan Singh are keeping the tradition alive.

As for the pace, Indian had nothing to show except Shute Banerjee. He bowled and bowled his heart out. And since he loved fast bowling, he bowled fast, yet he was given only one test to play. He played, and he bowled as best as he could claming 5 wickets in the test match against West Indies in 1948 at his favourite Eden Gardens at Calcutta. But since he had claimed five wickets in the match, surcastingly it seems, he was packed out for ever and with it ended the history of fast bowling for India. This was in the 1948-49 series against West Indies at India. There were fast bowlers in that team who bowled as badly as compared to Shute Banerjee, but the selectors made Banerjee to lick the dust.

The West Indies team had four pacers playing for them against India. And believe me, they were all praise for the performance put up by Shute Banerjee in this test. But no sooner he was dropped, Everton Week was heard saying that he had scored four consecutive test tons at India, and by the time the series ends, he would have scored another 4 double tons consecutively.

Indian pace and its depth gave rise to the spinners. Vinoo Mankad was already there in the scene and assisting him was Chandu Sarwate, but between the period 1947-48, when India toured Australia for the first time, came Amir Elahi, Vijay Hazare and Gulam Ahmed. Vijay Hazare for the reason best known to the Indian think-tank then all of a sudden transformed into quickie. None of them except Mankad were the first class rated spinners. Everybody rolled his arm over to bowl "mediocre" spinners, however by that time a genuine medium pacer Dattaji Phadkar had arrived. Lala Amarnath was to assist him from the other end.

However, the problem with Lala was, he could not fulfil the potential that he possessed and he always kept himself surrounded in controversies, being in and out of the Indian team. From 1932-33 when Lala Amarnath first played for India, to 1951-52, when he played his last match for India against Pakistan, Lala had played or represented India in only 24 test matches. His figures would read as follow:

Batting:

M	I	No	RUNS	MS	100	50	Ave	Ct
24	40	4	878	118	1	4	24.38	13

Bowling:

O	W	5WI	10WM	Av
1481	45	2	-	32.91

In a nutshell Lala had played only 24 test matches in the two decades that he served Indian cricket. If one takes out the 4 years of war during the World War II, Lala had only 16 years of cricket to score 878 runs and claim 45 wickets. This truly disappoints everybody when one talks about Lala in terms of the treasure of cricket that was hidden in him, and the output that he could produce in terms of the fame for India.

Anyway, it became Dattaji Phadkar from 1947-48 to 1957-58, for a decade to spearhead the Indian pace attack. Phadkar was the heart of Indian pace in this period. However, he was left alone to handle the vagaries of quick bowling, as he did not have adequate support from the other end. Yet he did not give up.

His story of cricket is divided into two phases and it was all about his fast bowling. The first phase was between 1947 and 1954. Oh ! what a memory of Phadkar one would have, and the second phase was between 1955 and 1958. Oh! what a pity it was. Aided to his effort was his batting which made everybody feel that after Amar Singh, Phadkar was a real "fast" all-rounder that India has ever had in test cricket. This statistic would make an interesting reading.

Batting:

M	I	No	Runs	MS	Ave	100/50	C
31	45	7	1229	123	32.34	2/8	21

Bowling:

Balls	Maidens	Runs	Wkts	Ave	5wi/10wm
5975	275	2285	62	36.85	3/-

However, during this period, between 1946 and 1958, as said earlier there were Vinoo Mankad, Gulam Ahmed, Subhash Gupte, Chandu Sarwate, and the bulk of the bowling were done by them.

It was after Vinoo's break in Indian cricket that the selectors felt that time was over to encourage fast bowling. Vinoo made the Indians think and feel that if India had to win a test series, it should encourage the "tweakers" rather than the "seamers". This led to a revolution. The Board saw that since 1932 when India made the test baptism to 1951, almost two decades had passed by and India did not taste a "test" victory.

No nation till then, playing cricket, and till now, ever at this time, had gone in, for two decades, without a win at the test. This made the cricket administrators feel that it was high time that India encouraged the spinners and changed the "complex" of the pitches laid in India, so that it spun more and more as the game progressed.

The series of 1951-52 followed and Ted Dexter was to bring an M. C. C. team to India. This team played 5 test matches at New Delhi, Bombay, Calcutta, Kanpur and at Madras, and last two tests produced result. The first three ended without any result.

The leather city of Kanpur, where the fourth test was played saw the great Vijay Hazare bagging a "pair" for the first time in his career in test cricket. Having conceded a lead of 82 runs in the first innings, India were bundled out for 157 runs in the second innings.

The situation could have been even worst, had not Hemu Adhikari scored a fighting 60. This knock of 60 gave some respectability to the Indian innings, but it was England which ultimately went up to rattle the 73 required for victory losing only two wickets. In this match it was the deadly duo of the off-spinners Gulam Ahmed with figure of 5 for 70 and Vinoo Mankad with 4 for 74 which brought India back to the usual self, for taking the fight to the English camp, but as batting collapsed and as described earlier, the cheap dismissal of Vijay Hazare, who had bagged a "pair", took the game out of Indian clutch.

The last test was played at Madras on a turning track. The pitch was tailor made for spin and the duo of Gulam Ahmed and Vinoo Mankad with their tantalising spin and tormenting turn took the wind out of the English sail. Mankad had a figure of 38.5–15-55-8 in the first and 30.4-9-53-4 in the second, whereas Gulam Ahmed had 18-5-53-0 in the first and 26-5-77-4 in the second.

In this match, which was the first victory tasted by India, saw Pankaj Roy score 111 and Polly Umrigar score an unbeaten 130. A quick fire 61 came from Duttaji Phadkar, C. D. Gopinath and Lala Amarnath scored 35 and 31 respectively.

To come back to the game, as described earlier "this was the first test match won by India" and that too just immediately after the new year. There were 20 English wickets that had tumbled. The team had played with seamers, Duttaji Phadkar, Ramesh Divecha and Lala Amarnath. The combined efforts of our seamers were.

Name	O	M	R	W	O	M	R	W
Dattaji Phadkar	16	2	49	1	9	2	17	1
R. V. Divecha	12	2	27	0	7	1	21	1
L. Amarnath	27	6	56	0	3	0	6	0
Total	55	10	132	1	19	3	44	2

As compared thus read the figures of the three spinners Vinoo Mankad, Gulam Ahmed and Vijay Hazare

Name	O	M	R	W	O	M	R	W
Gulam Ahmed	18	5	53	0	26	5	77	4
Vinoo Mankad	38.5	15	55	8	30.4	9	53	4
Vijay Hazare	10	5	15	1	-	-	—	-
Total	66. 5	25	123	9	56.4	14	130	8

The figures and the statistics tell their own tale. In the first innings, V. S. Hazare the skipper used the spinners and the pacers in equal measures. Both the departments also conceded the runs in equal measure. However, the spinners claimed 9 wickets whereas the lone wicket went to Phadkar.

What was amazing was the confidence that Hazare had in Lala Amarnath. He gave him 27 overs to operate, just 10 less than Vinoo Mankad. And Lala had nothing to show for his effort, whereas Mankad had 8. It was here that Lala as a fast bowler, as the Indians would like to call it, was finished. Gone were his old sparks, gone were the chinks in his armour. If Lala was playing in the team, it was merely of his and for his cricketing brain and experience. Moreover, the control he commanded on the administration. His voice then in the cricket fraternity was termed as the Voice of Death. His orders were final and people would tremble when he took the situation under his arm.

It was not the Lala who would turn his finger over the seam to bowl his off cutters which would rattle the batsman's wicket. Lala as a bowler in this series was "dead". Not only that, in Kanpur, where India had lost the match he was not in the side. India were trailing 0-1 at the start of the Madras test and Lala was called to bolster the Indian pace attack. None other than the captain Vijay Hazare, requested the selectors and forced them to include Lala for the test at Madras.

So much so that Hazare pinned all his faith on him and gave Lala a total of 27 overs to bowl. But he disappointed everybody. Sensing that Lala had lost the magic of his arm to produce those deadly cutters Hazare fell back to Dattaji Phadkar, and the spin duo of Mankad-Ahmad which won the match for India.

Lala's vicious pace as a medium pacer had died with this victory and once again a "legion" of fast bowling died in India. It was here that the selectors took account of Lala's bowling figure in the series. It reads as

Name	O	M	R	W	5WI	10Wm	Ave
Lala Amarnath	111.5	26	207	3	-	-	69.00

Every wicket that Lala took cost him 69 runs. It was here that the pace revolution had gone. The Indian selectors really at this time felt and thought that Nissar and Amar Singh were the history. Shute Banerjee was a one match wonder, and Lala's deed of bowling was good only to be scripted in the pages of history. In other words, the cricket administrators did not see anything good for the quickies and plunged their thoughts and their actions on the tweakers.

Because of this, in 1952, immediately after this series, Lala was not selected for the tour of England. However, in the winter when Pakistan came here in 1952, for their first ever tour, the selectors fell back to Lala. He was 41 in age.

Lala by then had sharpened his reflexes, and his bowling skill at the nets in Burlton Park. He really wanted to show that he was not over, as a cricketer. Also basically hailing from Pakistan, and having settled in India after the partition he had a burning ambition to play for India against Pakistan.

India was beaten 3-0 by England under the leadership of V. S. Hazare, and when the team came back, Hazare was removed as the captain. Lala Amarnath was made skipper. The selectors did it finally to make full use of the administrative skill of Amarnath, to nullify Abdul Hafeez Kardar who was a stubborn autocrat.

It was for the last time that the world saw Amarnath that he was a fox in terms of leading a side. Amarnath won the rubber against a young, but raw and inexperienced Pakistan by 2-1. His captainship and once for a change, his "slow" cutters were vicious. His style of changing the bowling, and his shots, some orthodox, others wild, fetched him a couple of fifties, which helped India to win the rubber. But by that time, he was nearing 42 and that was the end of Lala. For the first time Lala felt the heat of the "Summer of 42", and for it, he anticipated his end, for he was not to play anymore for India. And with it ended a story, "a paradoxical history", about the fast bowling of India.

The spinners Gulam Ahmed and Vinoo Mankad, continued in the same fashion, and although Dattaji Phadkar was holding the "fort" for the pacers, he was left all alone. His partners, Gulab Ramchand, Polly Umrigar and Ramesh Divecha were only good in patches.

They were good abroad, because of the hard and bouncy pitches that they got to play. In India, the slow "turners" made these set of pacers, ineffective and useless.

Dattaji too could continue, at his fiery best till 1954. But from 1954, he started declining and he reached his nadir between the periods 1955 and 1957. He hit the rock bottom in 1958 against the series of West Indies at home.

He was included for the third test match which was played at Calcutta. And this was his "waterloo". Given to bowl 43 overs, he conceded 173 runs without a wicket and though he scored a fighting 35 in the second knock, he was "out" forever from the international cricket. Dattaji Phadkar career would read as

Batting:

M	I	No	Runs	HS	Average	100/50	Catch
31	45	7	1229	123	32.34	2/8	21

Bowling:

Balls	Maidens	Runs	Wicket	Average	5WI/10Wn
5975	275	22.85	62	36.85	3/-

The spinners on the other hand continued making waves. Vinoo Mankad and Gulam Ahmed were there to roll their arms over. In India, where the pitches were slow and "turners", they would spin a "web" around the batsman. However, at abroad, they did not disappoint, but were as less effective as their show in India. Agreed, they did not get those "turners" abroad, yet majority of the wickets which fell abroad were claimed by the spinners.

If the spinners were ruling the roost, the selectors it seems were raising the toast, at the "slow and unnatural" death of quickies, there emerged a spinner, a leg spinner who was born in test cricket in 1953. Yes, I'm referring to Subhash Gupte.

He was such a great cricketer, a great spinner, that, if at all a world team was selected by anybody, between the period 1953 and 1958, he would have "walked" into anybody's list, who would prepare the World team. To me individually, he has been the best spinner that was ever born to the international cricket.

And this too, in the face of the competition as that from our own Vinoo, and that from Lock, Tayfield, Benaud, Ramadhin and Valentine.

As said, with the inclusion of Gupte in the squad of India in 1953, it was for the first time that India had a "spin triangle" or the trio of spinners. Subhash Gupte was a class right arm orthodox leg spinner, Gulam Ahmed was a world class off-spinner, right arm of course, and Vinoo Mankad was a left arm world class tweak bowler.

From 1953 to 1959, when this trio was separated and broken, India had played 23 test matches, of which India had won 2, lost 4 and had drawn remaining of the test. As said earlier the bulk of the wickets, say about 90% of them, were claimed by the trio while the pacers hardly accounted for 10%, even not, because some of the batsmen of the opponent team got themselves run out.

The trio was broken during 1959, when for all practical purposes, Gulam Ahmed announced his retirement from all the form of cricket. A world class of spinner, that he was, he was touted as the best of spinner that India has ever produced till then. His international records read as:

Batting:

M	I	No	R	HS	100	F	Catches	Ave
22	31	9	192	50	0	1	11	8.72

Bowling:

Runs	Wkts	5WI	10Wn	Ave
2052	68	4	1	30. 17

So was the case with Gupte. One could not visualize a team before him, and it was practically impossible to form a Indian "test" team without him. From the first test at Port of Spain in January 1953 to the final test at the Oval in 1959, he had a run of 28 test matches. He just did not miss any of the test matches that India played till then.

Now, if this sequence was broken, it was not because of any injury, or any illness. It was because he went for a coaching assignment to "earn" some extra money in cricket, at West Indies in 1959. He came back to India in 1960, to represent India against Pakistan and England.

To describe Subhash Gupte, is to describe, what amount of hot gas could be present in the "sun", and to describe his deliveries... well it would be a futile exercise for a chum like me. Like Vinoo Mankad, in the earlier period, and a decade later, the smiling assassinator, Erapalli Prasanna, made the batsman look like a clown in a circus. To spot his googly was to find a black cat, in a dark pitched black dark room. As it would be to a student of management, to describe the differences between "sales" and "marketing, " to differentiate between Gupte's leg spin, "and a googly", was the most difficult "exam", for a batsman facing him.

Vinoo Mankad however continued playing for India. He played till the end of the 1963 season, and from 1959, when he lost his able partner Gulam Ahmed and later Subhash Gupte, was accompanied by Chandu Borde. But during the home series, against West Indies in 1958-59, Mankad was finally "Mankaded", by the selectors. His days with cricket had come to an end. He was asked to lead India, in the ill-fated Madras test against the West Indies during 1958-59, when he was told about the captainship, only 10 minutes before the match. And in the final test at Delhi, he had the mortification of conceding 167 runs in 55 overs without taking a wicket.

As said earlier, he continued playing cricket till 1963 in the Ranji Trophy, as a "professional", with Salim Durrani for Rajasthan. He died in 1978, when he was 62 years of age.

Mankad – Lords 1952 – 72 and 184 and 73-24-196-5 as well as 42-12-35-0, a perfect salute to the most perfect cricketer that India had ever produced, for whatever Mankad gave it to the Indian cricket in the test matches.

Actually it was during this period, Gulam Ahmad calling it a day after the English tour of 1959, Gupte going to West Indies to seek a greener pasture, and Vinoo Mankad bidding goodbye to the game of cricket, that saw a great "void" being created in the spin department of Indian cricket.

I shall be grossly doing injustice to myself, and to the entire universe, if I do not put Mankad in figures. His record reads as under.

Batting:

M	I	No	Runs	HS	Ave	100/50	Cat
44	72	05	2109	231	31-47	5/6	33

Bowling :	Balls	Maidens	Runs	Wickets	Ave	5Wi/10wi
	14686	777	5235	162	32.331	8/2

God would'nt have spared me if I did not put Mankad's record on paper, and that's why I did. Till 1959 when he retired from the game, he had two double centuries, and two different spells of 8 wickets in an innings, which later on was broken by Kapil Dev, as Kapil had four different spell of 8 wickets in a single innings.

He was also the fastest cricketer to score a double of 1000 runs and 100 wickets. He achieved this distinction in his 22nd test against Pakistan. This in fact is a record still unbroken in the annals of Indian cricket.

As described earlier, the place left behind by the exit of those three musketeers had created a "void" in Indian cricket. Indian cricket, a year before that had also lost Dattaji Phadkar, retiring from the test cricket with four cricketers of that tremendous quality gone, the backbone of Indian cricket was broken. It needed young guys, specially the bowlers to emerge. A second generation of pacers and tweakers was the need of the hour for Indian cricket.

It was this time that three quickies again, and three spinners took "birth" in Indian cricket. The quickies were Ramakant Desai, R. Surendranath and Vasant Ranjane, on the parallel line, the tweakers were Chandu Borde, Salim Durrani and R. G. Nadkarni affectionately termed as "Bapu" of Indian cricket. Salim Durrani was a cricketer of a different breed altogether, and Vinoo Mankad had spotted his talent and groomed him initially. Salim Durrani completely aped Mankad in his bowling.

When something fresh and a good change takes place in the surrounding, it always becomes the necessity to take care that the good things remain static and survive. It was to the credit and the good luck of both, Ramakant "tiny" Desai, and Surendranath, that they did not get "baptized" at India. For they were lucky that they made their respective debut at England in 1959, where they not only found a favourable English condition to help them, but a "true" solid, hard and bouncy pitch to exhibit their valour. Both of them were successful. Surendranath on this tour had emerged very successful with two haul of 5 wickets each in an innings in the series. So was Ramakant Desai who had one haul of 5 wickets in an innings. The individual effort by these two bowlers at the end of series read as:

Name	O	M	R	W	5Wi/10wm	Ave
Ramakant Desai	189.4	40	602	12	1 -	50.16
R. Surendranath	203.4	75	426	16	2 -	20.66
Total	393.2	115	1028	28	3-	36.71

Out of the 58 English wickets that fell, 28 were claimed by these two medium pacers, whereas the three spinners, Subhash Gupte, Bapu Nadkarni and Chandu Borde, between themselves had clamied 30 wickets. So almost 48.27% of the wickets were claimed by the pacers. However Desai looked very exhausted and unimpressive because of the umpteen number of catches dropped of his bowling.

Compare this with the performance of the Mohd. Nissar and Amarsingh. They had, in between them in 7 test matches, accounted for 53 wickets for a percentage of 64% and now we had a pair of bowlers who on their first tour of England had claimed about 48% of the wickets which fell at England.

After the combination of Mohd. Nissar and Amar Singh this was for the first time that a pair of young fast bowlers had set their feet on the "test" cricket in India. The third seamer, Vasant Ranjane, who was making a wave in the Indian cricket scene was playing in the Ranji Trophy matches for Maharashtra, thus honing his skills on the dead and flat turning pitches at India. V. M. Muddiah, the third seamer, who was in the squad of England in 1959, and the only Coorgi to make it to the Indian team then, has not played in England.

However, this series was a major disappointment for India, as they were blanked 5-0 by England. The English pace trio of Brian Statham, Freddie Trueman, and Alec Bedser carried too many guns and ammunition for India. For most of the time, the Indian batsmen had no answer to the swings and cuts of the English bowlers. Also some of the deliveries bowled by the English paceman Freddie Trueman were out of the world, really unplayable.

The only redeeming feature of this series was a classical 118 by Polly Umrigar at the fourth test at Manchester, besides a century on debut by Abbas Ali Baig. He was a student at the Oxford University and was summoned to play for the country on an emergency call by the team management.

When the team reached home after the tour, its Manager submitted a report about the necessity of exposing the Indian batsmen in the test matches, to the pace bowling. The report contained certain contents where it was described that the Indian batsmen at some stage did not want to face Freddie Trueman at all. The report lavishly praised the effort and the deeds of R. Surendranath and Ramakant Desai and mentioned that if India was to do better, it had to encourage the pacers.

The suggestion also included the change of the "face" of the pitches laid down for the domestic matches. Green top and lively pitches were the need of the hour. The report also suggested that at abroad, India was never going to have the "sleeping beauties", or the slow turners, but the fast, hostile, and the bumpy tracks. Hence, it was necessary for India to have an overhauling and revamping the pitches at home, so that the batsmen equip themselves for a better technique to face the pacers abroad.

A good suggestion it was, and for the first time, the Board invited five fast bowlers, four from West Indies and one from England to play in the Duleep Trophy matches. Every zone got a bowler each to play for them, and East Zone had the services of Roy Gilchrist to serve them.

However, all the four "imported" pacers were not happy with the condition laid for them to bowl at their "fiery" red hot pace. Bowling pace requires a lot of green grass on the wicket, beside a proper rolling of the pitch and watering it. The grass on the wicket has to be taken care of. Proper watering, and "cutting" of the blades too requires expertise, and this was not done properly. The result was, after a season, Roy Gilchrist, who was a fearsome fast bowler of West Indies, lost his interest to play in India, and he never came back after it. The others too, followed his suit, and went back slowly.

This was the first occasion in the annals of Indian cricket that a "demand" for promoting pace was generated. It happened after Desai and Surendranath were to wake up the Indian selectors about the growing necessity and grooming of the pacers, after their stupendous show at England. It was also the first time that the five pacers, like a business, were invited, but were not royally treated, to stay here for ever.

Every demand meets its end because the want ceases, and the law of diminishing returns, too, holds good. The demand of the pacers too met the same fate. By the mid of 1961, it ended as the "import" pacers were never to come back to India.

By then, in Indian cricket, Chandu Borde and Salim Durrani had started cracking the wickets, and hitting the headlines by their slow armours. With them came in

Erapalli Prasanna and B. S. Chandrashekar from "Mysore". By the start of the season, in 1961 these two Mysorean had served their notice to the cricketing fraternity of this country and to the Indian selectors that the wizard of the spin was to conquer this game in India.

Came the Pakistan tour of 1960-61, India showed that the responsibility of her pace bowling, was to be equally expedited through Desai, Surendranth, Muddiah and Rusi Surti. The spin was to be taken care of by Subhash Gupte, Chandu Borde, and Bapu Nadkarni. The series ended without any result. Personal ego of both the captains, coupled with the national prestige involved, saw both the teams playing safe, though India was at times taking the chances through their skipper Nari Contractor

The series of 1961-62 against M. C. C. again changed the course of history for cricket in India. Ted Dexter, whose England annihilated and humiliated India by 5-0 in 1959, had to lick the dust this time.

A "protege" of Vinoo Mankad, named Salim Durrani, and his able partner Chandu Borde, were to sweep England of the floor and of the toes. Both of them were to score 316 and 189 in the test series. But it was their bowling where Durrani's 23 wickets, ably supported by Chandu Borde who claimed 16 wickets haul, were instrumental in helping India to chalk out a 2-0 series win for India. It was in this series that Nawab of Pataudi made his test debut at Calcutta, scoring a fluent 64, and immediately in the next at Madras he scored his maiden test hundred. It was here in Calcutta that Sharmila Tagore, witnessed a "test" cricket, first in her life along with Satyajit Ray, and four years later, Nawab and Sharmila were to tie the "knot". How quickly does the "MAUSAM" change in cricket, is it not.

Also important it was that in the Madras test, in this series, Erapalli Prasanna had made his debut. He did not get to bowl much in the match as the Indian skipper Nari Contractor, used Salim Durrani and Chandu Borde in a "sweeping" manner to reflect blow-after-blow to the English men. But Prasanna in the limited spell that he got to bowl and within that "limitation factor", claimed his maiden test wicket and gave a notice about his flawless talent as an off-spinner who could be a wizard in the making.

However the importance of series lay in the fact that THIS WAS THE FIRST SERIES WON BY INDIA AND HERE AGAIN OUT OF 71 ENGLISH WICKETS THAT FELL 49 WERE CLAIMED BY THE TWEAKERS AND THE REMAINING BY THE QUICKIES.

The percentage of success for the quickies was confined to 31, but the two pacers, Vasant Ranjane and Ramakant Desai spared no effort to provide the important breakthrough, whenever it was needed. By this time Surendranath, who had played only 11 tests, was considered too old and weak to play for India by the selectors and he was discarded. He was a bowler, who could have gone a long way to serve India purposefully, but after this series, his services were done away. His test career reads as follow:

Batting:

M	I	No	RUNS	HS	100	F	Ave	Ct
11	20	7	136	27	0	0	10.46	4

Bowling:

Runs	Wkts	5 Wi	10Wm	Ave
1053	26	2	-	40.50

However, it was the credit of Surendranath, and his bowling in the series in England in 1959 that the world of cricket realized that India too can create terror and havoc with their fast bowling. After the duo of Amar Singh and Mohd. Nissar, the world of cricket had imagined that "pace" in India had died for ever, but this cricketer Surendranath proved that it was not . He actually in plain words "gave the birth of pace in India", after Independence.

SALUTE TO THIS PACER, WHO WAS KILLED BY THE INDIAN SELECTORS.

Making his debut against England, in 1959, Surendranath's career came to an end by the mid of 1961. His place was taken by Vasant Ranjane from Maharashtra.

The maiden test series win against England in 1960-61, and the role of the spinners, especially the magic of Salim Durrani, once again casted the belief of the selectors on the spinners and it was once again felt that India cannot do anything of noteworthy without spin. So spin it was once again and between the period 1962 and 1964, there were three spinners, Srinivas Venkatraghvan, B. S. Chandrashekar and B. S. Bedi who had emerged on the Indian cricket scene.

Since Chandu Borde and Salim Durrani were a permanent feature in the Indian team, the "trio" of Bedi, Chandra and Venkat had to wait for a bit long, till they got their chances. Of the three Bishan Bedi had to wait for a bit long, till 1967, before being rechristened and baptized in "test" against West Indies in 1967.

Between 1962 and 1964, the Indian pace attack was in the hands of Ramakant Desai and Vasant Ranjane. Ranjane looked and appeared too thin and fragile in health, but he was the first "pocket dynamo" as termed by the late Sir Frank Worrel, during the Indian tour of 1962 at West Indies. He had a fang but not so much of pace.

After this tour, Erapalli Prasanna had to leave cricket to pursue his studies in Engineering at Mysore. Actually Prasanna was a second year engineering undergraduate when he took the tour of West Indies in 1962. On returning back, he lost his father. He pursued his studies in Engineering till 1967, when he completed his Masters of Engineering from the National Institute of Engineer, at Mysore.

Prasanna's exit made the way for B. S. Chandrashekar, to make his debut against England in 1964. By that time Vasant Ranjane, the "pocket dynamo" was considered weak, and fragile by the Indian selectors and after the series against England, Vasant Ranjane was told to look for some other job as a "career" to mend for himself. Vasant Ranjane cricket career reads as follow.

Batting

M	I	No	R	HS	100	50's	Ct	Ave
7	9	3	40	16	0	0	1	6. 67

Bowling

Runs	W	5WI	10Wn	Ave
649	19	-	-	34. 15

In fact Vasant Ranjane was good and could have continued to play till 1967, when India toured England. But the growth of spin, like mushroom in India, made the pacer to eat the humble pie. Nobody cared for pace though India needed them badly.

It was to the credit of "tiny" Desai, that in spite of so many adversaries and tough opposition, he continued to survive as a pacer. The tour of West Indies in 1967, asserted Bedi's place in the side, as he made his test debut. Moreover, after finishing his studies and earning his Master Degree in Engineering, Prasanna too came back to the Indian cricketing scenario.

In the matches against West Indies, when South Zone were playing against the West Indies, Erapalli Prasanna, in a spell of flowing and flighted deliveries, produced a spell of 8 for 76 that nearly brought the defeat of the West Indies, and Prasanna to the test fold. Till then, the off-spin department in Indian cricket was held by another engineer, who had passed his engineering from the Guindy Engineering College, Madras, named Srinivas Venkatraghvan.

There emerged a "sensation" in the bowling, especially the pace bowling department. A pacer, good in bowling the cutters and swing, but growing in age, known as "football wonder" in India, under whose captainship, did India win an "Asiad Football Gold" in Djakarta in 1962, known as Chuni Goswami, cut through the Sober's West Indies in 1967, in a match at Indore where the Windies were playing against a combined Central-East team on a matting wicket. The team led by Hanumant Singh cut the West Indies and Gary Sobers into size by bowling them out within 175 runs in both the innings. Subroto Guha had a dream spell of 7 for 27 in that innings. In all he had a match spell of 11 wickets for 114 runs. Goswami had a 25 and 8 scalps for 97 runs to show for his effort. Guha had made it to England for this effort.

Chuni Goswami, on the basis of his performance just about made it to the team, but lost out to Bishen Singh Bedi, as the selectors needed a spinner to persist with.

> *Had Chuni Goswami made it, he would have been the second sportsman, in the world, after Dennis Compton to have represented both the football and cricket teams for his country.*

With the series of West Indies in India in 1966-1967, ending with West Indies chalking a 2-0 victory over India, the situation became too piquant for India to open its attack.

There were times thereafter, when Ajit Wadekar had to open the attack with Budhi Kundaran, despite the fact that Subroto Guha had been there always in the side, warming the bench.

From 1967 to 1968-69, India had toured England, Australia and New Zealand, and there were some "comics" performed by the Indian selectors. Considering Ramakant Desai, as a factor "constant" for pace bowling, the Indian selectors kept on changing the "other pacer" of the side; and the axe kept on falling on Subroto Guha.

From nowhere in 1968, Umesh Kulkarni was pitched for the twin tours of Australia and New Zealand, only to fizzle out. Thereafter that tour, where did Umesh Kulkarni go, well nobody knows. Also the tours of Australia and New

Zealand saw the end of Ramakant Desai. He had the distinction of being a "quickie" by the Indian standard, and having the distinction to represent India for nearly a decade as a pacer after Phadkar.

He was the first "quickie" to survive for nearly a decade in a country, where pacers were considered to be a third class bogie.

It is to Desai's credit that he went about his task less selfishly and willingly, always desiring to get wickets for India. His chances had come and he grabbed them. Now it was his turn to go. His record reads as follow.

Batting:

M	I	No	Runs	HS	100	F	Chs	Ave
28	44	13	418	85	0	1	9	13.48

Bowling:

Runs	W	5Wi	10wm	Ave	B.B
2763	74	2	0	37.34	6 for 56 vs N. Z

Desai also had a tryst with destiny for his batting against Pakistan. In the 1960-61 series against Pakistan at Bombay, in the first test, he added 149 runs for the ninth wicket, which if memory serves me well, is in fact a record for India. It was sad to see Ramakant Desai bidding his farewell from Indian cricket.

From that moment, when Desai had left cricket, an analysis was made about the contribution which the trio of Surendranath, Desai and Ranjane had contributed to Indian cricket bowling and it reads as

Name	Runs	I	Wkt	5Wi	10wm	Ave
Surendranath	1053	11	26	2	-	40. 50
Ranjane	649	7	19	-	-	34. 15
Desai	2763	28	74	2	-	37. 34
Total	4465	46	119	4	-	37. 52

From it, one gets to learn that the trio had played 7 tests more than Karsan Ghavri, who played 39, and had claimed 10 wickets more than Ghavri, who had claimed 109. It was the condition in which the three seamers bowled in India. They played not to run through the batting, but to "fill in the blanks" about the position, in the Indian team, and to just remove the sheen of the ball to make the way for the other spinners.

Yet, whenever they got a chance, they grabbed it with both the hands, or bowled their heart out to "break" through. The figures could have been better, but for the "quality" of deteriorating fielding that "ruled the waves" in test cricket in India then. So many catches in the slips would go abegging. Specially Ranjane had to suffer the most. In the 1962 series against West Indies, as many as nine catches of his bowling were dropped in the slip region, in the only match which he played at Jamaica. Yet he had the figures of 19-2-72-4 in the first and 28-3-81-2 in the second of the 19 wickets he claimed in his career, 6 came in this match, but he was not to play for more than six "test" matches afterwards in his career.

The exit of Ramakant Desai in 1968, after the twin tour of Australia, saw a "void" being created in the Indian team. Rusi Surti, the other pacer, an all rounder of course, was to make Australia his permanent home and Budhi Kunderan, who was basically a wicket keeper but who had opened the bowling for India, had decided to settle down at Scotland for a green pasture.

The red cherry was to be shared by Abid Ali, along with Solkar, sometime with Ajit Wadekar. The purpose was to remove the sheen of the ball and hand it over to the spinners to do the rest.

With Abid, the others to share the new ball were Subroto Guha, Eknath Solkar and Mohinder Amarnath, but except Solkar, nobody stayed and nobody could maintain their place permanently in the Indian squad. The result was, India could not find a real opening combination to open their attack.

However, between 1973 and 1975, there was a complete change in the scenario. To "neutralize" the four spinners, the domestic cricket threw four pacers, Pandurang Salgaocar, Karsan Ghavri, Madanlal Sharma and Kapil Dev Nikhanj. Kapil was only 14 years of age when he first made his mark in the Cooch-Behar Trophy and two years later, when 16, he hit the headlines, again in the same tournament, claiming first hattrick of his career.

Kapil in fact has a record in cricket, which no cricketer in the world would have it in the future, or has it of late, to boast about it.

He is the only medium pacer of India, and in the world to have claimed hattrick in school cricket, Cooch-Behar Trophy in 1975, in Rohinton Baria Trophy, for Kurukshetra University in 1977, in Moin-ud-Dowlah Trophy, in a first class game for Mohan Meaknis in 1977, for North Zone in Duleep Trophy in 1978 and for India against Sri Lanka in Asia Cup, in 1990, in an one-day international match.

However, it took three years for Kapil to cement his place in the side in 1978. Till then, from 1972 to 1977 till the end of the India test series against Australia, it was Abid-Solkar, Solkar-Gavaskar, Solkar-Wadekar, Abid-Madanlal, Madanlal-Solkar, Ghavri-Madanlal, Ghavri-Gavaskar, Madanlal-Mohinder Amarnath, and all sort of the various permutation and combination from the players mentioned above, which opened for India.

The fieriest, quickest, and venomous of them all, Pandurang Salgaocar, did not play a test for India. And in 1978 when Kapil Dev made his "debut" for India, the wise Subroto Guha and Abid Ali, virtually hanged their boot, because they knew that their days of being a "jackal" in Indian cricket were over. The record of Abid Ali and Subroto Guha in batting and bowling reads as under.

Batting									
Name	M	I	No	Runs	Hs	100	50's	ct	Ave
Syed Abid Ali	27	49	3	956	81	-	6	30	2078
Subroto Guha	4	7	2	17	6	-	-	2	3.40
Bowling		Runs		W	5wi	10wm	Ave		
Syed Abid Ali		1820		46	1	-	39. 57		
Subroto Guha		311		3	-	-	103.67		

Subroto Guha's anyalysis might reflect a very poor image of him being a test cricketer, but to be frank, he was never given a fair chance to prove his "mettle". He was in the Indian team to tour England in 1967, but he did not play even a single test, also he was unnecessarily "hoofed" out of the Indian squad for their twin tour of Australia and New Zealand in 1968-69. If he was utilized properly, and if he was taken to the twin tour of Australia and New Zealand and exposed properly, Subroto Guha could have contributed much "more" to the Indian cricket. He was very accurate, and a tremendous mover of the ball, both the ways. But he was treated shabbily.

The series against Pakistan in 1978, saw the total crucification of the famous spin quartet at Pakistan. Zaheer Abbas and Javed Miandad, in that series, proved that Indian spinners were over the hill and finished. Together, Zaheer and Miandad finished the Indian spinners by crucifying the Indian spin trio.

Actually looking into the combination of the spinners of India, the Pakistan Board had prepared a kind of wicket at all the test centers where the spinners of India had nothing to "buy" for, but to bite the nail and from here, Erapalli Prasanna's destiny too had deserted him.

Immediately next, Bhagwat Subramanayam Chandrashekar was to go out for ever against the series of Kalicharan's West Indies. Six months later after this series, Bishen Bedi's name was cut off from the muster roll of Indian cricket, and Venkat was "now-out", and "now-in" of the Indian team then.

It was in 1978 against the Pakistan, at the last test at Lahore, that Karsan Ghavri had bowled in tandem with Kapil Dev. And from here, it was Kapil Dev till 1994, who was to hold the pace of Indian cricket team with aplomb.

Kapil and Ghavri from the Lahore test against Pakistan to the test series against New Zealand in 1981, were to play 31 tests together. And whenever they played, the selectors did not think to break this combination. A change of thinking had erupted at the "national" level about the pace and it got set in the minds of the selectors.

This pair brought about 6 victories on the basis of their bowling alone, beside 543 wickets combined. Kapil had 434 to show for himself, while Ghavri had 109.

Kapil Dev went on to become the first pacer of India to claim 100 wickets in the test matches, and Ghavri followed him next, as said earlier, this pair together had played 31 test matches in all, unseparated, and bowling more than 70% of the overs that the Indian bowlers would bowl, without getting injured at any time either in the match, or in the series.

> *What was more! This pair did not allow any opening batting pair, that existed then in the world of cricket, to put on a century stand till it lasted in Indian cricket.*

The pair was popularly known as "Jai-Veeru" of Indian cricket. Many believe that this was the pair, from 1978 which had brought about a change in Indian cricket. The spin age became the "age of the fast revolution" in Indian cricket, because of this pair. People now-a-days think in this manner.

However it is not. The performance of R. Surendernath and Ramakant Desai in 1959 at England had sown the seed, and did it by virtue of their performance. Twenty years later in 1979 the tree bore the fruits in the form of Karsan Ghavri and Kapil Dev.

For it was from the World Cup at England in 1979, and the series thereafter against England, that Karsan – Kapil express started running fast on the Indian cricket track.

The pace revolution, hence, had started in 1959 after the deed of Surendranath and Desai at England. Karsan and Kapil later pulled it, and carried on as the legacy of Surendranath and Desai.

The country should salute R. Surendranath and Ramakant Desai for the same, always. For it was their "pace" in 1959, which had brought about a change in the "face" of Indian cricket, besides a change in the line and length of thinking of the Indian selectors.

If I were to pay my praise, then I would go to the extent of saying that the World Cup winning cricket squad of 1983, which ran "full pace" in the finals was the culmination of the pace set by Surendranath and Desai during the 1959 tour of India to England.

The seed of pace was sown by the duo in 1959, but the fruit was reaped in 1983 by Kapil's "Devils". The spin had won us some of the world famous, the outstanding series, the pace the World Cup 1983.

The record of Karsan Ghavri in the test match is as under-:

Name	T	I	NO	Runs	HS	Cen	H/C	Catches	Ave
K. Ghavri	39	57	14	913	86	-	2	16	21.23

The above average pertains to his batting. His bowling analysis in the test match would read as under-:

Name	T	Balls	Runs	Wkts	BB	BBM	5Wkts/I	10Wkts/M	Ave
K. Ghavri	39	7036	3656	109	5/33	7/120	-4-	-0-	33.54

Out of these 109 test wickets Karsan Ghavri had claimed ten wickets as a spinner. On two different occasions he bowled his tweaks with "CHINAMAN" as his forte, and on both the occasions he claimed a 'FIVER'. That was the dual or the two-in-one kind of a bowler that Ghavri was.

Ghavri was dropped from the Indian team in 1981 after the twin tour of Australia and New Zealand. He thereafter played for Bombay till the end of 1982 and from 1983 he switched his base to Saurashtra in Ranji Trophy for whom he continued playing till the end of 1985.

His performance from 1981 till 1983, when the World Cup was held, in the Ranji Trophy was good, yet he was not selected for the World Cup, and the coot who was selected in his place was Sunil Valson. He was converted into a spoot by the think-tank immediately thereafter. Neither was he considered even to play a single match in the World Cup, nor was he given any chance after it, though chums like Bharat Arun and Venkat Ramanna played some game for India afterwards.

Here again the selectors, oh the great selectors, played their game much more than the players could play. Karsan Ghavri too was "played on" by the selectors.

There is a song in a movie, the movie - which is famous by the name of "Kabhie Andhera, Kabhie Ujaala". The movie has a very hard song sung by the great Kishore Da. It is as "Surma Mera Nirala, Ankhon mein jisne dala, Jeevan hua ujaala, Hain yeh kaun nazarwala." The music was composed by the great O. P. Nayyar, and Shri Majrooh Sultanpuri had penned the song. Tremendous hard song made very easy by Kishore Da using his youdling and cudling, and so very sweet to listen, the song was a tremendous hit during the mid sixties.

If the song was made a parody and if Kishore Da had to sing it, the song would be thus-:

Selector mera niraala

Chayan ka kiya ghotala

Bharat ka hua mu kala

Selector hai kaun nazarwala.

O selector oodi, oodi, oodi, yeh hi liiii

Selector odli, odli odli, odli uuuuuu oli oli oou eeeee

Really this would have been the tune of Kishore Da for this song if he had to sing for the Indian selectors.

8

GAVASKAR OR VISHVANATH: I'M THE GREATEST

IT was the year 1967 and the Ranji Trophy season for 1967-68 had just begun. Karnataka known as Mysore then, had travelled all the way from the "garden city", Bangalore to the city of "ghee and milk" Vijaywada to play a Ranji match against Andhra Pradesh.

A young baby-looking guy, very humble and modest, had but valour, aged about 18 was travelling with the Karnataka team. The team was led by V. Subramanyam known affectionately as "Subbu" to his mate, was a test player.

The team arrived at Vijaywada, about three hours late of its scheduled time, and "Subbu" and his boys had already lost some valuable net practice. The next day Mysore had a bit of net practice and the players were off to a reception.

Mysore, besides having V. Subramanyam, Erapalli Prasanna, B. S. Chandrashekar and Beerala Raghunath, had nothing more to show as a team. However, within 12 hours from the reception, it had to offer a complete "little master", who was to shine in the world of cricket, either like a "twinkle star" or like a "milky way".

It was the fortune of Mysore that they had lost both the openers quickly, being forced to increase the tempo of the scoring quickly. In strode a 5 feet 1 inch lad, after the fall of the second wicket. And by lunch he was almost in his fifties. By the tea he was nearing his century. By the end of the play, he was near to his 150. Next day came the declaration, and before it he had hammered the Andhra bowlers for 230 runs, unbeaten. The declaration came soon after.

Gundappa Ranganath Vishvanath, born at a village near Shimoga, on February 12th 1949, in the state of Mysore then, was born in Indian cricket with an unbeaten knock of 230 against Andhra. This score remained the highest individual score by any batsman on debut in Ranji cricket till 1994 when Amol Majumdar of Mumbai surpassed it.

Vishvanath's next venture was against Hyderabad which had Nawab of Pataudi, Abbas Ali Baig, M. L. Jaisimha, Abid Ali, P. Govindraj, Nausher Mehta, P. Krishnamurthy and Sultan Saleem in its rank. Vishvanath, played in this match. He did not score many. He scored only 69 and 38 in that game. The Nawab was left clapping at his stroke. It was during the lunch time that the Nawab asked Subbu "where did you get that midget from", Subbu replied "from the Kolar Gold Field". Well, very shortly that gold of yours will be mine, said the Nawab jokingly, but in a very pensive and serious mood and voice.

The season went on-and-on, and it was not before the semi-finals that the entire world of media came to know about Subbu's "Gold" and his cricketing deed.

Mysore had to face Bombay in the semis. They got out within 250 and Vishvanath's contribution was 30 in the first innings. This total was meager, as compared to Bombay and with the like of Ashok Mankad, Ajit Wadekar and Dilip Sardesai in Bombay's rank, 250 odd was not a huge target to surpass. Bombay had secured the vital first innings lead. The point of interest was whether Karnataka could save themselves from innings defeat.

Yes, it did, and did it in style. The two openers from Mysore gave them a flying start. However, came the moment and came the man. In an awe inspiring performance, the two Mysore batsmen, Vishvanath and Brijesh Patel, produced such a sparkling demonstration of batsmanship that the cherry was changed as many as five times during the course of this partnership. Both of them had collared the Bombay attack and had reduced it to ash. Bombay had been winning the Ranji Trophy since 1958 and it had won this time too, but for the first time it appeared that its days were going to come.

In a manner, which one would describe as classical and phenomenal, Vishvanath and Brijesh Patel saw Mysore, not only avoid the innings defeat, but both had scored their respective tons. The high quality of the strokes played by Vishvanath, with superb timings and the placement of the balls, aided by the geometrical dissecting shots kept the entire fraternity of cricket world stranded. It was a "dream" as K. N. Prabhu had to describe this innings.

The very next season, New Zealand under Graeme Dowling had to tour India, and the Board President's XI was to take on the Kiwis at Indore. Here it was where Mushtaq Ali and Vijay Merchant together had sat for the first time, to watch the game together. Board XI was led by Chandu Borde. In that game the selectors were to decide about a few positions that were needed to fill in the breach for the Indian cricket team.

The choice of course was between Vishvanath and Borde. They both batted together in this game. Borde had about 55 test matches experience behind him and Vishvanath was a novice in test matches till then.

Started the competition and Vishvanath started with two rasping "square hit" of Richard Collinge, and Mushtaq Ali jumped off his feet. "Like me! Vijay", is it not. No, replied Merchant, I see some shade of Hazare, and some of Niel Harvey, though he was a right handed batsman. Borde followed the suit with two extra cover drives of Dayle Hadlee. The two started matching each other stroke for stroke, however, within no time, Borde found that he could not match Vishvanath for his repertoire of strokes. Borde gave it up, soon. He fell back to his basics of cricket. Vishvanath, with a perfect example of compact cricket, took the control of the game.

Strokes followed one after another, and the way he hit the ball was an abject lesson for all who watched the game. He had so many alternatives for a single delivery. He would watch the ball till late, very late, and then play the strokes, late-very-late, with perfect balance of the bat and his body, and hit it, as per his wish, with sweet timings and perfect dissection of the field. When the declaration came, he was undefeated, scoring 68 with 14 hits to the fence. He had conquered Merchant, the Chairman of the selection committee. What was more, he had the uncanny ability to change his stroke at the very last minute. This was something very unique, which nobody in India till then had possessed.

The young Vishvanath, hardly 19 then was summoned to Nagpur along with Ambar Roy, Gopal Bose, Ramesh Nagdev, Subroto Guha, Surender Amarnath, Mohinder Amarnath, Ajit Gandotra, Ajit Pai, Dilip Sardesai and Nausher Mehta. The reason was the Indian test bowlers would bowl to these youngsters at the net, and two batsmen would be selected from this batch. The two to pass their test with "merits" were Ambar Roy and Gundappa Vishvanath. No other than Vijay Merchant chose them.

Ambar Roy, being a left handed batsman, was preferred to play and for the first time Gundappa Vishvanath was in the 14 for the test. Thus Nagpur it was, which brought

Gundappa Vishvanath, in the reserves, for the first time in Indian cricket.

From the first test in Nagpur in 1968 to the second test in Kanpur in 1969, against Australia, was a matter of only two months and four test matches. Vishvanath carried the lemon juice and the drinks for these three test matches. Came the Kanpur test against Australia in 1969, it brought a "gem" to the Indian cricket.

The New Zealand tour was followed by the Australians. India were lucky to hold New Zealand to a 1-1 draw. Thereafter the Australians outplayed us in the Bombay test. Next followed the test at Kanpur. And that was the place, the leather city which saw Gundappa Vishvanath, at Kanpur, making his test debut.

He came to bat at number four, and the first ball he flicked off Sheahan, a typical bullet shot, that came of his wrist, for which he had anticipated a boundary, was napped by Ian Redpath, flew himself like a dove and got to the ball, in his last ditch effort, like a panther getting the neck of the gazelle, and held the ball, for his dear life. With it ended Vishvanath tenure at the crease. He was out for a blob. "Never mind" said Pataudi, "I'will give you another chance." That was the consolation.

He got another chance, and this time he did not let go abegging. Immediately after he was out for a blob in the first, he took a binocular from Pataudi, and he watched every Australian; Mckenzie, Sheahan, Mallet and Connolly, minutely about their bowling and their tactics. He had come to know their tricks.

After Australia got out for 348, securing a first innings lead of 20 runs, his chance to bat had come. And this time, there was no stopping him. He just ran very fast for his first run in test cricket. For this was his first run to open his account.

Thereafter what followed was rains of boundaries and a feast of very high classical variety of strokes. Mankad, Wadekar, Pataudi and Gandotra were to come and go. He first shared an 80 runs partnership with Ashok Mankad, who scored 68, and was out. Vishvanath remained unbeaten on 68 on the day when play was called of.

The next day, he in the company of Eknath Solkar, added 110 runs for the sixth wicket. Solkar's contribution was only 35, before he was out. In the meantime, Vishvanath completed his first test ton. Call it any stroke that a book of cricket would have, and name any part of the field where you could place a fielder, Vishvanath's bat put the ball to all those points and parts of the field where the fielders could be placed, but there was no stopping Vishvanath. He finally got out for 137 and 100 of them exactly had come through the boundaries.

The President of India then, Mr. V. V. Giri, was watching the proceedings of the final day at Kanpur. He came back to Delhi and announced the list of Padma Shri award winners. Gundappa Ranganath Vishvanath was recipient of the award. That was awarded to him in 1971 as the award for 1970 was already decided and it went to Erapalli Prasanna. Vishvanath had come to stay in Indian cricket since then.

If there was Vishvanath, who had made cricket a "sensations", there was another from Bombay then who was inching his way to the world of cricket. Like Vishvanath, he too was given a chance to prove his mettle against the New Zealand, for the Combined University against Graeme Dowling team in 1969. The young little batsman had scored 25 then and he had found the bowling of Daylee Hadles and Richard Collings too hot to handle.

Thereafter, ocean of runs came in from his bat, and came the Ranji Trophy. In the finals against Rajasthan in Ranji Trophy match in 1970, he and Ashok Mankad put a 271 runs partnership for the first wicket, his individual score was 114 runs.

When the Indian team was selected for West Indies in 1971, he was included in the squad as opener. He scored 65, 67*, 116, 64*, 1, 117*, 124 and 220 runs in his very first series against the West Indies aggregating 774 runs on the tour. This brought another Indian, 5 feet 3 inches in height, to the Indian cricket. He too was a little master. And Sunil Manohar Gavaskar was to cement his place in the Indian squad.

The two little masters toured together to West Indies for the first time. Vishvanath was born on 12. 2. 1949 whereas Sunil was born on 10.7.1949. Vishvanath was two inches short of Gavaskar in height. Both were the masters of the game. Vishvanath did not stretch his studies beyond matriculation and Sunil Gavaskar was an Arts Graduate from Bombay University. This was a major difference.

However, when it came to the game and stroke play, both were a class of .their own. During the tour of West Indies in 1971, Gavaskar had missed the first test and Vishvanath the first two. M. L. Jaisimha and Salim Durrani were a miserable failure in batting for the two test matches that they had played. But the "two dream" balls of Durrani, that got rid of Sobers and Lloyd in the second test at Trinidad, where India had beaten them for their first win over West Indies, saw Durrani retaining his place for the third test.

Jaisimha's place went to Vishvanath in third test, and Sunil kept his place intact. This was for the first time at Guyana in West Indies, that the two little masters were involved together playing a test.

They batted together, and had a partnership of 112 runs for the third wicket in this match. This was the first partnership of over 100 runs that the two little masters had produced in the test. Seven years later, these two little masters were to be involved in one of the biggest partnership on 27-3-1978. It was on that day that Vishvanath had got married to Kavita Gavaskar, the youngest sister of Sunil Gavaskar.

While batting with Vishvanath, in that test at Guyana Gavaskar, like Chandu Borde tried to match Vishvanath, for stroke-to-stroke, but very wisely, he gave it up soon thereafter. He realized very soon that it was not easy to match Vishvanath for his repertoire of wonderful strokes. Vishvanath had so many different alternatives for varying his strokes, and no batsman in this aspect of batting could have matched him.

Sunil gave the chase soon, and he concentrated very heavily to focuss on staying at the wicket and graft his runs. He immediately, during the course of his partnership, got to learn that unlike Vishvanath he should have two options, either to go forward or to fall back to play his stroke.

He also had noticed that unlike Vishvanath he had a very mediocre reflex and he could not match Vishvanath for the kind of lightning strokes that Vishvanath could play because of his reflexes and the kind of a wristy steel that he possessed.

This was the place, and this was the moment in that partnership, at the crease, where Sunil with Vishvanath, learned that he has to be a grafter, or an accumulator, as well as a straight bat cricketer, if he had to rule the world of cricket.

The object lesson with that partnership with Vishvanath, which Sunil Gavaskar learned, had a telling impact on his performance, and for the remaining of the series, Sunil had scored 64*, 1, 117*, 124 and 220.

The partnership of 112 runs got Vishvanath his first 50 at the Caribbean, but it got Sunil his first test hundred, 116 to be exact, at the Caribbean. Vishvanath till the end of his career, scored four centuries against the Caribbeans, but Sunil Gavaskar scored a dozen thereafter. The total of 13 centuries out of 34 scored by Sunil Gavaskar against the West Indies, is the highest number of test centuries scored by any cricketer against the West Indies. However, the 112 runs which Gundappa Vishvanath scored at Port-of-Spain, Trinidad, where India went on to chase a total of 406 runs to win the match, was in the comments of Clive Lloyd and Viv Richard, "the best" they had seen anybody scoring against West Indies at the Island and that too against an attack, which had the fiery of Michael Holding at his very best. The two square cut off two rising deliveries of Holding, which Vishvanath produced, raising off his toes, and picking a gap, between the cordons of eight fielders to send both the deliveries to the fence in the word of Tony Cozier was "the best" that he had seen as a cricket commentator, and it was very hard for him to describe the two shots.

Between 1971 after this series, and 1974, India had won three "rubbers", two against England and one against the West Indies, and both the little masters had featured in the series. But the moments of glory were mostly shared by the spin quartet of Prasanna, Bedi, Venkat and Chandra.

Whatever little was left, either went to Salim Durrani, or to a genious-cum-debonair named Farokh Engineer. However, in between Gundappa Vishvanath got his second test hundred, in his 15th test against England at the Brabourne Stadium on 7th of February 1973.

That very day Brabourne stadium saw a kind of batting which the crowds of Bombay, then witnessing the match would not like to forget, till the end of their lives. Salim Durrani and Vishvanath joined together, after Sunil Gavaskar was out cheaply, and Farokh Engineer (121) and Ajit Wadekar (87) left the scene. That was on 6th February 1973.

The next day, as it would happen on Feb 7th, 1973, Salim Durrani started with a bang. He hit a six of Tony Greig to start a partnerhip that was to produce 150 runs. Vishvanath started playing from where he had left at Kanpur (75*) in the previous test.

There were twenty runs, which separated Vishvanath from Salim. But 16 runs plundered in two overs by Vishvanath against Chris Old and Pat Pocock brought him together, on par, with Salim. Thereafter, it was a race against the time. What Vishvanath would do, Salim would do it better, and what Salim did thereafter, Vishvanath would do to outbeat him, for the better. The result was that the 45,000 spectators were treated "lavishly" to drink the "Fantas and the Colas" to put their throat, back into their places. Every money spent by the crowd, was got back to them with dividend.

In between the break, Durrani jokingly told Vishvanath "apeing me isn't", but "what about the six I hit of Tony," could you match it.

Well, the play started, and within no time, both reached 49 runs. "I'll be the first", said Salim to Vishvanath to get that fifty, "and you follow me". In the very first ball of the next over which Gundappa Vishvanath faced from Chris Old, he hooked the ball in the manner, which Salim did and send the ball hurling to the square leg region. The ball sored so high that it fell into the swimming pool of the Brabourne Stadium.

Vishvanath had hit the first "six" of his life in test cricket. The game was held. "Why did you do it", asked Salim. That was my job. "Well, if I had not hooked the ball, that delivery from Old would have hit me on my face and my youth would have turned old", said Vishvanath. The ball was replaced, and pat came the answer from Salim. The first delivery of the next over was sent by Salim Durrani to packed crowd of the north stand of the stadium. Somebody had chanted, from the crowd "we want a six, Durrani", and Durrani exactly hit the ball, from where the voice had come.

After the end of the over Vishvanath went to Salim and said "nobody had matched me till this day for my stroke play". Salim giggled and replied "because nobody by the name of Salim Durrani" had played with you then. From 55, there onward to 73, both kept matching each other in strokes for strokes. It was really a wonder, a surprise to see a 38 years old Salim, matching a 24 years old Vishvanath both in reflexes and in stroke play. To be frank, many a times it appeared that Durrani was far more balanced, power packed and solid in his stroke. Vishvanath was steely, wristy and reflexive. It was like a dad wrestling with his young son and matching the skill of the son with his experience.

What was flattering was that even at the age of 38, Salim Durrani had the vision and eyesight, as clear and sharp as a hawk. For never did he err once, picking the deliveries to be hit, and never did he miss a single delivery which had to be smashed and punched.

At 73 then, Salim Durrani went once more chancing his arm, for a big one against Pocock, and he holed it out to Underwood. This wicket had raised on 150 runs. Actually once again, there was a loud shout, a demand for six from the crowd–Durrani went out for it and eventually holed it out.

> *This was perhaps one of the best partnership in terms of the class of stroke play, and from the value of entertainment, that was played in the test match for India.*

It was the age of Salim Durrani and finally his vaning stamina which broke the partnership, and not any kind of a good, or a bad delivery. Had Durrani been five years younger in age, he would have got his century if he was not injured. Actually, he was playing with a groin injury, and his movements were restricted. Else his individual score would have been more than 73. He might have missed taking as many as fifteen singles.

However, after the exit of Durrani, Vishvanath produced a kind of blitzkrieg, which only a batsman of his class would do. His eyes being set, he tore apart the bowling of the hapless English team to add a quick 40, and reach his second century of his test career, in the process.

No sooner did he achieve this big feat, Tony Greig ran upto him and like a baby lifted the "baby" of the team in his arms and planted a kiss. Such was the mastery of the knock that Vishvanath had played which had won the hearts of many including Greig that day.

Before Gundappa Vishvanath, there had been Lala Amarnath, Deepak Shodhan, A. G. Kripal Singh, Abbas Ali Baig, Hanumant Singh and after Vishvanath, there had been Surinder Amarnath, to have scored a century on their debut in test cricket. But it was only Vishvanath, who could break this hoodoo of scoring a century, again, after a test ton in debut in test cricket.

Before the Kanpur test in 1972-73 against England, the selectors were planning to drop Vishvanath from the Indian team. But after this test in 1973, no selectors could even dare to think about dropping Vishvanath from the test squad till 1983. The unbeaten 75 runs at Kanpur against England prolonged his test career, but this knock of 113 against England was to cement his place in the squad for ever.

The Salim Durrani-Gundappa Vishvanath combination had a similar role to play, once more during the second innings. Salim Durrani was to score a quick 37, with three towering, but sizzling sixes, and Vishvanath scoring 48. This time too they added 66 runs in about 58 minutes of play. The crowd went into ruptures then.

To be frank, it was the Irani Trophy in 1970 when the world of Indian cricket saw the deeds of these two cricketers, massacring the Bombay bowlers at the Jawaharlal Nehru stadium at Poona. In the second innings in that match, Durrani had scored 109 and Vishvanath 104. They had a partnership of over 175 runs in that game. And this one against England was a repeat of the same.

Sunil Gavaskar in the series next was to get his first test ton abroad at England, outside the American continent. In the series of 74 which saw England humiliating India by 3-0, Gavaskar, Vishvanath and Farokh Engineer kept the Indian flag flying high. Bits and pieces of good performance came from Abid Ali and Solkar, but the Indians were washed out at the first half of the English summer.

Came the West Indies under Clive Lloyd in 1974-75, and India were 0-2 by the end of the second test at New Delhi. Pataudi had come back for the third test at Calcutta, after missing one at New Delhi and after the Bangalore test, where India were screwed down and jacked by 163 runs, Sunil Gavaskar was not to play again, till the final test at Bombay.

A delivery from Pandurang Salgaocar had broken his thumb in a Ranji match at Pune and Sunil was out till the last test at Bombay. The onus of batting fell on the broad shoulders of Gundappa Vishvanath. Till then he had the scores of 29 and 22 at Bangalore and 32 and 39 at New Delhi.

Before the Culcutta test, it was a toss up between Pandurang Salgaocar and Karsan Ghavri, as to who would play for India, and Pataudi preferred to choose Ghavri because of his all-round ability. Madanlal on the basis of his knock of 56 against West Indies in an upcountry match was called to accompany Ghavri and young Anshuman Gaekwad who had scored a 104 for the Universities at Indore against West Indies, was baptized at "test" at Calcutta. December 27th 1974 was the day when Karsan Ghavri made his test debut for India along with Anshuman Gaekwad.

This was the turning point in the annals of test cricket in India with Gundappa Vishvanath taking the charge, scoring a fluent 52. India rattled up a mediocre 233 in the first, with Madanlal contributing 48, and Pataudi and Gaekwad contributing 36 apiece, India conceded lead of 7 runs to West Indies in the first innings with Madanlal claiming 4 for 22.

The Indian pacers after the England sojourn in 1974, were at their dead end. In this match at Calcutta, Pataudi noticed that the two pacers Karsan Ghavri and Madanlal, were very enthusiastic, full of promise, but raw. They had in them to deliver.

He had a very encouraging sessions with both the pacers, and told them to believe that they in-between could rattle the West Indies. He assured them full support and help in this match, and promised that both the pacers would be given 15 overs at least in both the innings, individually, to bowl at the Windies. But they had to produce the result.

Pataudi had, and was injecting, some spirit in the quickies, which till then was dead. The result was for the people to see. Both Ghavri and Madanlal were really devastating, and Madanlal had an impressive spell of 4 for 22.

It was here in this match that Pataudi observing the reflexes that Vishvanath possessed "ordered" him to stand at the slip. This was Vishvanath's 21 test match. From here till his last test match, 70 best in a row, he held the first slip position during fielding and had 68 catches in total, 63 of them in the first slip.

However, if it was his those 3 brilliant catches in the slip, and a run out in the match, it was his thumping 139 runs which knocked Clive Lloyd and the West Indies, for the first time in India.

Ever since the West Indies had toured India, for the first time in 1948, it took India 27 years, exactly on January 1st 1975, first day of the New year, for India to beat West Indies for the first time on their soil

At one stage India were 192 for 6 with only Ghavri, Prasanna, Bedi and Chandra remaining to bat. A rest day followed and thereafter Vishvanath, who was batting on 75 overnight, joined Ghavri and produced 91 runs for the seventh wicket. The only blemish of Vishvanath was when on 83, he hanged his bat to an outgoing delivery from Bernard Julien, which went between Kalicharan and Lloyd in the slip.

From 86 to 139, it was vantage Vishvanath. Karsan Ghavri held dourly for about 137 minutes to score 27, which included a six off Alquemedo Willet. Ghavri left at

283 and Vishvanath was the last man out, bowled by Holder for 139. Even Chandrashekar had contributed an unbeaten 7.

Thereafter Bedi (4 for 52), Chandrashekar (3 for 66) Ghavri (1 for 18) and Madanlal (1 for 23) bowled India to a historic win. The two pacers Ghavri and Madanlal set the rot for West Indies. Gorden Greenidge was lbw to Ghavri for 3 and Madanlal, who had taken 4 for 22 in the first innings bowled a perfect inswinger that uprooted Viv Richards mid stick for 47. Little resistance came from Kalicharan along with Clive Lloyd, but no sooner that Vishvanath snabbed a "gem" of catch to dismiss Kalicharan of Chandra, the writings were on the wall for West Indies.

This catch of Vishvanath was similar to that of Wadekar which he took of Bedi to dismiss Underwood against England in 1973. In both the cases, both went to their right first, but the ball broke back sharply in both the cases, and took the outer edge to "fly" to the wrong ends. Wadekar as in that catch and Vishvanath in this, moved very late, on the left, and in both the cases, they flung themselves to get their fingers on the ball to clutch it and hold it for their dear life. Both the catches then and now, turned the complexion of the game. The difference was, Wadekar used his diving skill to a great extent, and Vish used his reflexes to the maximum. This catch was, like the one in 1972-73 which Wadekar held, turned out to be the "turning-point" of the match. Thereafter West Indies succumbed to the guiles of our spinners to be beaten hollow–and –square, for the first time in India.

The victory at the Oval in 1971, was fashioned to a large extent by Vishvanath, who had featured in a 48 runs partnership for the fourth wicket with Dilip Sardesai (40) and again with Farokh Engineer, with whom he added 36 priceless runs for the sixth wicket. Finally when he was out for 33, then India needed only four for the victory.

And now, at Calcutta in 1974–75 it was his 91 runs partnerhip with Karsan Ghavri, which laid the foundation for India's first victory over West Indies in India. He not only scored 52 and 139, besides holding 3 catches in the slip. In the first essay, the way he anticipated a cut from Richards, used his reflexes as to stop that shot in the slip, and grabbed the ball, like a hawk to hit the wicket to run out Richard will be etched well in the memory of the cricket lovers for a very long time to come.

> *This was the victory which changed the face of the Indian cricket after being battered 3-0 by England in 1974. After that English wash, the Indian cricketers had lost all their hopes on them. This was exemplified by the manner in which they had lost the first two tests against West Indies at Bangalore and Delhi. But the clever planning of Pataudi, his faith in the speedstars Madanlal and Ghavri, and his words of encouragement to Vishvanath and Gaekwad really did the trick. It floored the West Indies. The spin trio of Bedi, Chandra and Prasanna was at its flighting best.*

It was from here till the end of the series against Australia in 1977-78 that Indian cricketers were to fight like wounded tiger and turn the table on their opponents. From the fourth test at Chepauk in January 1975, to be exact 11th January 1975 to the final test against Australia in Sydney, India had notched as many as 8 victories in the 22 tests that they played against New Zealand (twice), West Indies, Australia and England.

The percentage of the victory was 36.36

However, just after the Calcutta test in 1975, it was the Madras test in which one saw Vishvanath in full gloom. The Chepauk stadium had a lot of green grass on it. The Indian skipper won the toss and decided to bat first. Lloyd was happy. He had Andy Roberts, Keith Boyce, Bernard Julien and Vanburn Holder in this match to share the new ball.

The Indian camp was stunned at Pataudi's decision to bat first on such a lively green wicket. And Lloyd proved correct. For, by lunch India were tottering at 76/6. Vishvanath was batting on 14 then.

During the lunch break Engineer reprimanded Pataudi for his decision, but Pataudi's reply was "just watch from here". And how correct Pat was.

From 76 for 6, in the company of Ghavri, Vishvanath added 41 runs, with Ghavri accounting for 12, Prasanna was out at the same score and the score board read at 117 for 8. Thereafter Bedi joined Vishvanath and took the score past 169, adding 52 runs for the ninth wicket. Bedi scored 14, and was out. Came Chandrashekar and with him Vishvanath added 21 priceless runs. All those 21 runs were scored by Vishvanath.

He shielded Chandra for an hour till tea. Twenty minutes after tea, Chandra facing Roberts for the first time, was out thus denying Vishvanath to complete one of the classic, very classic test ton of his career. Vishvanath remained unbeaten on 97.

Vishvanath had showed the world how to play a real "fast" bowler correctly with full and flawless technique. Andy Robers, on this pitch, which got very slow after lunch had claimed 7 for 64. If Vishvanath batting display stood out, it was because he met Robert's extreme pace smack in the face. Tony Cozier has said:

"The sight of any fast bowler repeatedly beating the batsman with sheer speed is always an exciting phenomenon for him to be confronted by a batsman equally hostile and belligerent is the stuff of which discerning cricket followers, dreams are made. As Vishvanath plundered Roberts with his team in desperate trouble after lunch, there was a memory of Ted Dexter playing a similar innings in a similar situation at Lords in 1963 against the fury of Hall and Griffith. England's total was meager then, as was as India's when they were placed at 76 for 6. Dexter's 72 will always be talked of as one of the non-century finest innings. So will Vishvanath 97* for he met force with force in an amazing display of supreme batsmanship – he deserved a century, but the quality of his batsmanship was in no way diminished by the fact that he felt short by three runs. It is on the contrary, that this knock, though not a three figure knock, will be above all the three figures knock, that has truly been played by any batsman in India."

Andy Robert bowled at his fastest. He used his judicious bouncers, and the effect was devastating. His best ball, the sharpest breakback had trapped Gaekwad and Pataudi. A wicked bouncer had claimed Mankad, and he sent Ghavri's midstick to the distance one really finds the fast bowler can. Actually in this test Roberts showed his true colours. Vishvanath's fight–to-the finish 97* put the final stamp on him as a batsman of class. For 57 of the 97* runs that Vishvanath had scored had come of Andy.

Getting out for 190, India got Windies out for 192 with Erapalli Prasanna claiming 5 for 70. Batting second, India did a shade better with Vishvanath (46), Anshuman Gaekwad (80) and Karsan Ghavri (35*) to score 256 runs. Prasanna again turned his arm over to claim 4 for 41, Bedi 3 for 29 and Chandra 2 for 57 to skittle out West Indies for 154, thus helping India to win by 100 runs and to square the rubber.

This was the first time in the history of Indian Cricket to win two matches in a row against West Indies. Thirteen years ago under Nari Contractor, India had notched two back–to-back victories against England, the venues then again were Calcutta and Madras.

Well, the inauguaral test match at the Wankhede Stadium at Bombay in the same series saw West Indies scoring 604 runs, which was possible due to a unconquered 242 by Clive Lloyd, 104 by Roy Fredricks, 98 by Kalicharan and 91 scored by Derry K Murray.

India replied it with 406 with Gavaskar scoring 86, Solkar getting his maiden test century (102), Gaekwad 51 and Vishwanath 95. Gaining a lead of 198 runs, West Indies rattled it up with 205. All the West Indies batsmen got into their thirties within no time; and declared their innings. Needing 404 to win, India lost the match, then and there on the last day when they were all out, just after tea for 202.

Actually the match was lost by India immediately after Vanburn Holder bowled a beauty, a very very late in-swinger, which broke back so lazily, but sharply, that it castled the mid stick of Vishvanath. This in fact was the ball of the test series. The second ball of the entire tour was when Andy Roberts had bowled Anil Deshpande at Nagpur where the wicket of Deshpande had cartwheeled for 23 stick at the VCA ground.

Though some resistance came from Anshuman Gaekwad (42) and Brijesh Patel (73), it could not prevent India losing the test by 201 runs. This series, by so far, has seen the best series played on the Indian soil. Gundappa Vishvanath performances read at the end of the series as:

M	I	No	Runs	Ave	100	50	Ct	St	Run out
5	10	1	568	63.11	1	3	7	-	2

To what extent did Vishvanath dominate the series could be gauged by the fact that the second in batting average was Anshuman Gaekwad who scored 220 runs in six innings with an average for 36.66. And whenever Vishvanath got out within 40s, India lost the test matches in that series.

At Bangalore and at Delhi, he did not score over 40 and both the matches went out of India's grasp and here in the Wankhede stadium after scoring 52, 139, 97 and 46 he failed once to get past 40, and with it India lost the test. This proved Vishvanath solidity as a batsman in the Indian team.

The twin tour of New Zealand and the West Indies were to follow soon. This was for the first time in the annals of the game in India that somebody, not from West Zone, or South Zone was leading India. It was Bishen Singh Bedi who led the Indian team.

It was also for the first time that as many as six cricketers from Karnataka and four from Delhi were representing India.

The stranglehold of the maximum number of cricketers from Bombay representing the Indian team had broken. The tour had some surprises to offer.

Karsan Ghavri, who had displayed remarkable valour, grit and determination during the previous tour of West Indies to India was dropped for the reason best known to the selectors.

However, the tour of New Zealand saw India making a remarkable and achieving a wonderful feat. In the first test against New Zealand played at Auckland, India was led by Sunil Gavaskar.

The match which was to be played between 24th and 29th January 1976, ended on January 28th with India beating New Zealand by 8 wickets with Gundappa Vishvanath hitting the winning run. Sunil Gavaskar at the other end was unbeaten with 35.

This was the first test match that India had won under the captaincy of Sunil Gavaskar.

Gavaskar himself had scored 116 in the first innings and remained unbeaten with 35 in the second. Surinder Amarnath, the Lala's 'colt' got a thunderous 124 in his debut match, whereas the Lala's second 'colt' Mohinder, who was staging a comeback after seven years of wilderness in Indian cricket scored 64.

However, the highlight of this match was a spell of 25-5-64-3 and 23-9-76-8 by the offspinner Erapalli Prasanna with a match figure of 48-9-140-11, Erapalli Prasanna had overtaken Vinoo Mankad's haul of 162 test wickets, to become the leading wickets taker for India at the end of this match.

It was a flying start by India, but as the series took its way, and prolonged further, India were reduced to the pulp.

The second test match which was played at Christ Church saw India scrape through, just avoiding to escape from the clutches of defeat. Gavaskar had failed in the first, and so did Vengsarkar and Amarnath. The innings was held together by Gundappa Vishvanath, and he was helped in a large measure by Mohinder Amarnath and Syed Kirmani. Vishvanath again rose to the occasion by scoring 83, an innings which was termed as "gem" by some of the stalwarts of New Zealand. He came at the wicket when the score board read 41 for 2, and left at 196, of the 155 runs that were added while his tenure at the crease, he himself scored 83 of these runs.

New Zealand scored 403 to gain a lead of 133 runs. The Indian spinners were a total failure, and the mediocre pace of Madanlal (5 for 134) and Mohinder Amarnath (4 for 63) somehow did not allow New Zealand to score over 450 plus.

Mohinder by his performance once again proved the selectors that how fool they were to ignore his talent from 1969-70 till the start of this series. Also Ghavri's exclusion was very much felt by the team.

It was to the benevolence of the Almighty that both Mohinder and Madanlal did not break or get injured in this series, or the series which was to follow next against the West Indies. Else, perhaps India might have had to open with Gavaskar, Vengsarkar, Brijesh Patel, for their bowling. How short-sighted could our selectors be!

Well, in the second innings of the same test, India did better with the team thwarting New Zealand for the victory. The opening pair of Vengsarkar and Gavaskar put on 60 runs. Thereafter, there was a mini collapse, and by the time the score read 100, Surinder Amarnath too had gone.

A defeat was in sight. But Gavaskar (71) first with Vishvanath, and then Vishvanath in the company of Mohinder Amarnath (30) stemmed the rot. By the time

Vishvanath was out, scoring 79, the time ran out and India had saved the test.

This knock by Gundappa Vishvanath, again was described as one of the finest innings of craftsmanship and exhibition of highest class of technique, played by any batsman in the gruelling 'chilly' conditions at New Zealand.

The two in-laws in between contributed 255 runs out of the 525 runs scored by India. In terms of percentage, the two had scored 48.57% of the runs for India in this test. Vishvanath alone had contributed 32% of runs with his bat in this test.

If the Indians had thought that they would get away with the series, somehow, they were in for a rude shock. For, the last test played at Basin Reserve at Wellington brought about their waterloo.

India won the toss, and for the first time in the series, both Gavaskar (22) and Vishvanath failed, and India were all out for 220. It could not have been possible but for a painstaking 81 by Brijesh Patel and an enterprising 49 by Syed Kirmani.

> *Kirmani in the previous test at Christ Church created a world record for the most victims in an innings of test match by effecting 6 dismissals.*

He had gone from strength-to-strength to regularize his place in the squad and his 49 was a testimony to his being getting matured as a cricketer. New Zealand replied with 334 and when India had come to bat in the second knock, it was a rude shock.

Sunil Gavaskar could not bat, as he was out due to an injury and Richard Hadlee in a dream spell of 8.3-0-23-7 and with a match figure of 22.3-1-58-11, had sent India packing to lick the dust.

> *This was the start of Richard Hadlee, and he went on, having to claim 432 wickets in 80 test matches in his career, to become the highest wicket taker in the annals of test matches, which was broken in January 1994 by Kapil Dev.*

In this test, only Vishvanath scored a fighting 20 in the second knock, while Surinder Amarnath got a 27. The moment Vishvanath was out at 62, the entire team could only add another 19 before being folded off.

It was evident that if Gavaskar and Vishvanath did not get runs the Indian cricket team would crack and get shattered. The batting started with Gavaskar and would end with Vishvanath.

What was more was that the Indian batsmen in this series had scored 1311 test runs with an average of 27.89 to New Zealand's 1218 with an average of 30.45, yet it lost the test to level the series.

In the bowling, Prasanna after his 11 wickets haul in the first test could not add any in the remaining two tests, yet ended on topping the bowling average with 11 wickets for an average of 20.27 per wicket. He was overwhelmed by Richard Hadlee whose 12 wickets in the series had cost him 16.41 runs per wicket.

There itself the series was decided. Though the series ended in a 1-1 draw, India's shortfall and shortcomings against the real quickies and the hot stuff had surfaced once again and except for Gavaskar and Vishvanath nobody could face the 'genuine' pace properly and the remaining batsmen in the Indian squad were not adequately geared up to face a real 'red hot' stuff from the quickies.

The scenario in West Indies in 1976 was no different. Our vulnerability against the top notch pace and the inadequacy of our batsmen except Gundappa Vishvanath and Sunil Gavaskar, to face the real quick stuff was evidently exposed in the first test at Barbados.

But a little had to be written before I come down to this series. Clive Lloyd had beaten Australia in the World Cup in 1975. The West Indies, in a thriller had beaten Australia by 17 runs in the finals at Lords and were crowned as the undisputed kings of cricket.

Hence the Windies tour of Australia had aroused a fire spread enthusiasm amongst the cricket fans in Australia, and the world over. The series ended in a disaster and West Indies were beaten 1-5 by Australia.

However, the series saw Lance Gibbs claiming 309th test wicket of his career and thus he became the highest wicket taker in the history of the game. This record was later broken by Dennis Lillee of Australia.

It was here that Clive Lloyd's captainship was under a scrutiny and in no case did he want to loose it. The Indian team after its tour to New Zealand had arrived at West Indies.

Actually, to be frank again, the Indian team just did not do and perform to its potential. Except for the first test at Auckland, where India had won, the team was found wanting. The bowling neither had the venom nor the fang, leave apart the question of having any poison. New Zealand clearly dominated, but were distinctly unlucky to share the honour. This was possible due to some superb display of tenacious and determined batting by Sunil Gavaskar, and the wristy attractive batting display of Gundappa Vishvanath. Yes fringes came from Mohinder and at times from Badpaji, Surinder.

Against this background, when the team landed at Barbados for the first test, nobody had given India a semblance of a chance to stand up to the fiery of Roberts, Holding, Holford and Julien.

And how true it was. The wicket at Barbados was a green top and from the first look, it appeared that the wicket would play true and fast. Also that it would last for the entire 5 days.

Winning the toss, India elected to bat and till the score of 51, Clive Lloyd was a worried man. No sooner did Holding claimed his first prey in the match, getting Parthasarthy Sharma out for 6, the collapse triggered and one after another wickets started tumbling.

Except for Madanlal (45) and Mohinder Amarnath (26), nobody could hold his fort properly and West Indies packed the entire Indian team for 177. That was just before tea. It was here that India had lost the match.

West Indies went on a hunting spree with Lawrence Rowe (30), Roy Fredricks (54), Vivian Richards (142), Kalicharan (93) and Clive Lloyd (102) hitting the nails, one after another, in the Indian coffin to score a mammoth 488 for 9 declared.

There wasn't any chance that India was going to save this match. The academic interest was how long India would prolong the fight. All the chances diminished immediately when Sunil Gavaskar (1) was out, holed by Jumadeen of Andy Roberts. By 66, three more wickets fell.

The pace of Holding and Roberts were too hot to handle and with the wicket playing true and fast, it appeared that India would be bundled out for a score even less than 100.

Gundappa Vishvanath once again rose to the occasion. He arrived after India had lost both the openers Gavaskar (1) and Sharma (1). He took the charge of the situation.

Flicking the balls, off his toes, between the fine leg and the mid wicket region, and judiciously falling back to square cut Roberts and Holding, he made the batting look very relaxed and easy.

It was to his belligerence and his command over his shots that he made the batting look very easy, which otherwise was not. The pitch was playing real fast and Roberts was at his truly best. Holding was seen at his fastest ever. But nothing could deter Vishvanath, who once again batted with supreme authority and exhibited his true colours scoring 62. The score stood at 117 for 5 then.

This gave a lot of confidence to the batsmen of the lower order and it helped Madanlal (55) and Mohinder Amarnath to prolong the battle. However once Amarnath was out to Raphick Jumadeen at 146, the game was over. India were out for 214, eventually losing the test by an innings and 97 runs.

The next test was at Port-of-Spain at Trinidad. And whenever a test had to be played at Trinidad Sunil Gavaskar would have to score. At Port–of–Spain, it was in 1971, where Salim Durrani produced two 'deadly' deliveries to show Gary Sobers and Clive Lloyd the way to pavilion and open the victory gate for the Indians to get in.

The wickets during those days used to be slow and it helped the 'turners'. And India always had the turners in abundance, much more than her population may be, to show.

The test started with no play possible at the first day. The game started off on the second day and West Indies were 237–7, Vivian Richards had blasted 130 of these. The next day, West Indies were packed for 241. It was Bishen Singh Bedi who had a spell of 34-11-82-5.

As said earlier, if a match had to be played at Port-of-Spain, how could Sunil Gavaskar let the moment and the test go scot free. For he regained his touch and class, may be just looking the wicket, and made up all his failures of the previous test by scoring 156.

Brijesh Patel's only century of his career also was to come here as he had hammered a 115. With Sunil Gavaskar, he had added 205 runs for the fifth wicket. Later Madanlal gave good company to Patel and saw India declaring at 402 for 5. Madanlal (33) and Patel (115) remained unbeaten.

West Indies had fallen in arrears by 161 runs. And in the second innings, by 137 runs, they had lost five crucial and important wickets.

At this stage, Lloyd chanced his arm of Venkatragavan. The ball beat him in the air and of the pitch. It took a turn and kissed his outer edge of the bat and flew to Solkar. Solkar was underneath it, and the catch, it appeared would be completed. But from nowhere, did Brijesh Patel come, without any call to catch it. He dashed with Solkar, only to spill the bean. This is what Lloyd needed. He later banged the Indian spinners for a quick fire 70 and by the time the play ended, Lloyd was out and so was the time. West Indies had saved the test match.

Had Brijesh Patel allowed Solkar to take the catch, West Indies could have lost the match there itself. However, it was the 'no-play' on the first day which saw this test petering out into an exciting draw. The Indians had their tails up and at no stage, did they allow West Indies to take the situation and charge of the game.

The next test was slated to be played at Georgetown and as it would rain heavily, and very heavily at Georgetown, the venue was shifted to Port-of-Spain once again after the rain played a spoilsport.

Again, as described earlier, if a test match is played at Port-of-Spain at Trinidad, even god, if it had willed, would not be able to stop Sunil Manohar Gavaskar. 64, 67*, 156 were the ventures of Sunil Gavaskar's first three visits to this strip. And now a history was to be created in the annals of Indian test.

Here again, looking into the decisive turn the wickets take, West Indies included two spinners, Imtiaz Ali and Albert Padmore. Clive Lloyd had called correctly and elected to strike first.

He appeared to be correct as a lambasting 177 by Vivian Richards, and a bulldozing 68 by the Windies skipper, let the tone set for West Indies to score 359. B. S. Chandrashekar had a figure of 32.2-8-120-6 and Bishen Bedi's spell read as 30-11-73-4.

India, by the time they could reach 50, had lost both the openers. Gavaskar was out leg before to Holding for 26, and this was the first occasion that the Indian opener, who had made Port-of-Spain, his home could not score over 50.

The innings was later retrieved, and set in order, once again by Gundappa Vishvanath who scored a fluent, a well stroked 41, but once he was out, bowled by Imtiaz Ali the entire batting except for Madanlal, who scored 41, collapsed. The innings came to a close at 228, thus conceding a lead of 131 runs.

Aided by a masterful stroke play of 103 by Alvin Kalicharan, and bits-and-pieces of contribution coming in from the other batsmen, West Indies declared at 271 for 6. This time the majority of the wickets was claimed by Venkat whose analysis read as 30.3-5-65-3.

Needing 402 to win, India started their second day with Anshuman Gaekwad (28) and Sunil Gavaskar putting on 69 for the first wicket. Having the company of Lala's second colt, Mohinder, Sunil went on to add 108 with him for the second wicket and was eventually out for 102. Mohinder by that time was into his 40s.

This was once again Sunil Gavaskar, who had laid the foundation. His venture till then at Port-of-Spain read 64, 67*, 156, 26 and now 102. His batting average till then at Port-of-Spain read 415 runs, two centuries, two fifties with an average of 100.37 runs per innings.

In strode the little master Gundappa Vishvanath and by the time he could set his eye in and could start stroking fluently, Mohinder had got past 60s. He was 67.

Almost for an hour, Vishvanath could not get past 10. He was badly held up like the cabbie being held at the jam. The Windies' spinners Albert Padmore, Imtiaz Ali and Raphick Jumadeen, had casted a spell with spun web in the neighbourhood of Vishy's bat that there was a time when the skipper Bishen Singh Bedi felt so humiliated that he had preferred the 12th man Parthasarthy Sharma to go to Vishy and ask him to come back to the pavilion, on the pretext and pretence of stomach upset.

Here went a move wrong by the Windies skipper Clive Lloyd. He claimed the new ball and felt that if a wicket tumbles than the series and the match would be over by then and there. He packed the off side with as many as eight fielders, and ordered Holding to bounce every alternate deliveries.

It had been the habit of Vishvanath always to score runs when there would be a cordon of 8 to 9 fielders on the off side. It happened when he scored 137 at Kanpur, it happened when he scored 113 against England at the Brabourne Stadium in 1973, it also happened at Eden Gardens against West Indies in 1974-75, and history was to repeat here itself.

The first two deliveries which Holding bounced at Vishvanath were dispatched by him, in a manner which characterizes Vishvanath. The ball consecutively zoomed to the boundaries. The shackles were broken and the chain which had tied Vishvanath, it seemed, either got 'loose' or it opened up.

For the next two hours, it was vintage 'Lord Indra', at Port-of-Spain, showering runs, in the form of Vishvanath's 'blade'. Mohinder, who was into the 70s by then, could move upto only 77 and there he remained stationary, as not only did Vishvanath catch him but outclassed him to reach his century, for the first time in West Indies. This was fourth of his career and the first at the Caribbean.

Eventually, to shield Mohinder, he ran himself out for 112. The drives, the square cuts and the square drives were all to be seen and believed. The famous 'Vishvanath's delight', half pull half cut, were executed in a manner which would have put the sculptors of Ajanta and Ellora in great shame. The perfect artistic nature of his batting was once again revealed, and the disdain of Holding was put to shame.

This was for the first time that Michael Holding did not have a wicket to his name in test cricket. His analysis read 21-1-82-0, and of these 82 runs, 50 were taken by Vishvanath, 36 of them by boundaries, in the region between cover point and the third slips.

His bat wielded like a sword, and it slained whatever the Windies bowlers could have, either in terms of pace or turns. Nobody could claim Vishvanath, the way he gained the command on his batting that day. The best way was to get him run out. And the West Indies did it.

When he left at 336, there were 66 runs required with only 68 minutes remaining.

Brijesh Patel, in the company of Mohindar Amarnath, took it to 392, when Mohinder was run out for 89. The formalities were completed soon, when Madanlal and Brijesh Patel in one over from Padmore hit 11 runs, Brijesh himself was unbeaten with 49.

> *This was the second occasion when a team had chased over 400 runs in test cricket to win a match. The first was the Donald Bradman's invincible Australia in 1948 against England.*

This was Vishvanath at his very best. This time there were no tears falling from Chandras' eyes. In 1974-75 when Vishvanath had played that out of the world 'glorious' innings of unbeaten 97, Chandra could not hold his tears when he got out, thus denying Vishvanath of scoring a ton. Chandra cried like a baby that day, for about half-an-hour then. But this time, there was no stopping his laughter. Perhaps 'laughter was the best medicine' for Chandra and for the entire nation on that day. The Indian team had made the Windies a fool to believe that it was impossible for any team to score over four hundred in the last innings of the match.

> *This also was the first occasion, where the two Indian greats Sunil Gavaskar and Gundappa Vishvanath, had scored centuries in the same test match.*

This was the last time that the spinners or any spinner played under the stewardship of Clive Lloyd. After the defeat in this test, Clive Lloyd decided to go in with four fast bowlers for all the tests that West Indies were to play thereafter. If at all any spinners were playing for WI after this test, it was purely for their fielding and their authority for batting.

The last test at Jamaica was 'bloodshed' test, where Clive Lloyd and Michael Holding played to "kill" the Indians. As many as 5 Indians were hurt by Holding and sent to hospital. Some had their cagerib broken by Holding or some had their wrist broken into pieces.

The batsmen to fall in these categories were Anshuman Gaekwad, Gundappa Vishvanath, Brijesh Patel, Bishen Bedi and B. S. Chandrashekar. India eventually lost the series by 2-1.

This match would go into history of the game, as one of the bloodiest and dirtiest test ever played against India by any team, as in the first innings itself, India had easily declared their innings at 306-6. Where were the batsmen to bat! Most of them were languishing in the hospital.

Again the twin series of New Zealand and England followed at home. The series against New Zealand saw India beating them by 2-0. It was Sunil Gavaskar who scored 117 in the first test at Wankhede Stadium.

The 117 runs scored by Sunil Gavaskar, was his first test ton at home after eight centuries abroad.

If Sunil Gavaskar had scored his first test ton, Gundappa Vishvanath too had scored his first century against New Zealand at Kanpur. The fading light and the dark cloud had made the stage a bit impossible for India to force the pace of the run quickly.

But within two hours of play at Kanpur, from the lunch to the tea, Vishvanath dissected the New Zealand bowling and made it look a rotten egg in the basket. He had scored an unbeaten 103 in this match.

The next test at Madras, which was played under the rain and a soggy outfield, he started from where he left at Kanpur. In a demonstration of 'slain' batting, he pulverized the Kiwi attack, clipping their wings to score 89. In the process he completed his 2500 runs in test cricket. India had won the series 2-0.

But disaster was to struck Gundappa Vishvanath and India thereafter. England under Tony Greig visited India during the second half of 1976-77 and there itself, India was floored.

The loss of form of Gundappa Vishvanath dug India in. He could score only 177 runs in this series, and his batting average was even poorer as compared to Madanlal and Ghavri.

The only test, where he hit a characteristic 79 (n.o.) at Bangalore saw India winning the test match. Besides it, he had nothing to show for the entire series. Though Sunil Gavaskar had a test ton to show, it could not prevent India losing the series 1-3 to England. However, this series could see the re-emergence of Karsan Ghavri as an all-rounder. This was also the series which saw Sunil Gavaskar reaching the mark of 1000 runs in a calendar year for the first time.

By that time the Kerry Packer rage had hit the world of cricket, and India was off to Australia to take on a very poor and weak Australian team led by Bobby Simpson. He had come out of retirement at 42 to lead a young and inexperienced kangaroos.

The first two tests were very closely fought and the honours went to Australia.

The first test played at Brisbane was won by Australia by 16 runs and 2nd at Perth was also won by Australia by one wicket.

In the first two tests, which India lost, Sunil Gavaskar got two centuries, all in the second innings of the two tests. Mohinder had scored one, exact 100 in the second, and missed out one, getting out at the nineties, in the second test. Vishvanath's contribution, for the first four innings of the two tests was 45, 35, 29 and 1.

The second test at Perth was all ours, but a valiant test hundred by Tony Mann, who scored exact 100 took the match from us.

For the history of the game, Tony Mann is the first night watchman to have scored a 100 in the test.

The destiny changed from the third test onward and, from there the runs started coming from Vishvanath's blade. Two fifties, 59 and 55 and a century from Sunil Gavaskar, his third consecutive, aided by two spells for identical bowling by Chandra in this match, 6 for 52 each in two innings, saw India beating Australia to narrow the lead to 1-2.

This was for the first time that India had beaten Australia on their soil, in test match.

The next test at Sydney saw India beating Australia by an innings. Though Sunil Gavaskar had failed, the combined effort by Mohinder Amarnath, Chetan Chauhan, Dilip Vengsarkar, coupled by a fluent 89 by Gundappa Vishvanath, and once again a superb spell of off-spin bowling by Erapalli Prasanna, aided by Bedi saw India beating Australia by an innings. Prasanna had a bowling analysis of 4 for 16

This was the first time that India had beaten Australia by an innings in a test match.

The last test at Adelaide was a cliff hanger. India needed 445 to score in the last innings to wrap up the series. Once again Sunil Gavaskar had failed. But with Mohinder scoring 89, Vengsarkar 73 and Vishvanath 87, and a little resistance which came from Syed Kirmani, who scored 52, Ghavri and Prasanna in batting tried everything to pull of one of the sensational victory for India in the test but India failed by 45 runs to end the series losing 2-3. Slipshod decision of the umpires which clearly favoured the Aussies went a long way for them to win the series.

Whereas Sunil Gavaskar scored his consecutive test centuries in this series, Vishvanath scored five consecutive half centuries. His score was 45, 35, 29, 1, 59, 55, 89, 73 and 87. He had scored 473 runs to head the batting average with 52.55 runs per innings, as compared to Sunil Gavaskar who stood third in batting average despite his 3 consecutive test tons.

Between the period 1978 to 1983, India played 9 test series, totalling about 47 test matches, and it included a World Cup match at England in 1979.

There were two series against Pakistan (1978 and 1979-80), one against the West Indies (1978-79), two against Australia (1979-80) and 1981, one against England (1979) beside the Golden Jubilee test, one against New Zealand (1981), beside a full fledged tour of Pakistan (1982–1983).

The batting of India was totally held up by the combination of the two 'in-laws' Sunil Gavaskar and Gundappa Vishvanath, but in between, one could see, Dilip Vengsarkar breaking the shackles and scoring heavily to make his presence felt, but overall it would be the two batsmen, 'the little masters' who would hold the sway.

However in this period between 1978 to the mid of 1983, out of the 38 tests played by India, in which Sunil Gavaskar and Gundappa Vishvanath had paired in all, India had won 6 test matches.

In these six test matches that India had won Vishvanath had scored 4 test centuries in them. In retrospect, Sunil Gavaskar had scored more centuries than Vishwanath, but his centuries did not help India at any time to win the matches. India was mostly on the losing side whenever Gavaskar scored a ton, then in those 38 matches.

The two memorable test centuries, out of the four which Gundappa Vishvanath hit were a score of 124 at Madras against the West Indies led by Kalicharan and a classical wristy 114 at Melbourne against Australia.

The two centuries ensured that India went ahead to beat West Indies in 1979 to clinch the rubber at Madras, and beating Greg Chappel led Australia by 57 runs to square the rubber at 1-1. The thrashing of Greg Chappel team has its own importance in the annals of Indian cricket.

In that match at one stage India had virtually pulled out when Gavaskar was adjudged out leg before by Lillee.

There was an altercation between the two greats and Lillee, it is said that he had used certain foul mouthed words against Gavaskar and Gavaskar was off the world. He pulled Chetan out of the game. Only a last minute intervention by Col Shahid Durrani, Manager of the Indian team, made the match move forward.

Needing 143 to win, India bowled out Australia for 86. Replying to India's 237, Australia were 417 in the first, and a requirement of 143 seemed a fun play for them, with that kind of a batting with Allan Border, Doug Walters, Graeme Yallop, Greg Chappel, Doug Walters to come. Two splendid deliveries by Ghavri, first getting out John Dyson and then bowling out Greg Chappel round his leg for zero, knocked the sail out of the Aussies. Dilip Doshi took it over from then, and soon the Aussies half side was back to the pavilion.

Next morning it was Kapil Dev to start with, who had taken many doses of pain killers, the previous night. Absolutely breathing fire, he bamboozled the Aussies to roll them off for 86. Kapil's efforts were 5 for 26 and no sooner that he entered the pavilion, he was to raise a toast with the legendary Sir Don Bradman, who had personally ordered a big champagne especially for Kapil to uncork the same and raise the toast.

Ghavri was a big support to Kapil whenever Kapil had to bank on somebody for the kill. Immensely dedicated, Ghavri was a perfect team man. In this series, he claimed Greg Chappel for all the five times that he was out. But everytime Greg would blast him before falling to him. This time, however, Ghavri unruffled him by bowling a few short, and all of a sudden bringing one from round the leg to the off. Greg had vanished and with it vanished the Aussies. Only a semblance of resistance had come from Allan Border who had scored 124 in the first innings, Douglas Walters who scored 78 in the first, was unbeaten with 18 in the second innings, the rest were clueless against Kapil. It was Gundappa Vishvanath's 114 and 30 in the match which saved India. The century was of a very classical order. He was forcefully and wrongly ruled out for 114 whereas actually he was not out.

Over it the unnecessary verdict to rule out Gavaskar had totally unnerved Gavaskar, and when he had that altercation with Lillee, he completely lost his cool to pull the team out for the test. Somehow, Shahid Durrani was there to play cool and save the day for India and Indian cricket.

There was another memorable innings which Vishvanath had played at Lords between these two countries. It was after the World Cup 1979, where after being beaten by England at the first test, India were bowled out for 96 at Lords. England batting first had seized a lead of over 250 runs, and thus it had enforced a follow on.

With Sunil Gavaskar out cheaply, and Chetan Chauhan gone thereafter, a vision of England's victory was raised. But an stubborn 113 by Dilip Vengsarkar, aided with a scintillating 113 by Vishvanath who along with Vengsarkar had added 213 runs for the third wicket saw India through the match. The British media had hailed this partnership, as equal and as enterprising, to the partnership of Mushtaq Ali and Vijay Merchant, during India's tour of England in 1936. They then, too had added 213 runs for the opening wicket.

One of the best innings played by Vishvanath was against the West Indies in the World Cup in 1979. With Andy Roberts, Mike Holding, Malcolm Marshal and Joel Garner in their rank, West Indies had tore the Indian batting with the score reading at 76 for 6.

But again like in the Madras test in 1974-75, Vishvanath chose the occasion to rise, first, partnering with Kapil, and then with Ghavri, and for the last, Bedi to steer India to 190. The total was same, as in Madras in 1974-75. Vishvanath went on to score 75 runs, which was perhaps best innings played against the West Indies in that World Cup. This 75 remained the highest Indian individuals score for almost 4 years for India in the one-dayers till Yashpal Sharma's 89 and then Kapil Dev's 175 overtook it in the 1983 World Cup.

In 1982-83 series of India against Pakistan, Pakistan was the last when these 'in-laws' were seen together again. Sunil's performance was good on that tour. Whereas Vishvanath apart from a breezy 53, and two glorious innings of 37, could not do anything and it saw him out of the Indian team thereafter.

Actually the two 'cheat' series, one against England in 1976-77 at India, and the last against Pakistan in 1982-83, saw Gundappa Vishvanath failing very badly. The last against Pakistan saw his waterloo.

The Vaseline used by John Lever, swung Vishvanath out in the 1976-77 series against England, but it was to his luck that he survived playing that stupendous knock of an unbeaten 79 which saw India win the match, and prolong his career. However, the "reverse swing" series at Pakistan in 1982-83 saw Vishvanath fortune being reversed. The "unholy" ploy used by Imran Khan to use a bottle cork and cut the seam of the cherry to swing the ball reverse like a rainbow curve, was something new that the Indian cricket was facing.

Over it, Vishvanath's reflexes had gone down. He was also plagued very badly by his 'problem', and along with his problem crept in the problem of his batting, the Pakistani Umpires became a helluva problems for him. On five occasions on that tour he was clearly NOT-OUT, but was ruled out. He even went to Lala Amarnath to speak his heart out, and find a solution to his problems, yet he could not overcome by any of his problems.

Once he felt that he had found it he got into his groove, scoring two consecutive score of 37, but every time he found his touch, the umpires' little finger would go up. The four decisions that went against him, when he had scored 24, 53, 37 and 37, would have put a "shame" about the standard of umpiring, anywhere in the world, but not in Pakistan.

Whenever there would be any kind of appeal against Vishvanath, the little fingers of the Pakistani umpires would point upward and Vishvanath would understand that ALLAH UPAR HAI, ie the God stays up over the sky so high, like a diamond in the sky.

His foundation and determination of waging a fight back was gone then and there. The Pakistanis targetted him, and could succeed in getting him out. Thus his 91st test played in Pakistan, proved to be his last test.

From the George Town test played at West Indies in 1971 to his 91st Test, he played 87 tests in a row which stood as record for any cricketer to have played these many tests consecutively without a break, till his in-law Sunil Gavaskar broke the record.

From 1983 to 1987, Sunil Gavaskar played as many as eight series which included a World Cup too. He played all these series without Vishvanath. The 'partnership' of Gavaskar–Vishvanath for the test matches was finally broken.

Sunil Gavaskar, in between the time from 1983 to 1987, went to beat Sir Bradman's record of highest individual centuries, beside winning the World Cup in 1983 and the one-day tournament at Australia in 1985. He played like his in-law Vishvanath, his last series in India, and his last test match at Bangalore, in his sister-in-law's place to score a magical 96, against Pakistan, which could not help India to win the match, and he retired from test cricket thereafter.

The two, from the Georgetown test, in 1971 against West Indies till the end of the Pakistan test series of 1982-83, had played in 89 tests together, a world record of any 'relatives', playing so many tests together without being separated.

Together they paired in 19 tests which brought victory for India. From November 1969, when Vishvanath first played for India till the end of his Pakistan sojourn,

Gundappa Vishvanath had carved 21 tests win for India, and in all the twenty-one tests that he had featured, he contributed either a fifty or a hundred, beside his catches in the slips Sunil had two tests victories, less to show.

After 1983, when Vishvanath left the company of Sunil Gavaskar, Gavaskar had played 26 test matches, but he could not win even a single match for India, even while he was setting all kinds of personal record in test matches.

This shows how important was Gundappa Vishvanath to Sunil Gavaskar, for his plans, for winning the test matches for India. The two test victories overseas, against England had come under Kapil Dev's leadership, but Gavaskar's contribution in those victories were as good as a COCK LAYING THE EGGS. In all fairness and with all the tribute to this great Indian legend, Gavaskar in the World Cup 83, and in the series of 1986 against England was a terrific headache to the lovers of cricket as he was an abject failure in both these outings.

India did not loose even a single test match, whenever Gundappa Vishvanath had scored a century.

Five of Gundappa 'Vishvanath' test centuries came at a moment, when India really needed them, and it earmarked India's victory in test matches. The other nine came at a juncture when India needed it to force a draw. In terms of percentage about 35.71% of test tons by Vishvanath had brought victory to India, the balance 64.29% of centuries saved the matches for India.

Also, on the 'deadly' fast pitches, where Vishvanath's five test hundred brought India the win, Gavaskar had failed in three of them, miserably, and did not take part in one. The exception being in Port-of-Spain in 1976, where India had to chase 402, Gavaskar had scored 26 and 102, whereas Vishvanath had scored 41 and 112.

Unofficially, Vishvanath holds the world record of putting the highest runs for any wicket, for the third wicket, adding first an unbeaten 136 runs with Vengsarkar (injured 70) and then 316 runs with Yashpal Sharma

(130) in Madras in 1981-82.

This was the test he scored a gallant 222, where Sunil Gavaskar had failed. His knock was embellished with 32 hits to the fence, this is a record which he shared with Budhi Kunderan, to hit the maximum number of boundaries in an innings, which was later, if I'm not mistaken, was broken by V. V. S. Laxman at Calcutta, when he had scored 281 against Australia.

Vishvanath's runs came, always, at a condition, which used to be critical. He had forty half centuries to his credit which at one stage was a world record, for the highest number of fifties hit in test cricket by any cricketer. This record now perhaps stands in the name of Stephen Rodgers Waugh.

In terms of 'technique', Vishvanath was very perfect and absolutely compact. Being very natural and possessing the habit of having so many alternatives to play a single delivery, and seemed with the natural ability to play his stroke, very-very late, beside to adjust his stroke accordingly, he always chanced his arm, which Sunil did not.

The two in–laws, together had played 215 test matches, had scored 16, 202 test runs, have held 178 catches, had taken 2 test wickets, had hit 48 test centuries together, had notched 88 fifties together and had 'etched' 21 victories for India in test cricket, will always be remembered as "the two best to have played test cricket for India". Vishvanath's solitary wicket was Jim Higgs of Australia in 1979 at New Delhi, whereas Gavaskar had claimed Zaheer Abbas at Faisalabad in 1978

Hereunder is the performance of the two great cricketers of India.

Name	M	I	NO	Runs	H	Cen	H/C	Ave
G.R. Vishvanath	91	155	10	6080	222	-14-	-40-	-42.32-
S.M. Gavaskar	125	214	16	10,122	236(n0)	-34-	-45-	51.12

But, who amongst the two is the greatest, my vote would go to Vishvanath. First for those 35.71% of wins for India in test matches, whenever he scored a ton, and secondly, without Gavaskar at Delhi in 1969 against Australia, he led India to seven wickets win, he himself had scored an unbeaten 44, and the two tests win against Clive Lloyd's Windies in 1974-75 series, at Calcutta, and at Madras.

Without Gavaskar, he scored 52, 139, 97 and 46 to help India square the series at 2-2 at the end of the Madras test then.

Another contribution of Vishvanath's greatest contributions to Indian cricket was 'the run chase at Port-of–Spain' in 1976, which fetched India a 6 wkts win over West Indies. This had changed the 'face' and the character of India's run chase and its habits. On many occasions, thereafter, India had scored over 400 in test cricket in the second innings, either to chase a victory, or to save a test match.

Gavaskar, without Vishvanath, could not win any test match for India on the basis of his batting alone.

However, one thing that stands for sure is "NO OTHER RELATIVES TO COME WOULD CONTRIBUTE SO MUCH TO INDIAN CRICKET."

A lot of cricket enthusiasts have always asked me one question, and it was "if Vishvanath was better than Gavaskar, why it is that he scored less runs compared to Gavaskar".

My logical explanation has always been "the difference between them was how to play and 'when to play the shots' "!

Vishvanath always knew "how" to play the shots and he played them at will. He accumulated

6080 runs in 91 test matches. But it was Gavaskar, who knew, "when" to play the shots. He played his shot only "when" needed. For that's the reason he scored 10,122 runs in 122 test matches which included 34 test tons, and 13 against West Indies.

For one thing, which I would like to make it very clear to all and sundry, India will never, in its history, again, will have a Gundappa Vishvanath, or a Sunil Gavaskar.

A rare breed of cricketers were these two in-laws but a sportsman of a rare breed was GUNDAPPA RANGANATH VISHVANATH. May be Vishvanath has scored only 14 test centuries and only 6080 runs in test cricket, but when it comes to being asked who was the best Indian batsman from 1967 to 1987, the answer will always be GUNDAPPA VISHVANATH, though the highest run getter would be SUNIL MANOHAR GAVASKAR.

Sunil Gavaskar is being termed as the head, body and the soul of Indian cricket. However I would like to say that Vishvanath was the MORROW in the bone of Indian cricket. The morrow gets converted into sperms after remaining in the bone for fourty days. Scientifically only three drops of morrow gets converted into sperms. There lies the importance of morrow in the living body. The rest goes waste. NO DOUBT THEY SAY THAT THE MANAGEMENT OF FERTILITY IS THE MOST IMPORTANT MANAGEMENT IN LIFE.

That's what Vishvanath knock made us to feel about the importance of the sperms and the blood. He got those runs for India at a very critical juncture when the others failed, for his innings were always like the extra drops of blood infused into the Indian team for its survival or the extra drop of sperms which was necessary for fertilisation, for producing the victory, it always etched VICTORY for

India, or saved them from an ignominious defeat. It kept the Indian team to exist.

To me he was the BLOOD of Indian cricket and rightly, Dennis Swanton had referred him as the BLOODY BAT of Indian cricket, when he scored those 33 runs at the Oval in 1971 which killed England in that test match.

There is something more I would like to add to Sunil Manohar Gavaskar. He in a blaze of sensation, dropped Kapil Dev from the Indian team for the third test which was played at Calcutta in 1984. This was something unbelievable and it raised many an eyebrows in the country. The reason cited was an uncharacteristic and irresponsible shot by Kapil. India had lost the match then.

Look at the score. In that match there were only three fifties scored by the Indians. Mohinder (64) and Kapil (64) in the first innings and only Sunil Gavaskar (65) in the second. Nobody else could get into the fifties. So how was Kapil's performance in any way irresponsible. If there was anybody who aggregated more than hundred runs in the match, it was Mohinder Amarnath, who had aggregated 105 in the match, rest nobody could aggregate more than ninety in the match.

The selectors at the insistence of the captain then, who I would not have to name because everybody by now knows who was the captain then, had hoofed Kapil's name out for the Calcutta test which was to follow then. This was for the act of indiscipline.

Let us look into Gavaskar's performances from 1983, from the start of the Windies tour to the World Cup. Gavaskar had scored 5 and 9 in the first, 2 and 24 in the second, 0 and an unbeaten 148 in the third and was an utter flop in the remaining two.

His batting analysis reads as follow after the series: He had scored a total of 243 runs in that entire series with an unbeaten 148 as his highest. He stood sixth in the final analysis on the tour in the batting.

His poor form continued in the World Cup and his scores were 19, 4, in the first two matches in that tournament of the 1983 World Cup. Now add to that was a very poor strings of scores in the one-dayers that were held on the previous tour of the West Indies sojourn which was held just before the World Cup 1983.

Looking into his very poor score, the Indian think-tank had dropped Kapil as the skipper for the next two games against the West Indies and Australia, which India lost. There was a huge outburst of temper and some untoward incidents. All of a sudden Kapil was made a villain. "Just see, the two matches that Gavaskar missed playing in the 1983 World Cup, and India had lost both of them," were the people's comment. What was his contribution in the first two matches that India had won when he was in the squad, is my answer.

Well he was back into the squad after Dilip Vengsarkar had received a serious injury in the match against the West Indies which India had lost. What was again Gavaskar's contribution, one might ask.

Well the readers, here it is : 0 and 9 in the next two matches. He was again a failure against the England in the semis and then a super-duper failure in the finals against the West Indies. My question is–WHAT KIND OF RESPONSIBLE BATTING WAS IT.

Neigh and NAY, the Indian selectors did not have a heart to drop Gavaskar. Kapil had it. He showed and he demonstrated and demonstrated it in a large and in a huge manner. He had to pay the penalty for it.

Gavaskar again in the series against England in 1986 did not fare any better under the leadership of Kapil, but was a shade better than what he scored in terms of average against the West Indies in 1983. He scored 34, 22, 35, 1, 23 and 54 in that order to score 169 runs to stand fifth in the final batting analysis. He maintained his batting average thereafter from this tour to the last series and the last match he played against Pakistan in 1987 to announce his retirement from the test scenario, and also from cricket.

Gavaskar in his playing days was also the front runner in the matter of ad endorsement. At one point of a time he alone was doing 15 ads endorsements. The companies were not the hanky–panky ones. The instant food, the fast food, the ball pens, the cold drinks, the auto makers, the suitings and shirtings, the razors, the travel–you name them and you had Sunil Gavaskar endorsing them.

My question is–where are those companies now. The YAMAHA MOTORS continue to exist, but have a market share of less than five percent, the THUMBS-UP has been turned into the thumbs down. The Cokes have gulped it. None of the instant and the fast food companies that he endorsed now exist. These have either gone with the wind, or have made the way for the Kentucky Fried Chickens and the McDowells. The ball point pen that he endorsed do not write now, because they have wond up their business, and the travels (Air-India) is in a state always to decide whether it should continue to do the business or should it merge with the Indian-Airline to survive.

What shall I call it–a MIDAS TOUCH IN REVERSE or THE CRUEL HAND OF DESTINY which has killed all these companies. In both the cases here I have referred him as a God. It is because I respect him.

Now we find him doing a kind of consultancy to the BCCI. My point is–If Gavaskar was a midas touch, why the companies he endorsed for, had gone with the wind. Yes my dear readers, and yes the BCCI – Sunil Gavaskar is not the ultimate victorious verdict of the almighty. He too has had his parts of failures and his association with the high names and the fames of the Indian organisations then and even now has brought about a disaster to the companies. It can happen in the same fashion to the BCCI also.

He may be heard but his words may not be taken as the final decision and the final outcome coming from the mouth of the Lord Shiva always. Why give him the unnecessary importance always. There are others who have a better credentials than him and one of them is Erapalli Prasanna. The other whose name readily comes to my mind is B. S. Bedi. What fantastic record do they have in their career in the job. Even Gundappa Vishvanath had a fantastic career with the State Bank in the security department and so had Roger Binny in the Public Relations department. Why can't the Board listen and act to their advice.

Sunil Gavaskar to me is the best opening batsman that India has ever produced, but a poor ambassador, specially when it comes to public relations. There are many instances when he needlessly spoilt his relation –both on and off the field with the players that he was playing against, or with the umpires, or the people who had nothing to do with him.

Sunil Gavaskar to me is an OVERHYPED entity altogether. He likes to remain in the limelight. Whether be it "PREMACHI SAVALI" or anything out of it, he has enjoyed the light. He knows his way in and his way out and he always had people who would help him to be in the limelight. Whether he deserved it or not, that is and that never had been his consideration.

In this age of the electronic media, there are some who have stuck to him like a leech, to always place him high on the cloud number nine, for their own advantage. That he has under-performed after his playing days were over to help his cobbers at the time of their dire strait, it seems it is something not very special to him. He is always busy now talking more about the game, rather than putting his best effort to solve the problems that surmounts the cricketers who have played with him. Gavaskar can do a lot being off the game, rather than being with it. But it seems that those things are not in his agenda.

Gavaskar possesses a uniqueness to enjoy the three bagsfull and the authority, but it never seems that he likes to shoulder the responsibilities. In this matter also I have had an experience. After spending about Rs 1,000 from my pocket to various authorities, I had written to the genius master to help Salim Durrani to be conferred with the Padma Shri award. With his authority I felt he could move the things. Pat came a reply to me, he suggested me to write it to the Secretary of BCCI. I got my answer as the God had replied to my answer.

For, whatever he has done and for whatever he did to us we with an open heart accept him as a legend. Also he had some kind of a role to play to shape the destiny of the Indian cricket so we do excuse him. BUT HE WAS NOT THE ONE AND ONLY ONE. There have been many, and this book is about them. Being elder in age, and with the Bengalis in 1971, readily agreeing to adopt him as a son to play the Ranji Trophy for them which did not happen, Sunil Gavaskar, you are a BORODA to us, and we have taken your outburst as the burst of our elder brother to say the least.

My only request to you is : fight hard, like you fought on the ground and get that Padma Shri award conferred to Salim Altaf Durrani, to Dilip Sardesai, and to Eknath Solkar, poshthumously in that order. Be fast, be quick.

It is said that handsome is what handsome does and greatness is what a great does. You will be a greater than the life figure to us if you can lay a way out for Durrani, Solkar and Sardesai to be conferred with the Padma Shri.

Do not again say to me or write to me that you are wondered to know that Salim Uncle has not received this award. If he has not, it is your duty to channelise the path and the way for him to get it. Do not forget the help you got from Salim Durrani at the time of your tour to the West Indies in 1971. That would be a feather in your cap.

Sunil Gavaskar at least has shaped the destiny to some extent as far as the Indian cricket is concerned. Some of them who are seated with him in the commentary box will never be able to do it in any capacity. And how can they. They do not even know the A, B, C, D of the Indian games and sports, neither they know the history, civics and the geography of it. Yet these commentators have made the people here in India to believe that they are to the sports, what James Irvine Livingstone was to the Suez Canal. Their's way of talking, flouting the others at times, and the kind of words that they use at times, had propelled the bobbies of England to swirl their stick on one of them, once at London, for which he had registered a complaint with the English police authority. This kind of acts will only put them into trouble, will some day get them into a helluva problem. Better watch out the commentators.

Anyway, when we were studying the management, I remember our Professsor for Personnel Management, teaching us that, it is and it should be JUDICIOUS REJECTION always, rather than the EFFECTIVE SELECTION in the process of recruitment and selection.

Gavaskar's mindset then to induce the Indian selectors to reject Kapil Dev for one test match as a suspension was not judiciously correct, if Kapil's performance is taken into account.

There was a movie, named "Mere Jivan Saathi" starring Rajesh Khanna and Tanuja released in 1973. The movie had as many as seven fantastic songs which made the movie an all time hit. There was a song in it : O MERE DIL KE CHAEN, CHAEN AAEY MERE DIL KO DUA KIJIYE: sung by the GREAT, Kishore Da.

Yes this is a song which puts the likes of me into normalcy, when I go into the state of reminiscene, and then of depression about the Kapil's dropping affair for one test. There are many like me who loose their composure when they are reminded of this, what puts them into normalcy and composure is not known to me, it could be anybody's guess.

Kapil in himself is an institution, and by dropping him then the selectors had demolished that institution. For in the eyes of God they are the sinners...

Thanks, Kishore Da, many a thanks to you for that song. There is one more song in that film sung by Kishore

Da, "CHALA JAATA HOON, KISI KI DHUN MEIN". Yes this is the song which keeps us going when we are subjected to any nonsense in our life, be it the office affair, be it anything in our life, or be it the BCCI, it administrators and its selectors.

THANK YOU KISHORE DA FOR THAT OUT-OF-THE-WORLD song which was simply "MAGNIFICIENT". That is the song which helped us to keep our composure, when Kapil was kicked out of the B.C.C.I. But for you Kishore Da, and but for that song, we would have died of the pain to learn that Kapil was kicked out by the B.C.C.I. troupes. Today he has been totally outcasted from the society that belongs to the B.C.C.I.

Yes CHALA JAATA HOON KISI KI DHUN MEIN......that DHUN keeps me alive.

9

EKKI: THE FIELDING REVOLUTION

IT was the year 1967-68 and the Indian team had embarked on a tour of Australia and New Zealand. This was the first twin tour taken by India in the annals of the Indian cricket. The Indian team was led by Mansur Ali Khan Pataudi and Chandu Srikant Borde was his deputy.

The team had as many as 7 players from Bombay besides Chandu Borde from Maharashtra. So as many as eight positions had been vacant in the West Zone squad for Duleep Trophy.

A left handed batsman-cum-left arm spinner by the name of Eknath Dhondu Solkar was then making a large wave in Indian cricket. He was the captain of the "first" national Indian school cricket team which had toured Ceylon in 1965. Imran Ali of Nagpur, a solid middle order batsman was the deputy to Solkar in that school team.

As West Zone were without their regular "stars", who had boarded the plane for the Australia and New Zealand sojourn, West Zone included eight new members for their Duleep Trophy campaign against the North Zone.

As mentioned earlier, one of them to get the nod of the West Zone selector was Eknath Dhondu Solkar. He was in the side to play against the North and he made full opportunity that came to him.

He scored a patient 148 in the match against North in his first essay to the first class game of Duleep Trophy. Not only that, when his chance came for fielding, he had grabbed as many as seven catches in the match, standing first at the forward short leg, and then in the covers.

He had equalled a world record for snapping those 7 catches, and if he had taken one more in the same matches, the world record of as many as eight catches in any first class cricket game would have been to his name.

He was informed by the team Manager of the West Zone about this, and when the dolliest of "dolly", a turn of his legs by K. S. Inderjit Singhji, came to him, he floored it. This chance to script his name in the records of book had gone, but his knock of 148 beside those seven catches made Eknath Solkar a rising star of Indian Cricket overnight, and Solkar had come to stay in Indian cricket.

Further good knock came to him in the Ranji Trophy matches and beside this, his fielding which was a magic, a treat to watch, cemented his place permanently in the Bombay Ranji squad. Born in 1949, in the same year as that of Gundappa Vishvanath and Sunil Gavaskar, and along with Eknath Solkar, were making news and hitting the headlines in the domestic cricket.

Vijay Merchant it was, who had a good look at him, and when the New Zealand squad under Grame Dowling arrived in India, he took the chance of putting Eknath Solkar, along with Gundappa Vishvanath, Ajit Gandotra and Subroto Guha, in the reserves for the Indian team.

After losing the test at Nagpur to New Zealand by 107 runs, Eknath Solkar was included in the Indian Squad for the first time. This test match was a disaster for India, and it was the rain which saved India from losing the series.

New Zealand, in the last and the final test at Hyderabad in 1969 had scored 181 and got India out for 89, and again in their second knock, declared their innings at 175 for 8, thus setting a target of 268 for India to win. India were reeling at 76 for 7 when the rain interrupted and the match ended without result. Eknath Solkar first essay at the wicket ended with a "blob", thus emulating some of the great, who had started their career with a "zero", and in the second knock, he was fighting to save the match for India with Venkatraghvan supporting at the other end. Solkar had an unlucky 13 to show for his unconquered effort.

Thus a "mix" of "unlucky badge and a great patch" had strucked him in the debut, and this was to stick with him till the end of his test playing career.

The Australians under Bill Lawry were here immediately after the tour of New Zealand and though, Solkar, Vishvanath, Surinder Amarnath and Subroto Guha were in the squad, for Bombay test none of these teenagers had played in the first test at Bombay, which India lost by 8 wickets.

However, it was here that the Indian Skipper Nawab of Pataudi took a deep liking for Eknath Solkar. In this test, played in Bombay at Brabourne Stadium, Dilip Sardesai had torn his muscles in the thigh and he went back to the pavilion, and Solkar took the field thereafter.

It was here that Solkar had matched Pataudi for every move after move for his fielding at the covers. India had never had a fielder who could match Pataudi in the out-field at the "cover" region then, and Solkar had just arrived.

The next was a request of Bedi which Pataudi heeded. Bedi wanted a fielder in the forward short leg region and Pataudi having watched Solkar's agility in the field ordered him to take that position. He brought off a great catch, a "quarter chance" in term of Sheahan himself of Bedi, in the forward short leg to send the entire Brabourne stadium into ruptures.

Earlier, India had lost the first test at Bombay by 8 wickets. Obviously there was a change in the squad for the next and once again Solkar was fielded in the next at Kanpur. He was in the test squad once again.

Along with Solkar, who had regained his place in the squad, Gundappa Vishvanath and Ajit Gandotra were to made the debut. Vishvanath like Solkar, started with a "blob", as described earlier, that some of the greatest in test had started with a blob, but ended with a 137 in this test. Ajit Gandotra, started with "13" runs, and this is a number, unlucky for some, for after this test, Gandotra was never to play again for India after the third test at Delhi where India beat Australia by seven wickets.

The Kanpur test would always be remembered for two incidents. The first for Gundappa Vishvanath's 137, his maiden century in test, and then, in the second innings, when it appeared that Australia would break through for a win, it was a 110 runs partnership with Vishvanath, that Solkar had added, for the sixth wicket, that saw India through. Solkar's own score was 35. This partnership had saved India and Solkar was, since then a permanent feature in the Indian squad. In this match in the first innings Solkar scored a well strucked 44.

The next test at Delhi saw India beating Australia by 7 wickets and right from the day one of this test, till the match lasted, Pataudi had made the forward short leg position, a permanent home for Eknath Solkar.

He had helped India to triumph in this test by holding two sharp chances in the same position, beside scoring an unbeaten 13 in the first essay. This five knocks in test cricket by then were 0, 13*, 44, 35, 13*. It was observed that Solkar had the capacity to score a 35 and grab two catches in the test. This had ensured his place permanently in the side.

The other change which one saw was that he had started opening the bowling for India. A slow left arm leg spinner to start with, Solkar had changed himself to bowl the slow off-cutters for India.

The Australian sojourn ended with India losing the series 1-3, but Solkar, by his own standard had cemented his place in the squad. He had scored 178 runs in the series with an average of 29.66, not a bad start to a cricketer, who would come down to bat at a lower order, just above the tail-enders.

The West Indies tour of 1971 was the next in that order. And here for this tour, another 'yourself' cricketer by the name of Sunil Manohar Gavaskar was to join the wagon of Vishvanath and Solkar. Also Dilip Sardesai had staged a comeback. Bombay's Ranji captain, Ajit Wadekar was to lead the side and it had the three 'S'; Sardesai, Solkar and Sunil in the side. These three 'S' were to create a history and bring about a change in the face of Indian cricket then. The fourth 'S' Salim Durrani too was to join them to script a "Golden chapter" in the history of Indian cricketers and Indian cricket.

The first test of that series was played at Jamaica and India were tottering at 76 for 6. Joined by Solkar during that stage, Sardesai added 137 runs for the sixth wicket. Solkar's contribution was 65.

Next Erapalli Prasanna was to add 122 runs with Sardesai for the ninth wicket, Prasanna between the period from 1967 to 1973 was regarded as the best night watchman by the world of cricket, and then 52 runs were added by Sardesai and Bedi for the last wicket. Dilip Sardesai was eventually out for 212, his second century of his test career, and this was his highest individual score in test matches.

The match was reduced to a four days affair as the first day play was lost because of rain. Prasanna with 4 for 65 and Venkat with 3 for 45, held the West Indies for 217, West Indies were asked to follow on and it was for the first time in test history that West Indies were forced to follow on against India. The match ended without result.

In the second test, Sunil Gavaskar was to make his debut at Port-of-Spain, Trinidad. After Ashok Mankad

(44), Sunil Gavaskar (65) gave India a flying start, and West Indies had been bowled out for 214, Dilip Sardesai in the company of Eknath Solkar, laid a very strong foundation for India.

They together, once again added 114 runs and ensured that India secured a huge lead. Sardesai had scored 112 and Solkar contributed 55. India took a lead of 138 runs.

Here it was a drama that started. West Indies fought back gallantly through Roy Fredricks and Steve Comacho and at one stage they were 150 for two wickets.

It was here that Eknath Solkar came into the picture. He first took two stupendous catches at the forward short leg to remove both the openers in the first innings, and held two more to grab 4 catches.

Thereafter, when Gary Sobers and Clive Lloyd had come to the wicket together, Dilip Sardesai, who had a terrific cricket brain, requested Ajit Wadekar to introduce Salim Durrani. Durrani, who was Sardesai's room partner during that tour, was put into the attack. Durrani had promised Sardesai on the close of the previous day's play that he would see to it that he gets Clive Lloyd out and would bowl out Sobers for a blob.

Salim Durrani, first got Clive Lloyd out, caught by Wadekar at the short square leg, and immediately next, bowled Gary Sobers, shattering the bails which was placed on the off and the mid stick, through a beautiful armour for which Sobers had no clue at all.

From 150 for 2, it was 169 for 4 and finally 256 all out. Eknath Solkar had two more catches in this innings to swell his total number of catches to 6 in the match.

Needing 124 for victory, India again got to a fluent start with the opening pair of Mankad (29) and Gavaskar putting on 74 runs. Between 74 to 84, India lost two more wickets of Salim Durrani and Dilip Sardesai, before rattling up the match by 7 wickets. This was the first time in the history of Indian cricket that India had beaten West Indies in test match. Syed Abid Ali who had scored an unbeaten 21 had hit the winning shot, a boundary of Sobers to inscribe one of the sensational and historic win for India.

Solkar had many a things to do in this victory. He scored a valiant 55, took as many as six catches in the match and effectively bowled his slow off-cutters to contribute to the Indian victory.

However it was Solkar, his six sharp acrobatic catches which turned the match in India's favour. Four of them were of the world class.

Solkar by then had set a standard in the field at the forward short leg position, that nobody before him, in the world could ever imagine of doing it.

The most to be benefited by it were the Indian spinners. Specially Erapalli Prasanna and Bishen Singh Bedi became very dangerous-killers to be frank because of Solkar's gallant deed at the forward shot leg position.

Secondly, till then, the standard of the fielding of the Indian cricket team, which was the "worst" in the world till 1968, all of a sudden appeared to be the best. Solkar made a lot of difference in this arena of cricket for India. With Sunil Gavaskar at first slip, Wadekar in the second, Venkat in the gully, Abid Ali in the backward short leg, and the "hero" of them all Eknath Solkar in the forward short leg. Oh where would the batsman place the ball to keep it out of the stump, anything in the air would be snapped and swapped by this deadly pentagon of the close fielders.

The man to lead it from the front was Eknath Solkar, and he individually, by his own standard, had raised the standard of the Indian fielding to eight, on a scale of ten.

This victory at Port-of-Spain was simply due to three factors. The first was the effort of Dilip Sardesai to hit 112 and a "request" to Ajit Wadekar to bring in Salim Durrani to bowl when the Windies score read at 150/2. Secondly the Silver medallion effort of Eknath Solkar, who scored a valiant 55 and grabbed 6 catches in the match. And the last, but not the least, the two Golden "balls" of Salim Durrani to get rid of Clive Lloyd first, and them Gary Sobers, whom he bowled for a blob, successively.

The series went from strength to strength, and this "trio" of Sardesai, Sunil Gavaskar and Solkar, by the end of this test, also had added same good flesh to their arms by their act and display at the Caribbean.

For, Sunil Gavaskar went on to notch his first career century in the next test which ended without result. In the fourth test at Barbados, West Indies amassed a huge 501 for 5 declared. That was the do or die test for the Windies. Once again when the score stood at 70 for 6 at Barbados, in the fourth test Dilip Sardesai came to the Indian rescue. He along with Eknath Solkar added 189 for the seventh wicket. After Solkar was out for 65, Sardesai added 62 for the last wicket with Bishen Singh Bedi, who remained unbeaten on 20 to save the follow-on for India. Dilip Sardesai was the last man out for 150.

After a quick declaration by the West Indies at 180 for 6 it was Sunil Gavaskar again with an unbeaten 117, who saved this test match for India. The match ended with India scoring 221 for 6, and Eknath Solkar was in the company of Sunil Gavaskar, who fought tooth-and-nail to save India, from facing a 99% defeat in this test match.

No sooner the last test got over, in which Sunil Gavaskar had scripted 124 and 220 runs in the match, the history had to show that India had beaten West Indies by 1-0 on their soil for the first time.

This was India's first victory and the first series win at West Indies.

This brought to the forefront, the three dimensional qualities of Eknath Solkar. He had scored 224 runs in the series with 3 fifties and had taken 9 catches beside 6 wickets in the series. The phenomenon if it was, anything but his brilliant fielding.

There were a few occasions in the series where he was asked to stand in the cover region. He had matched

Pataudi from moves by moves in India. So how could one think that he would stand next to Clive Lloyd. For at the end of the series, the debate was not whether Lloyd or Solkar was good at the cover region. The debatable question was 'where was Solkar good, in the covers or in the forward short leg'.

The next series against England saw India beating England by 1-0. Here too Solkar had a good time with the bat and the ball. He scored a 67 and an unbeaten 6 in the first test at Lords, a fifty in the second and in between he would chip in with one or two wickets here and there, when he was asked to turn his arm over.

But his crowning glory came in at the Oval. England got out for 355 and restricted India to 284. Wadekar (48), Sardesai (54), Engineer (58), and Solkar (44) helped India to swell their total and with Abid and Venkat also scoring 26 and 24 respectively, India had narrowed the lead to think of putting a stiff fight in this test.

However, in the second knock, the "one" catch which swung the pendulum of the match in favour of India was the one which Solkar "clutched" to get rid of Alan Knott of Venkat for 1.

No sooner did the floater from Venkat hit the faint edge of the bat and then the pad, and was about to kiss the ground one feet away from Alan Knott's left leg, Solkar anticipating the flight of the ball, flung himself, stretched to the maximum, got both his hands beneath the ball and scooped the catch. This was a magic, a miraculous catch in the annals of test cricket.

From there onwards with the score board reading at England 54 for 5, India and Eknath Solkar were to tie a "knot" with the destiny at the Oval. Chandra who had till then taken 4 wickets, removed the English tail to finish with 6 for 36 and it required 172 runs for India to win the match.

It cost 6 wickets for India to taste its first test as well as the first series win over England at England.

As said earlier, if it was one moment to be picked, which turned the scale in our favour, it was the catch of Alan Knott, which Solkar held of Venkat to pulverise England and reduced its image to a burnt carbon paper. Solkar was by then not the best close-in fielder, but perhaps the world's best fielder in the world of cricket.

The next sojourn was against the same opponent in India. Here too, the pendulum started to swing the either way, and till the Madras test, the contest was tough on a even keel, however, India went 2-1 up by the end of the third test.

This was possible largely due to the debonair batting of Farokh Engineer, and the blitzkreig of Salim Durrani. Whenever the English bowlers took control of the stock of situation, Durrani would come out to hit them out of the ground. Durrani was in his real element in these series, and was perhaps the best Indian on the view. Had it not been of him, the result of the series would have been England-3, India-0.

If the batting performances of Engineer and Durrani combined, was the "trial balance", the catches of Eknath Solkar, who had 12 by the end of the Madras test, was the "Profit and Loss account." There was a one test loss as the New Delhi test was won by England, and two tests gain, with most of the gain coming from those twelve catches that Solkar had accounted for, and hence Solkar's account as well as the balance sheet of India, showed an asset of two wins, with an outstanding surplus of 12 catches. These twelve catches had made the difference then.

Till then, he never knew about the fact that he had equalled a world record. Now in the next test at Kanpur, he was told by a statistician that he needed one more catch to individually script the record of the highest number of catches, in a series, in his name.

After fielding for 357 runs, at Kanpur came England to bat and with it came a dolliest of a dolly catch offered by

Graeme Roope to Solkar. When everybody expected him to catch it he, to the surprise of everybody, spilled it.

This was the match, where for the first time, Eknath Solkar did not have a catch in the test match against his name to show the world.

Well, none came to him in this test, and no other catch would visit him even in the next test at Bombay and Solkar's chance to script his name in the books of world record for bagging the maximum number of catches, individually, had gone.

It was here that with the catch of Graeme Roope, having come and gone, the luck of Solkar too had started playing "eyes – spy's" with him.

For he was to play 4 series after this. This included two against England, one against New Zealand and one against West Indies. These four series saw Solkar playing 9 test matches. He scored a century once in the inaugural test match at Wankhede Stadium, and then finally against England at Eden Gardens at Calcutta, in 1976-77, then he bowed out of test cricket.

After spilling that catch of Graeme Roope, Solkar somehow was not the Solkar whom the world had seen, as quick as a gazelle on the feet, as supple as the snake to twist his body, and as sharp as the "Gillette" twin razor blade to hold the catches in an electrifying manner.

As a batsman, he seemed to have reached the hit-or-miss stage of Rusi Surti, as a bowler he looked a parody of Bernard Julien, as fielder he looked a Solkar who had come down a peg or two.........

In his entire career, he held 57 catches. Four of those 57 came in as a substitute. Fifty three catches in twenty seven tests, by any standard, was a performance, which was above all the standard set till then, made him and gave him the pride of place, and a place in "Hall of fame" in the fielding department of this game. Add those four catches, as a substitute that he had held, and he made the script to write that he was the best close-in fielder.

A total of 57 catches, with an average of 2.07 catches per test is something which will never be broken by any standard in the world of cricket. This will put Eknath Solkar as the best close-in fielder in the world that the game of cricket has produced.

It is, and it was Eknath Solkar, whose fielding and the standard of the close-in fielding, which he set and the sharp catches he took off Prasanna, Bedi, Chandra and Venkat, made these spin quartet look very invincible.

Those three-in-a-row victory, which saw Solkar, holding 26 catches, took India's cricket to the highest pedestal and put India on the "Zenith" of the world cricket, for the period between 1971 and 1973.

The face of Indian fielding had changed and Solkar was the one who transformed it. Eknath Dhondhu Solkar will always be remembered for bringing about a revolution and a change in the face of Indian fielding.

Along with his fielding was the runs that he had scored in the test matches. There was a time during his career in the test matches that he played, he was given the nickname-Mr DEPENDABLE for his stoic, stubborn and staking bat. He would rise up to the occasion whenever India were in the doldrums.

He was a very honest and a true cricketer, who knew only one thing, that cricket was his religion. He lived for cricket, ate it, chewed it and swallowed it, beside breathing it. Nay, he never missed an opportunity to play the game, whether for India, West Zone, Bombay or his office team Mafatlal.

If at all the one man who had changed the face of the standard of the fielding of this game in India, it was Eknath Solkar, who was equally brilliant, both at the covers and at the forward short leg region.

India will never ever have a fielder like him in the days to come, like India will never ever have a Mansur Ali Khan

Pataudi, Vishvanath, a Sunil Gavaskar, a Kapil Dev, a Salim Durrani, a Farokh Engineer, a Syed Kirmani, a dogged stubborn opener like Chetan Chauhan or like the spin quartret, who went on to change the face of Indian cricket in the way that they could. Players of that species are born once in a thousand years and fortunately we at our lifetime were very lucky to see them performing in front of our naked eyes.

Solkar's fielding and the standard that he set should be a milestone and an inspiration to the future generation, and it would teach them always, CATCHES WIN MATCHES.

SOLKAR'S 53 CATCHES IN TEST:

Year	Opponent	Test	Total	Chandra	Bedi	Prasanna	Venkat	Others
1969	N.Z	1	1	-	-	-	-	1
1969-70	Aus	4	10	-	2	5	2	1
1971	WI	5	9	-	2	3	4	-
1971	Eng	3	5	3	-	-	1	1
1972-73	Eng	5	12	7	2	2	-	1
1974	Eng	3	4	-	3	1	-	-
1974-75	WI	4	8	2	2	1	2	1
1976	WI	1	3	1	1	-	1	-
1976-77	Eng	1	1	-	-	1	-	-
Total		**27**	**53**	**13**	**12**	**13**	**10**	**5**

As for others, he has held one catch each of Abid Ali, Ghavri and Salim Durrani, and two of his own bowling. In addition, Solkar had held 3 catches as a substitute fielder, which are not counted in one's career.

These are two things which every cricket followers, who have studied the game minutely would agree. The first is the kind of unbelievable quarter chances and the half chance catches that he grabbed, would be very hard for the present generation of cricketers to even think of it, lest to try to catch them.

Secondly, India will never again have a close-in fielder like him. He perhaps will remain the finest and the best fielder that India has ever produced.

There are many pundits of the game of cricket, who would either choose a best Indian Eleven, or a best World Eleven. The players who find a place in these teams either get it on the basis of their batting, or bowling. There is only one who would make it to these teams, purely on the basis of his magnificient and majestic fielding. HE IS NONE OTHER THAN EKNATH DHONDU SOLKAR.

Oh! catches of those sorts! Oh! catches of those kind, MIRACULOUS. Oh! and again Oh! are those kind of catches that exist in cricket, and Oh! are those the kind of catches held! Well, I would'nt have believed it, if Eknath Dhondu Solkar had not caught them.

Solkar as a human being was a very simple man. He knew nothing about anything, but if he knew something it was how to maintain the friendship, and his friends were the cricket and the cricketers. Gavaskar, Parkar, Gundappa Vishvanath and Milind Rege were his best friends.

Later on the names of Karsan Ghavri and Salim Durrani were added to his list of friends. He literally would worship Pataudi, as he felt that without Pataudi he would not have been anything for what actually he was. He adored Durrani for the way he hit those sixes. He once had said to Durrani that he would like to have a century runs partnership with him to which Durrani had replied to him that it could be possible if Solkar played for Rajasthan. Solkar's reply was –Why don't you play for Bombay. That is what Bombay and Bombay's cricket was for him.

Nothing was more to him except cricket. He ate cricket, he would breathe cricket, he drank cricket, and he lived his life with cricket. He knew nothing without cricket except cricket, all that he knew was to be precise and perfect in his fielding and perfect it with grace which was again cricket.

He was a very poor eater. He always feared that if he ate a lot like Sardesai, his fielding would wane and would disappear in the air. So in order to keep himself trim, he ate very little and he would do a lot of running.

However he wished that he had added some weight. Once a great Indian cricketer, who would always pull his leg had told him that if one wanted to add some weight without eating, the best would be to keep a bottle of beer under the pillow and sleep. The fermentation process that goes into making a beer has its effect on the body and the body swells, without making a difference to the movement.

Solkar was to believe that he would put the beer uncorked under his pillow. It was Polly Umrigar during the twin tour of 1976 at the West Indies, who found that Solkar would sleep that way. He later explained Solkar about the entire joke. No doubt, when he was hit on the head by Sheldon Gomes of that fierce pull at Trinidad in a game against them, the game was over for the day and everybody of the team had gone to the hospital to meet Solkar, it was the worried team who put in a lot of question to the doctor and to him about his head. It was Sunil Gavaskar who had said that anyway what is in his head. Solkar then had kept quite.

When the Indian team had come back after the twin tour of Australia and New Zealand in 1981, Solkar then had called Gavaskar to inform him that he had won the Ranji Trophy for Bombay as a captain, and that is what was in his head ever since he started playing cricket for Bombay. As a friend Solkar was very close to Gavaskar and Milind Rege, though he was as thick and as thin as a cobber when it used to be Vishvanath as a friend. Everyday till he was alive he would call Vishvanath on the phone and talked to him.

On the day he expired, an hour before he had rang Vishvanath and asked about going to Sai-baba for his darshan and blessing, after the NCA fielding session of the camp would be over. That was Eknath Dhondhu Solkar. So very simple, so very pure and so very religious.

He was the one who had changed the face of the fielding first for the Indian cricket. Likes of Solkar.... in the forward short leg .... no, no, never-never to be seen again.

At last, the one catch of Eknath Solkar which got out Allan Knot at the Oval. That catch is described as the catch by the God through the hands of Solkar. My question is: What about the catch of Abid Ali in the 1968 Irani Trophy match of Uday Joshi against the South Zone? It was the same style, the same kind of a catch. No difference. Nobody talks about it, and neither did Solkar talk about it anytime, though he knew it and the records show it.

Yes Eknath Solkar was not a brooder, his catches and his actions made the people to talk about him. He preferred to keep quiet. If I'm speaking even a word, even a bit false about that Abid's catch, go ask Mr Rajan Bala about it, as Mr Raju Bharatan is not alive.

That was Eknath Dhondhu Solkar for you. Genious for the catches, else BHONDU as his cobbers who would keep on pulling his legs would refer him as to.

10

KAPIL DEV: THE ONE MAN DEMOLITION SQUAD

NO my dear friends, who are reading this book, nay the readers, I just do not have it in me to explain about this illustrious and a magnificient cricketer.

Can anybody explain to me what kind of aroma that could be there in the kasturi, what would be the quantum of water in the Pacific ocean, what could be the flux of light in the sun. These things are virtually hard to explain and describe.

In the same vein and the same manner, it is virtually hard to describe this institution of Indian cricket. I'm just making an attempt to do so, believing that I could be correct. Even if I'm, I might not be perfectly precise to write on this cricketer, the kinds of whom are born **ONCE in a thousand year**. Yes I'm trying to write about Kapil Dev Nikhanj.

It was the year 1974-75, and Ravindra Chaddha was leading the Haryana Ranji team to its first ever pre-quarter final match of a Ranji Trophy encounter against Madhya Pradesh at Indore.

There was a young, energetic, but a raw guy, who was hardly 16 years of age then, representing Haryana. He hailed from Chandigarh and he in that match had played with a little bit of impression that he was a promising bowler for the Haryana team then. After the match was over, he had five wickets to show. The guy was none other than Kapil Dev Nikhanj. Haryana had won the match and it threw two youngsters, Kapil Dev and Vijay Chander whose 87 had helped Haryana to win the match.

Two seasons afterward, Haryana went two steps ahead and lost to Bombay in the semis. But the quarter final match against Bengal was something which Indian cricket will never forget.

The star studded Bengal team was badly butchered and the Bengalis were bruised, first when Kapil Dev went on to claim 7 for 46, and then in the same match, Ashok Malhotra went on to score 86 for Haryana. The devastating spell of Kapil Dev brought him to the forefront of Indian cricket.

Kapil then by the end of 1977-78, had made it to the rest of the Indian team, and the Board President XI team. He nearly made it to the Indian team of 1977-78, which was to tour Australia, but narrowly missed it.

It was the tour of Pakistan in 1978, when Kapil Dev made the news. But before it, it was an Irani Trophy at Chandigarh in sector 22, the stadium where he hit the national headlines.

Playing for Rest of India against Karnataka, he took five wickets in the match. But it was his knock of unbeaten 66, which had 5 sixes and 7 boundaries, which caught the fancy of the spectators.

The Pakistan sojourn of 1978, saw Kapil Dev making his test debut for India. The series was lost 0-2 by India, but the two cameo knock of 59 at Lahore and 43 at

Karachi, besides the seven wickets he had captured in the series, made him a household name.

It was in this series, at Lahore where Kapil Dev, in tandem with Karsan Ghavri, bowled, as an opening bowler for India. The K-K express was born here.

As mentioned earlier, India had lost the test and the series by 2-0, and the next series was against the West Indies at home.

It was here in the series that Kapil Dev bloomed tremendously as an all-rounder. He got his first test ton played at the Feroze Shah Kotla at Delhi. In the entire series he captured 22 wickets. Ghavri had captured 27 wickets in the same series.

The series against Pakistan earlier in 1978 saw the end of Erapalli Prasanna as a test bowler. And at the end of the first test against West Indies at Bombay, saw B. S. Chandrashekar's destiny coming to an end as a test bowler for India.

Two genious and the exponent of spin bowling had evaporated and, from the Bangalore test match against the West Indies, two pacers from India had emerged to carry the burden of claiming wickets in test matches for India.

The series gave India a 1-0 lead over West Indies at Madras where India had defeated West Indies by 3 wickets. In a pitch which played fast, and true, and which behaved as the fastest wicket that the world ever could see and believe, and that too at Madras, Gundappa Vishvanath had scored 124 and 39 to give India the win.

However, it was Kapil's unbeaten 26 in the second innings which made the victory possible. Batting with a temperature of 104°C, he went to strike certain shots, which were beyond anybody's guess. It helped India to win the match. By the end of the series, Kapil had over 300 runs and 22 wickets to prove himself as an all-rounder with a great future.

It was the World Cup thereafter at England, and the test series against England, where India had lost the series

1-0 to England. Kapil Dev had failed with the bat, but had emerged the leading wicket taker for India with a personal best of 5-143.

It was here in this series that he had observed, with a keen interest, about Mike Hendrick swinging the ball from the leg stick to the off. Kapil till then had a natural inswinger, but from here he started learning to swing the ball outside.

The series against West Indies earlier, saw Kapil Dev and Karsan Ghavri, claiming 49 wickets amongst themselves.

The series against England saw them capturing 26 test wickets between them. This brought back the reminiscene of R. Surendranath and Ramakant Desai, who between them had captured 28 wickets in England in 1959.

The pair of Desai and Surendranath did not last long, but this pair of Ghavri and Kapil Dev, went from strength to strength and had cemented their place in the Indian test squad.

The Australian team under Kim Hughes was to tour India next, and immediately after this tour, Pakistan were to tour India.

The series against Australia brought the best from Kapil for he went on to capture over 30 wickets in the 6 test matches, and with Ghavri claiming 18, India went on to win the series 2-0.

This series, as said earlier, was followed by a home series against Pakistan. Pakistan, last had toured India in 1960-61 and had drawn the series by a whisker, the score was 0-0. It was after 18 years that Pakistan team was touring India.

This tour was a series of certain "personal" milestone for Kapil Dev. He single handedly won the series for India. He went on to capture another thirty plus wickets for India, with Ghavri helping him with 16 test scalp beside Kapil being an instant hit with the bat.

It was in this series that Kapil had claimed his 100 test wickets, when he had claimed Taslim Arif. Also he had completed his "test double" of 1000 runs and 100 wickets in this series.

A one "off" Golden Jubilee test against England followed and India were to loose the match by 10 wickets.

A sporting gesture by the Indian skipper Gundappa Vishvanath, to call back the English wicket keeper, when England were tottering at 56 for 6, changed the complexion of the game.

Ian Bothan with Bob Taylor, went on to build a partnership which turned the complexion of the game in England's favour. India had lost the test match then.

This was the first test that India had lost at home with Kapil Dev playing for India.

Between the series against the West Indies led by Alvin Kalicharan till this test match, played against England, Kapil Dev had created wonders after wonders both with the ball and the bat. His fielding was bonus, and India till then had won five test matches in the three series that it had played against her opponent. In all the series won by India, Kapil Dev was adjudged as the man of the series.

The Australian sojourn in 1981 was something which Kapil Dev and India would not like to forget easily. The series started with India losing the first test badly and just escaping a defeat in the second. Karsan Ghavri in the second innings of the second test batted stoutly and ensured that India does not loose the match and the series.

It was the third test at Melbourne that India had beaten Australia by 57 runs to tie the series 1-1. A century by Vishvanath who scored 114, in the test and some stubborn batting display by the Indian had set a target of 143 for Australia to win the test.

Needing 143 to defend, Karsan Ghavri produced two deliveries to knock out the sail of the Australian ship.

Taking a pain killing injection to ward off the pain in the right toe, Kapil in a devastating spell of 5 for 28, broke the backbone of the Australians to register one of the most exciting victories for India. Kapil had claimed 16 wickets in the series and Karsan Ghavri 10. This was the first occasion that India was able to finish squaring the series.

In the process, Karson Ghavri went on to claim 100 wickets of his test career. He thus became the second pacer from India to achieve the honour of claiming more than 100 wickets in the test.

The series of New Zealand followed thereafter and India were beaten 1-0 by New Zealand.

This was the last series where Kapil Dev had Karsan Ghavri as his new ball partner.

The hallmark of the bowling pair of Kapil Dev and Karsan Ghavri was, they did not allow any opening batting pair to add 100 runs for the opening wicket.

This is one feat which has never been achieved by any other opening pair of fast bowler in the world.

In his test career spanning to 39 test matches, Karsan Ghavri had accounted for 109 test wickets while in the batting, he had scored 912 runs with 88 against Australia as his highest. His best effort in bowling was the figure of 5 for 33 against England at Wankhede Stadium in 1976-77. Mind you all the five wickets that Ghavri claimed in this innings were from the tweaks and not from the "quicks".

Thereafter, Kapil Dev had to bowl with the like of Roger Binny, Mohinder Amarnath, Madanlal, Bharat Arun, Manoj Prabhakar, Subroto Banerjee and Javagal Srinath.

One pair had come, and gone thereafter, but none could produce the effect that Ghavri could produce it with Kapil. The result was Kapil was over burdened and over bowled. He started loosing his penetration, bite and the "dunk" that he had possessed once.

His glorious moment was the World Cup victory, and one of the avalanche of an innings that he played against

Zimbabwe, and his spell of 5 for 43 against England. All these helped India to move on to the finals of the World Cup.

Under his leadership India went on to win the World Cup held at England on 26-6-1983.

In the process, Kapil went to complete his 2000 runs and 200 wickets in the test cricket. He led India in the 1987 World Cup, but thereafter, he lost his captainship.

Kapil went on to play for India till 1994. In between he helped India to win the 1994 Hero Cup. The series against Sri Lanka also saw him capturing his 433rd wicket which made him the highest wicket taker of all time in test cricket.

This happened when he claimed the wicket of Haasan Tilakaratne getting him caught of Sanjay Manjrekar. Not only with ball, Kapil also had shone brilliantly with the bat, and the series of 1992-93 against England, at Madras, saw him completing his 5000 runs in test cricket. He had by then, joined the "bus" of some of the greatest all-rounder like Gary Sobers and Ian Botham in test cricket, to have achieved the distinction of scoring over 5000 runs and claiming over 200 wickets in the test matches.

The series before the West Indies sojourn to India in 1994 saw this great all-rounder, announced his retirement from the test cricket.

Kapil had represented India for 132 test matches, which is the highest number of test matches, till the moment of writing this book, played individually by any cricketer in India, and also by any cricketer, in this sub-continent.

He had claimed 434 wickets. This is the highest by any Indian cricketer till date and had also scored over 5000 runs in test cricket. The pair of Kapil Dev and Karsan Ghavri together had claimed 543 test wickets.

Kapil Dev will always be remembered for single handedly waging a war for the Indian cricket, especially after the exit of Karsan Ghavri in 1981 and when Gundappa Vishvanath left the scene in 1983.

For 13 long years since 1981, Kapil Dev accounted for 47% of output individually, of course, to contribute and help India fight its opponents in international test matches. He was rightly called as "One Man Demolition Squad".

The modern era of Indian cricket definitely would belong to Gundappa Vishvanath for his contribution with the bat to Indian test victory, to Karsan Ghavri for supporting Kapil Dev so magnificiently in bowling, to Roger Binny for supporting Kapil so brilliantly in bowling specially in one-dayers, and of course, this **"Hriday Yuvak Samrat",** Kapil Dev Nikhanj, for his deeds in the field of Indian cricket.

Unfortunately, Karsan Ghavri and Roger Binny, neither could win a Arjuna Award, or a Padma Shri.

Hey the administrators and the President of the BCCI, are you reading this book, are you listening? Act fast! and if yes! Please act fast.

Kapil Dev in journalistic parlance will always be remembered as the **One Man Demolition Squad**. There will never be another like Kapil Dev, as an all-rounder to play for India again.

If there was anybody who revolutionised the Indian bowling, transforming it from the spin to the pace, it was this HRIDAY YUVAK SAMRAT, a guy, a coot from Haryana. He completely changed not only the face of the Indian bowling, but he changed the face of Indian cricket with the World Cup that he won for India on June 26th 1983 at the Lords at England.

He was adjudged the INDIAN MILLENNIUM CRICKETER and that actually he was.

Kapil it was who along with Karsan Ghavri totally had changed the scenario of Indian cricket. From the "SPIN DOMINATION" he along with Ghavri had brought the

"PACE REVOLUTION". The analysis of both the players is as follow-:

BATTING

Name	T	I	No	R	HS	Cen	H/C	Ave
Karsan Ghavri	39	57	14	913	86	-0-	-2	21.23
Kapil Dev	131	184	14	5248	163	-10-	-27-	31. 05

BOWLING

Name	T	Balls	R/C	Wkts	BB	BB/M	5 W/I	10W/M	Ave
Karsan Ghavri	39	7036	3656	109	5/33	7/120	-4-	-0-	33.54
Kapil Dev	131	23,740	12837	434	9/81	11/146	-23-	-02-	29.64

Combined and if an effort is made to know what has been their contribution to Indian cricket, one finds that together they conceded 16493 runs and captured 543 wickets for an average of 30.37 runs per wicket.

Kapil is thus remembered very greatly by Indian cricket for this change, but to be honest with all and sundry, it was Karsan Ghavri also to a large extent to have supported Kapil for the same.

11

SALIM DURRANI: THE TURNING POINT OR PRINCE CHARMING

EACH OF HIS KNOCK HAS A CHUNK OF HISTORY ATTACHED TO IT AND HIS BOWLING HAD A REPERTOIRE THAT WAS THE TALENT HE WAS MADE OF.

WHEN I TALK ABOUT SALIM DURRANI I TALK ABOUT A GENIUS AND FOR THE GENIUS NO RULES APPLY. It was the cricketing year 1959-60 when Richie Benaud was leading an Australian team to India. The Indian team then was led by G. S. Ramchand. This series had many a historical landmarks and achievement for the Indian players who played in the series, but the important of them all was the first ever win against Australia at the test match at Kanpur. The series was lost 1-2 by India. Who can ever forget the Kanpur test where India had beaten Australia by 119 runs with Jasu Patel claiming 14 wickets conceding 124 runs for India.

However, one of the incidents of this series beside that famous test victory was that the world of Indian cricket would never forget, and would like to remember always was the debut of a young, handsome and a debonair cricketer named Salim Altaf Durrani, at the Bombay test.

One might like to know how this cricketer made it to the Indian team. Actually the West Indies team under the captaincy of Gerry Alexander was touring India for the 1958-59 series, in which they were to play five test matches. They played against the Central Zone team, then led by the late Vinoo Mankad at Jabalpur, at the Jabalpur University grounds on a matting wicket. When the Central Zone team came in to bat, they were totterring at 40 for 4. This was the time when he came on to hold the innings. His childhood dream Vinoo Mankad who had gone to open the innings, was batting with 20 odd runs at the other end.

He walked up to Vinoo, after taking the guard and asked, KYA KAROON. Vinoo promptly replied, WOHI JO SAURASHTRA AUR RAJASTHAN KE LIYE KARTE AYE HO. These words were like the balm to him which is applied on the forehead when the head is full of pain.

What followed was a classical batting, full of valour, character and style. The Guru-Shishya combination totally collared the strong West Indies bowling which comprised of Atkinson, Taylor, Sonny Ramadhin, Lance Gibbs, and Gary Sobers. His innings of 80 had 5 sixes, one each of all the bowlers mentioned above, and ten boundaries. He scored a mind lingering and a mouth licking 80. His Guru at the other end Vinoo Mankad had scored 88, but it was he who completely overshadowed Vinoo in the stand which was worth over 140 runs. He was very ruthless and completely brutal against Sobers and Ramadhin, and in fact Ramadhin looked very novice against him. Sobers was made to concede 20 runs in an over when he hit him for five consecutive boundaries, and on another occasion, Lance Gibbs was clobbered for 16 runs.

Three of his sixes landed out of the stadium, which was quite a big one, and two of his sixes smashed the window pane of the physics lab. That was the destruction he had caused to the West Indies bowlers. Not only that, while keeping the wickets, which he was doing that time, effected two magical stumpings, one each of Sarwate and Vinoo Mankad, to show that he was a star wicket keeper in the making. The pain to come for the cricketers, for the world over was born here at Jabalpur, on that day. And what a LOVELY pain he proved to the world over till he played his last test at the Brabourne stadium in 1973 against England. From here till the last test that he played, he was the PRINCE in whatever he did on the field.

It was here that Vinoo Mankad completely took him under his belt. The first thing Vinoo told him was, AB SEY WICKET KEEPING NAHIN. TO KYA, Salim asked him. LEFT ARM BOWLING, Vinoo Replied, MAIN SIKHAUNGA. THEEK HAI, he replied.

Vinoo made him to understand that there were Nana Joshi, Indrajeet Singhji, Budhi Kunderan, P. Sen and the evergreen Farokh Engineer awaiting in the wings, and as a wicketkeeper he would have very little chance. Vinoo thereafter made him a left hand tweaker, but not before his left hand got fractured for as many as five times, before he finally made a name as a whimsical and a magical left armer. Here in the chapter I would explain how, but let us move on to his exploits as a POOR MAN'S GARY SOBERS.

Absolutely handsome, tall, with his height measuring at 6 feet 4 inches, smiling and always the charm, which immediately made one to call him "charms", and since his name was Salim, people compared him with Salim of the Akbar's dynasty, and he soon was known as "Prince Salim" of Indian cricket.

There was a reason for the people then to call him Prince. The movie Mughal-e-Azam was released then. And it had a character named Salim. As this Salim would play and act as a prince, people nicknamed him Prince Salim. His game, his character on the field resembled to a prince. And off the field, he was a KING.

He was baptized at the Brabourne stadium against Australia in 1959-60 and in the only one test he played, in that series he batted at number 10. He helped Bapu Nadkarni to add 26 runs for the last wicket, his share alone was 18 with two towering sixes, one of Benaud and the other of Ian Meckiff. For no fault of his, he was later dropped by the Indian selectors. The reason was best known to the selectors. By his own standard, and his imagination, he was dumbfounded, lost but was not shattered. He promptly had declared to the Raja of Udaipur, who used to sponsor the Rajasthan team then, and who individually used to pay him for his services to the Rajasthan Ranji team, that he would be the best all rounder of the world rubbing his shoulders with the great Gary Sobers, in the days to come, and he proved his words, correct and true. He was the ONLY ONE of his kind, during those time, who used to promise and keep his words, like the great Romario of the Brazil football team. Romario might have failed a few times, but not this Prince. He never failed if he promised to deliver on the field. Here it was, that the dropping and chopping, and hiring and firing of Salim Durrani was to start, and it continued till he played his last test match for India against England at the Brabourne stadium in 1973. After the series against Australia, Salim Durrani was totally ignored till the end of series against Pakistan in 1960-61, which had ended in a draw. After the Bombay test against Australia, Salim Durrani was to create havoc with the ball, in the domestic cricket, besides he let his bat do the talkings. In a match against Pakistan at Jaipur, playing for Central Zone in 1960-61, Salim Durrani scored a century which only a cricketer like Durrani could afford. In a display of entertaining, sparkling and 115 minutes of batting, one saw him scoring 110 runs, yet he was not preferred to play for India by the selectors. When he bowled in that match, he bowled Hanif Mohammed with a dream delivery, which only a bowler of his calibre could bowl. During the course of the match, afterwards, Hanif came to him and complimented him saying in Urdu that, AAP KE WALID SAHIB, MERE USTAD HAIN. WOH JITNE UMDA USTAD HAIN, USSE BHI ZYADA BEHATRIN AUR UMDA AAPKA WHO GAIND THA. Besides that he had captured the wickets of Imtiaz Ahmed, Nazar Mohammed and Walli Mathais. Since Subhash Gupte was in the side and with Chandu Borde lending admirable support as a leg spinner, also Bapu Nadkarni assisting the bowling attack, it seems, the necessity of Prince Salim was never felt to include him in Indian team for that series and he was not included then. However, for his performance in domestic cricket, he was conferred with the Arjuna Award in 1961.

Salim Altaf Durrani was the first cricketer in the history of Indian cricket to have been the recipient of Arjuna Award conferred by the Govt. of India in 1961. One just cannot stop a genius for all the time and one could not stop this genius of cricket for long. Came the tour of England in 1961-1962, and came the man of the moment.

The English team was led by Ted Dexter and it had some of the best batsmen to play spin. In fact it was a very strong English side, and nobody had given any chance to the Indian team to beat them. It was also loaded with certain spinners, who had all the tricks and the ammunition to neutralize the Indian spinners. Nari Contractor was to lead the Indian team. The first three test matches played at Bombay, Kanpur and New Delhi were drawn. In these three test matches, Salim Durrani had only 126 runs and 5 wickets to show.

Durrani would come in to bat at number seven, only after Contractor, Jaisimha, Manjrekar, the Singh Brothers, A. G. Milkha and A. G. Kripal Singh and Borde would bat. Still he had left a mark on the mind of the selectors with a sparkling 71 which he had scored at Bombay. In this test, England had declared at 500-8, and at one stage a follow-on looked inevitable for India. But a ballistic stand of 142 runs that Durrani added with Borde saw India crawl to a "safer zone". Durrani had three towering sixes to augment his effort. This knock, in his second test ever, showed the glimpses of the Gary Sobers, and he after this knock was named as "Poor man's Gary Sobers". Borde had scored 69 runs in that innings

As described earlier, the first three test matches ended without any result. The Indian squad saw two changes for the next two test matches, and one of the Singh Brothers, A. G. Milkha Singh was dropped. Mansur Ali Khan Pataudi and Vijay Mehra were chosen. This further demoted Salim Durrani in the batting order. However, he was not to give up.

The advent of Pataudi and Vijay Mehra brought about a total change in the batting at Calcutta in the fourth test against England. Batting first in this test India had scored 380 runs. The prominent scorers were Chandu Borde (68), Mansur Ali Khan (64), Vijay Mehra (62) and the Prince of Indian cricket with 43. Writes Prasanna in his autobiography, ONE MORE OVER, that this innings of 43 was perhaps the best of the match.

Actually, the top order of India had collapsed, but the middle order gave the respectability. Durrani coming to bat at number eight just pounced on the English attack, and with the help of the tail enders, took the total to 380. He himself had scored 43. He would have scored more had he not got into a mix with the batsman batting at the other end, Chandu Borde, eventually sacrificed his wicket for Borde, during that run out mishap, and had he gone to bat two notch ahead, instead at number eight, he would have scored perhaps a ton in that innings. However, it was here that the fortune of Indian cricket and its destiny was to change for a better. India bowled out England for 212 thus gaining a lead of 168 runs. Bowling in tandem with Chandu Borde, he bowled a spell of 23.2-8-47-5.

After scoring 252 in the second essay, India through Salim Durrani, who had a figure of 33.2-12-66-3, ably supported by Ramakant Desai 2 for 31, Polly Umrigar 2 for

46, went on to bowl England for 233 runs to win the match by 187 runs and except for Alan Johnes, who had scored 96 in the second, none of the English batsmen could face Salim Durrani with ease.

Thus with this performance, Durrani had showed the selectors that they did not do any justice to his talent and from 1958 till this stage of the test matches that were played by India, he and his almost 3 years of test career was unnecessarily chopped off by the selectors. The next was the Madras test. Here again Durrani had a major role to play. Batting at number 9, he did not get enough chance for his bat to do the talking. But he stayed at the wicket very long to help India to swell the total by contributing 21. He had added over 25 valuable runs for the last wicket with Erapalli Prasanna, who making his test debut was unbeaten on 9. But it was his bowling which did the dancing, singing and tuning yet another great victory. In an exhibition of nagging accuracy at times, and flighting the deliveries, like a kite at the other, he made the English batsmen to dance to his tune, to floor six wickets. His analysis read 36-4-105-6. Chandu Borde admirably supported him with his figure reading at 30-9-58-2.

India had scored 428 runs in the first innings and the scintillating feature of the match was a ton scored by Mansur Ali Khan Pataudi (103). Farokh Engineer had scored 65, whereas Babu Nadkarni (63) and Nari Contractor (86) had something to do to butcher and collar the English attack. Pataudi and Contractor had added 104 runs for the third wicket.

Durrani turning his arms got a handsome lead for India with the score board showing that India had secured a first innings lead of 147 runs. In the second knock, except Vijay Manjrekar, who had scored 85, none of the Indians could stand up to the English spinner Fred Titmus, and India were out for 190.

England needed 355 to win, but another mesmerizing spell by Salim Durrani who had a figure of 34-12-72-4, broke the backbone of the England team and with Chandu Borde having a figure of 25.3-8-59-3, England were forced to hand over the "rubber" to India for the first time. Erapalli Prasanna had "opened" his accounts of wicket in this test with a figure of 11-3-19-1.

This was the first occasion in the history of test cricket that India had beaten England in a test series, besides this there was a maiden test series win for India against a team outside this continent.

Salim Durrani had 189 runs and 23 wickets to show. Vijay Manjreker with a score of 68, 84, 96, 189, 24, 27, 13 and 85, had amassed 586 runs to head the batting list with an average of 83.71 runs per innings, whereas it was Salim Durrani who had 23 wickets to show, besides those 189 runs to his effort to stamp his name as a true all-rounder. This performance of Salim Durrani made him the best all-rounder of the game and put him next to the great Gary Sobers then.

The Indian team thereafter was to tour West Indies and Durrani had booked his ticket to the Caribbeans. This series saw the end of the cricket career of Nari Contractor. In an upcountry game against Barbados, he got his forehead cracked by a "chucker" from Charlie Griffith and Pataudi took it over from there. However, it could not prevent India losing the series 5-0. The hallmark and the redeeming feature of this series was the fourth test which was played at the Port of Spain, Trinidad.

After conceding a lead of 247 runs against the Caribbeans, India were forced to follow-on, and India fought back gallantly to score 422 in their second knock. This was possible due to two centuries that India had scored. One of them came from Salim Durrani. This was for the first time that he was sent to bat at number three. Pouncing on the opportunity, he within two hours, by the end of the play, cracked 91 runs to remain unbeaten till night. The type of an attack he launched on the West Indies, most fastest the most dreaded bowler Wesley Hall was something, which was even worst than the plundering which Mahmood Ghaznavi might have done when he had to loot the Somnath temple.

Out of the sixteen boundaries and two sixes that Salim Durrani hit that day to remain unbeaten, he hit 10 of those boundaries besides those two huge sixes, of Wesley Hall, to hear from Hall, during the course of the drinks that "If you continue hitting me this way, I'll very soon loose my place in the West Indies squad". The next day, he spanked Hall for another 11 runs, of the 13 runs that he had scored, to get out for 104. It was an innings of a life time but that did not go well with the Indian skipper. The Indian skipper Pataudi had felt that with that kind of blazing start, Durrani should have stayed and kept his wicket intact for carrying the fight to the West Indies camp, rather than spanking the Indie's quickies. Another innings of a lifetime (172*) by Polly Umrigar brought the West Indies back to the crease to wipe off 172 runs from the Board to win the match. They did it, but not before Salim Durrani mesmerizing them with a spell of 33.2-12-66-3. For his effort, he came in for a lot of praise from players and the press, all over the world, but not a word of congratulations had come from the Indian skipper Pataudi.

This match could have been won by India, if and only if the Indian fielders would have accepted those 15 catches, that they dropped during the course of the match. The top scorer of the match for West Indies, Gary Sobers who scored an unbeaten 153 was dropped twice at zero by the Indian fielders of Salim Durrani, and after that he was dropped for another five times. Had the Indian team taken advantage of those catches tale of the match could have been different.

The moment Pataudi saw Salim Durrani playing in India, he realized that in terms of quality and talent, he had no "peers", nobody to equal him. On his day, he would be the monarch of all that he surveyed. But he was very casual, very negligent, and would not care of anything and anybody, if he felt to do something out of the world. The 1962 series of West Indies got over and India were bruised and battered 5-0. However, it was Salim Durrani's performance with 259 runs to his credit and 17 wickets at an average of 28.35 runs per wicket, that stood out in the series for India. He had castled Gary Sobers thrice in the first four innings that he bowled to him, and if the catches did not go abegging in the last one, he could have had Sobers for five times in the series.

This series saw Gary Sobers too producing and performing to his best, and the entire series was a clash between the two all-rounders, Sobers of West Indies and Salim Durrani of India. Though Sobers had more runs to show but Durrani had neutralized him in the series by claiming 17 wickets. It had become a hot debate then, to point, who amongst Sobers and Durrani, was the best all-rounder of the world. However, the conclusion was that Sobers and Salim Durrani were then the best all rounders of the world. Hereafter, the England team under Mike Smith was to tour India. India was led by Mansur Ali Khan Pataudi. The series ended without any result. This series was one of the most "spineless" series in which both the teams did not make any serious attempt to break the shackle of those spineless draw which killed the series.

Players of both the sides were interested to make an effort to write their names in the record book of cricket. A lot like Budhi Kunderan, Hanumant Singh, Mansur Ali Khan and M. L. Jaisimha successfully did it from the Indian side, and Peter Parfitt, Ken Barrington and Colin Cowdrey did it for the English team. Here it was in Bombay that Durrani got into test match of 90s and instead of batting patiently he once again chanced his arm to the English spinners to miss what could have been his second century of his test career. He did not care for it.

This attitude of the Prince had again 'furiated' the Nawab of cricket of India, but once again he let it go. The Nawab for the second time had a 'pep' talk with Durrani.

He let it go because he knew that this was the character of Salim Durrani though it harmed the team and the Indian cricket severely.

It was in this series at Kanpur, where the last test of the series was played. India were left with only 50 minutes when the series was to be over. In a display of swash-buckling cricket, Durrani hit a fifty in a manner which was unbelievable, in 28 minutes. He scored another eleven runs thereafter in two minutes to remain not out with 61. This fifty which he scored in 28 minutes is a world record in test cricket. This is the fastest fifty registered by any test playing cricketer, even till today the record stands.

Leave apart the spectators who were enjoying the game, even the scorers and the statisticians forgot in the moment of anxiousness and anxiety, to keep a check on the numbers of balls that he had faced to score this fifty. But to be precise, this knock of his had eight boundaries and 3 over boundaries. Two of them had cleared the stadium at the Green Park on that day. By the end of the series, Durrani had 230 runs and 11 wickets to show for his effort. While his 11 wickets were valued at 41.72 runs, his 230 runs came at an average of 28.74 from eight innings. It was till this stage that he was holding his place regularly as the India's best all-rounder, and one of the two best all rounders in the world of cricket, the other being Gary Sobers. However this was the beginning of Salim Durrani to face the worst of the time in cricket which he was to face in future.

The Australian cricket team had landed here immediately after the English sojourn and Pataudi was to lead the side. That was in 1964. The Australians were led by Bobby Simpson and had a team which was much stronger than their Indian counterpart.

Before the selection, there erupted a huge argument between the selectors and the skipper about whether to persist with Salim Durrani or to get rid of him. A section of the selectors were for his head. To some extent Pataudi too was not very happy about his casual approach where on occasions, he would become adventurous and throw away his wicket. Good sense prevailed and he was added to the list of the probables which was to play the Australian side. The surprise magic performed by the selectors for this squad was that Farokh Engineer was not considered to represent India, and his place had gone to K. S. Inderjeet Singhji. Anyway the series went on and in the first test, India lost to Australia by 139 runs. Replying to Australia's 397, India scored 276 through a knock of 128 by Mansur Ali Khan Pataudi. A sort of a record was held after this test.

This was for the first time that the instance of a combination of a father and a son had scored a century on debut against the same team. For, Iftikhar Ali Khan Pataudi had scored 102 in England, playing against them in 1932, and his son Mansur Ali Khan too accomplished the feat playing in his first ever test against Australia.

Just for a record, when the Pakistan team had toured India in 1979, Mudassar Nazar had hit a century at Bangalore and it was the second instant on the Indian soil where the father-son combination had scored a century playing against the same opponent in their very first test against a country. Australia after being out for 211 in the second knock, set a target of 332 for India to win it, but apart from Hanumant Singh, who scored a fighting 94 all in the second innings of the match, nobody rose up to the occasion.

The second test was a clift hanger at Bombay and the induction of B. S. Chandrashekar in the squad had a tantalising effect on the bowling. Getting Australia out for 320, India replied it with 341, and when Australia were out for 272 in the second knock, India hammered 256 losing eight wickets to square the series. Pataudi had two good knocks of 86 and 53, so had Manjrekar of 59 and 39, but the partnership which transformed the victory into reality was between Durrani (31) and Borde, whose unbeaten 30 made all the difference. At one stage India had lost seven wickets with all their front line batsmen back into the pavilion. It seemed to many that Australia would wrap up the match and the series, but a faithful and a fruitful partnership of over 50 runs for the eight wicket between Salim Durrani and Chandu Borde got us the win. This was the second occasion that the Indian had accounted the Aussies in a series. Durrani at a very critical juncture hit two towering sixes and brought India to the brink of victory, and in the final analysis his 31 runs made all the difference.

Chandrashekar in this match had a figure of 8 wickets for 123 runs. He had passed his test. After this test a scrutiny was done about Durrani's contribution. He had only 4 wickets conceding 246 runs till this match to showcase his effort. He was virtually out, but for that fighting 31 in the second knock which saved his skin, and the prestige of the Indians. The last test at Calcutta was a drab affair with both the teams adopting a "not to take a risk" approach. At one stage in this match, in the first innings on the first day, Australia at lunch, were placed at 123 for no loss.

However, in a dramatic spell of 23 overs in toto, and 15 overs after lunch, Durrani bowled in such a startling and tantalising manner, that the Aussies had taken the tea, after rolling over their arms a bit, to the Indian team batsmen. In short and to be brief, Pataudi had asked him to see that the Aussies go for the tea losing six wickets, he saw to it that the Aussies went for it bowling five overs to the Indian bats.

Between the lunch and tea, that day, Durrani spun such a deadly web around the Australian batsmen that from 123 for no loss, the Aussies were bowled out for 174. Salim Durrani had a figure of 27-11-73-6. The Australians found him very hard to read on the turning Eden's flat. What was more the first six wickets that he got were all bowled. It is the only and till this date, it has been the only occasion in a test match that the first six batsmen were out-clean bowled.

Though India had scored 235, gaining a lead of 57, the Aussies never took a chance thereafter and played it out to safety scoring 143-1. The rain also, to a large extent, played a spoilsport and killed the match in terms of enthusiasm. In the entire series, Durrani's contribution with the bat was 70, for an average of 14.00 runs per innings. His bowling had 10 wickets to show, but in the process he had conceded 428 runs, this made his bowling effort look so ugly.

This performance made the selectors feel that Durrani was not the same force of what he used to be a few years back. Moreover, he was reaching the 30's of his life. The selectors started thinking that he was getting 'old' for the game. However, due to the insistence of Pataudi, he was included in the side.

Next came New Zealand in 1965 under John Reid in India and Salim Durrani's place in the Indian squad went to Venkatraghavan after he was dropped midway during the tour. The four test match series went in favour of India by 1-0, and it was Venkatraghavan, in the fourth test, who was playing instead of Durrani, claimed 12 wickets in the match to bowl India to victory. By his own standard, Durrani had scored only 87 runs in the three test matches that he played. In the bowling he had nine wickets to show for his effort, each costing him 20.22 runs per wicket. The bowling was alright and upto the standard, but the batting was something which did not find any favour with the selectors.

Ultimately, when Gary Sobers and his team landed in India in 1966 it was the Bombay test which brought the waterloo for him and his career. In the Bombay test, India at one stage were well placed at 230 for 4 with Salim Durrani, who till then had stroked a wonderful 55. That was the last over of the day's play, and all it needed was to play out the over. Instead, the first ball from Gary Sobers of the last over, Durrani took such a heave at the ball, that he missed it and his wickets got shattered. When he came back to the pavilion, the Indian skipper Pataudi told him "enjoy this test for some more time as you will never play for India again". They saw only one mistake of Salim sweeping the ball. They did not see the fashion in which he scored those 55. It was a vintage knock, and a merciless one, specially against the bowling of Hall and Sobers.

He particularly had chosen and targeted Gary Sobers in this match and he literally had grinded him to dust scoring those 55. These acts of his went unnoticed by the selectors, what they noticed in him was his swipe, and that too, only that swipe. How lucky are the present days' – the present sets of modern cricketers like the Sehwags, the Gangulys, the Uthappas and the Gambhirs. THEY CAN PLAY THIS OR ANY KIND OF A FOOLISH AND UNWANTED SHOTS TO GET OUT, YET THEY CAN CONTINUE AGAIN TO COME BACK AGAIN AND AGAIN TO BE IN THE TEAM. THE TEAM HARDLY THINKS OF CHOPPING THEM OUT. For after this test which India lost by 6 wickets, Salim Durrani was a forgotten man in Indian cricket. From the season 1967-68, where he single handedly performed for Rajasthan, at times to take them to the finals of Ranji Trophy, to the season 1971, he was a forgotten man. However, like a tiger he fought back. Who can ever forget his bowling in the finals of Ranji Trophy against Bombay in 1960-61 at Udaipur, where he claimed 8 for 99. And who would forget his explosive and a cannon firing shot filled innings of 90 against England in 1964. It is said that tough men become tougher in the toughest conditions to bring out the best stuff out of them. And his performance proved the dictum to be true. He was a tough performer sincerely between the period 1968 and 1972, when at the age of 37 years, he staged a comeback to the national team in 1971 against the West Indies.

Who can again forget his belligerent knock of 119 he had played in the Ranji finals against Bombay. Thereafter, be it a Ranji match, a Duleep match, or a match which Central Zone would play against a visiting team, it had to be a Salim Durrani hitting the headlines. He was 37 years of age by then and old, but the sparkling eye of Vijay Merchant could see the fire burning in Salim Durrani. Merchant always had the notion that there was something, out of the world which was awaiting to come out of Durrani, and he preferred to give him all the chances so that he continued playing cricket.

He was selected for the Indian tour of West Indies in 1971. His Ranji Trophy performance was the ticket which booked his ticket to the Caribbean. And who could forget those "two" golden balls made out of a "dream" that Durrani had carried with him, to get rid of Clive Lloyd and Gary Sobers, to knock the sail out of West Indies, and put India to the path of their first test victory at West Indies. However, his bat did not favour him and he again lost his place in the team to tour England in 1971.

Between 1966 and 1969, India had played 17 test matches without Durrani. Though India had won five of them, the "Durrani special" was something which everybody in the team had missed, and missed it very badly.

Specially when the New Zealand team, first, and later when the Australians had arrived in India in 1969, one really had felt that if Durrani had played, specially in the series along with Dilip Sardesai, in the last two tests, perhaps the Madras test could have been won by India against the Aussies. At that juncture India needed somebody like Sardesai to carry and Durrani to punch the Australians. The short-sightedness of the Indian selectors did this to us. Moreover, Pataudi did not want these two seniors too. That made the difference.

However, after the series of West Indies in 1971, when

he was hoofed out of the Indian team, nobody gave Salim Durrani a chance to stage a comeback. He was nearing his 38th years of his life and at this age, everybody would hang his boots. But not Durrani. He knew that there was one last chance awaiting him. What he needed was an opportunity to don the Indian cap, rest he was confident that again a chapter would be scripted in the annals of the Indian cricket, and how correct he was, how correct he proved to be.

The Duleep Trophy season of 1972 was to start. He single handedly on the basis of his bowling alone, completely made a mincemeat, first of North Zone, then the South Zone in the semis and in the finals, the strong West Zone. In all he claimed 22 wickets, which is a record of the maximum number of wickets by any bowler in a single season in Duleep Trophy. Over it he scored 237 runs in his five essays to the wicket. He produced a performance which no cricketer from then to this stage of Duleep Trophy, has equalled it. For a moment, the Duleep Trophy was named as "Durrani's Trophy". This is how the Duleep Trophy of 1972 still now is known as. He had by then already celebrated his 38th birthday.

In that tournament at the Duleep Trophy, he averaged 78.10 runs to top the batting average amongst all the cricketers who had played in the tournament then, and his bowling, HE BOWLED AT AN ECONOMY RATE OF 1.85 RUNS PER OVER for his 22 wickets. This is in fact a national record which stands till this date of writing this book, as the most VALUABLE performance by any cricketer in terms of performance in a single Duleep season.

In the entire tourney, the entire Indian team and its players representing India who were playing for the other zonal teams, were BOWLED out by Salim Durrani, when they played against Central Zone. Out of the 22 wickets that he claimed in the tourney, 11 of them were clean bowled, which again is a sort of record. No bowler ever since then till date has the credit of getting fifty per cent of the wickets in terms of clean bowled, in a single season in the Duleep trophy. That was the kind of a form he was carrying when he was nearing the 39th birthday of his life.

When Tony Lewis brought his English side in 1972-73, Durrani, like a tiger, fought back to regain his place in the side. The M. C. C. were playing Central Zone at the Jawaharlal Nehru Stadium at Indore and it was during the lunch, that the skipper Hanumant Singh went upto him and told him that the selectors would be watching him very seriously for deciding to pick him for the Calcutta test. This was enough for the "Prince" to wield his bat like a sword.

Between the lunch and the tea, in that match, afterwards, the "Prince" played such an innings that it lit the entire city of Indore sparkling with the opinion that "why the hell the selectors had dropped him at all from the Indian squad".

In a show of the highest class of batsmanship, Durrani within a period of 95 minutes had butchered the attack of M. C. C. for 81 unbeaten "golden" runs. 64 of those runs came through the boundaries and two through over boundaries. In the second innings when England came in to bat, he claimed all the three wickets that fell, all of them clean bowled. The message was sent aloud and clear to the selectors, I'm ready, and dare if you can drop me.

Here in the match against the M. C. C. when Durrani hit that sparkling 81, everybody was awaiting to see him score a ton, but to the surprise of all and sundry, Hanumant Singh declared the innings. Salim was at the worst of the mood then and at the height of his temper. Actually he very badly wanted to come back to the Indian team, and a century would have made his job very simple, and his path very straight, he was well set for a ton. He was just waiting to get it and the way he was batting, it seemed to him that only another 10 minutes could have been enough to get that ton.

But that declaration completely brought out the animal

in him, and he was at his worst against Hanumant Singh. In that match Suryaveer Singh, brother of Hanumant Singh had scored a 102, and Durrani felt that Hanumant Singh, by declaring the innings, had made the way clear for Suryaveer to stake his claim for the test match, as the selectors were also looking out for a suitable partner for Sunil Gavaskar.

His temper was to be seen and believed.

He kept on yelling at Hanumant that IT WILL BE HIM AND NOT HIS BROTHER WHO WOULD GET THE NOD FROM THE SELECTORS. On every moment he shouted at Hanumant telling him that DUS MINUTE AUR NAHIN RUK SAKTA THA. APNEY BHAI KE LIYE YEH SAB KIYA. DEKH MAIN HI KHELOONGA, AUR KOI NAHIN. He was very upset and in the worst of his mood. Hanumant could not control him on that day. To make him understand some points, Hanumant gave him enough overs, when Central Zone came in to field and the three wickets that fell of the M. C. C., in the second innings, it was he who claimed it all. All the three were bowled of Durrani, and it was he who was recalled for the Calcutta test.

He was back into the Indian squad for the Calcutta test. Scoring 4 in the first knock, he was sent at number three to bat in second knock. This time he hit the English bowlers for a sparkling 53, which in a long way went and helped India to win the test and square the result at 1-1.

The next sojourn was the Madras test. After conceding a lead of 73, M.C.C. were very well placed at one stage. Durrani in a single delivery turned the match in our favour by claiming the wicket of Tony Greig whom he had brilliantly got caught by Eknath Solkar.

This was the turning point. Getting England out for 159, where Prasanna had a figure of 4 for 16, India went in to bat and were tottering 20 for 4, needing another 66 to win the game. Came Durrani and with it came two sixes and four boundaries. He scored 38 and he was in a way responsible to carve out the Indian victory. He had scored

38 in the first also. He was solely responsible in all the manners to put India ahead and up by 2-1, and he completely nailed the selectors for their foolishness. He proved to all and sundry how foolish they were to drop him from 1967 to 1971. But–Oh my God–the Indian selectors, at times, it seems that they are the consultants for all the Gods and came the ultimate magic immediately after the match was over. They created another magic without consulting anybody.

By the end of this test came the cropper. He was immediately dropped for the next test at Kanpur. Only when the selectors realized that how fool were they to drop him, and to what an extent the spectators were serious about not to allow to hold the test if he was not playing, did the jokers brought him back for the last match at Bombay. And the rest was a history.

The gates and all the entry points of the Brabourne stadium had the board displaying a slogan, NO DURRANI, NO TEST. This was a history once again repeated in the annals of the test series in India. It was the second instance, the first one being way back in 1948 against West Indies at Eden Gardens where the same kind of board and the placards were displayed at the test venue, no match to be allowed to be played if Mushtaq Ali was not allowed to play then, and now if Durrani did not play.

The crowd enjoyed every bit of 73 and 37 he had scored at Bombay and his association of 150 runs with Vishvanath was the "Kabab delight" at Brabourne, for those who were watching the match then. Again, after such a stupendous effort, everybody had thought and had formed an idea that he will be in the side to tour England in 1974, even though he was already 39 years of age by then. And add to it, he had a terrific domestic season to show. However, he was not considered and was dropped from the Indian squad. This test at Bombay proved to be his last test match of his career.

When Clive Lloyd and his men were here in 1974-75, he at an age of 40, representing the Central Zone, in a match against West Indies at Nagpur, was well set with a score of 23, and had almost signalled the selectors watching the game then that he was ready to take a position in the Indian team again. A nasty leg-before decision, which the umpire held it, very late, very late, L-A-T-E, upon the pressure applied by the West Indies fielders, saw his dream being shattered, his hopes dashed, his belief cut into pieces to stage yet another comeback. Many believed that it was a bad decision. And with that all the chances for him to stage yet another comeback were gone.

However, he was to play the two one-dayers in the "Bush Trophy" and in both the matches he hit 37 runs each. It was enough for him to send a signal to the selectors that he was ready for the World Cup 75, but the selectors did not favour him.

From 1975 to 1978, when he was almost 44 years of age, Durrani continued playing for Rajasthan and Central Zone with aplomb. In 1977, when he was 43 years of age in a bid to stage his claim to be selected for the Indian squad to play England, and tour Australia, he scored 71 runs in a Duleep game against North Zone, off the bowling of Bedi, Rajinder Goel, Madanlal, Mohinder Amarnath and Rakesh Shukla. Yet he did not find the favour of the selectors. At the age of 43, playing his last Ranji match for Rajasthan against Vidharbha in 1978, he gave up playing cricket for ever. His record is as follow:

Batting:

M	I	No	Runs	MS	Ave	100	50	Catches
29	51	03	1202	104	25.04	1	7	14

Bowling:

Balls	M	Runs	Wkts	Ave	Swi	10wm
6422	313	2657	75	35.43	3	1

He played 29 tests, whereas Engineer, Pataudi and Wadekar played 46. Durrani should have played 50 test matches. For, that was the caliber he had, and that was the talent he was made of. When one talks of him, everybody utters one word about him, and that is; he should not have been dropped from the Indian team to tour England in 1967, and in 1971, and the dual tour of Australia and New Zealand in 1968.

He was not handled properly and that was a loss to Indian cricket. That, his unique way of hitting sixes, and that too at the demand of public, could be an easy exercise for him, was profoundly demonstrated by Salim Durrani, both in the first class games, and also in the test matches. All his sixes that he hit only came, when the public demanded it from him, whether they be in the domestic matches, or in the test matches.

With that kind of a personality, and with that kind of a quality of playing game that he possessed, coupled with making the crowd so happy, fulfilling their demand to please them with a "six", Salim Durrani was the "Prince" of the hearts of the cricket lovers and "a poor man's Gary Sobers" for the cricketing fraternity.

He will always be remembered in Indian cricket, for those six victories, one each against Australia and West Indies, and four against England, where without his contribution, at a very vital moment, which gave India the necessary win in test match, India wouldn't have tasted victory at all. The journalism parlance for him was a man who hit those sixes at will, also had "SIXED" Indian victories.

His contribution in those 6 "test" victories were 22 wickets at an average of 18.09 runs per wickets and his 278 in twelve innings at an average of 23.16 runs per innings.

One might not be too convinced at these records, but his performance in all those victories has been the "turning point" of the India's win, in those matches, for he strucked vital blows with the ball, or somehow produced those punching strokes which had "punched" out the opponents while they were bowling to knock the Indian bat. His effort in batting, though small in number in terms of runs were very crucial always from the point of view of the Indian victory in test matches.

For, Durrani was never the statisticians' delight, he was always the crowds' "delite". He would always be remembered for the "sixes" he hit profoundly on public demand, a delight of Indian cricket.

For his deeds, and those deeds which transformed into Indian victory Salim Altaf Durrani, to me, would be the "turning point" of Indian cricket, though the press always considered him the "Prince Charming" of Indian cricket.

Durrani was a cricketer who always kept his words. He never uttered them just for the heck of it. He meant it and that was his business. To him his words on cricket were the orders served to him by Allah, and he had to obey them. It always came out of his mouth when his team would be in dire strait.

In the second test of the 1971 series against the West Indies, it was he who promised Dilip Sardesai first, and then to all the members of the Indian team after the finish of the day's play, when the WI total read 150 for 2, that he would get Gary Sobers and Clive Lloyd out cheaply, and he did.

He, during the course of the match against England at Madras in 1973, when the game was slipping out of the Indian grasp, and the grip, went to Ajit Wadekar and requested him to hand over the ball, "I will get out Greig in a span of twelve deliveries, give the ball to me". Wadekar first did not heed to his request. That really made his head TURN-OFF. It was Chandrashekar who came running to Wadekar and requested him to hand over the ball to Durrani. When Wadekar tossed the ball to him, he threw the ball back at Wadekar telling him that I'M NOT A FILL IN THE BLANK TYPE OF A BOWLER. I DO NOT NEED ANYBODY'S FAVOUR TO BOWL. GO ASK HANUMANT SINGH ABOUT MY BOWLING STORIES. But when

Chandrashekar kept on requesting him, he heeded to his request, and in the third delivery which he had bowled, got Greig out, turning a virtual out of the grip of India's match within his and India's grip.

He had planned with Eknath Solkar, about the first two deliveries that he would bowl to Greig, and then about the third one, in which he made it very clear to Solkar that he will spin the ball by turning his wrist, with the seam hitting the deck for an unpredictable bounce.

He exactly did it, and as per the planning Solkar had anticipated Greig playing the ball, had positioned himself for the catch. It was not an easy catch, but Solkar made it look easy, by clasping it with a forward dive. The catch was taken, and Durrani in his customary self, tossed the ball back to Wadekar telling that APNA TO HO GAYA. BULAO APNE BAKIYON KO. KHEL TO KHATAM HAI. MAIN AB AUR NAHIN KARTA. MOOD NAHIN HAI. WAISE BHI DARJON KA KAAM, EK CHOUTHAI MEIN KAR DIYA.

It was the persistent request of Chandrashekar and Prasanna, which changed his mood. Wadekar thereafter gave him 14 overs at a stretch. He completely checked the English scoring, his analysis was 15-5-24-1, allowing Prasanna to do all the bowling. And Prasanna who till this test was fighting to save his place in the squad, came up with another tantalising effort of 4 for 16, the analysis being 10-3-16-4. England were out for 159, and the wicket of Tony Greig was the GOLDEN SCALP. That was the turning point of the game. How seriously did Prasanna take the bowling at this test could be gauged by the fact that his finger was totally wrapped with bandage as he had badly hurt it, while fielding. Even worse was his spinning finger, which was totally bruised and under bandage. When he came on to bowl, the English batsmen, pointed this to the umpire and objected to his bowling. Prasanna went in the midst of the pitch, tore the entire bandage, and even with the fact that his spinning finger was oozing with blood, he bowled the entire ten overs without a fuss. England from 157 for 6, went down collapsing at 159 all out. Prasanna had a figure of 4 for 16.

The third occasion was the Duleep trophy semis against the South Zone in 1972. Playing in the sultry heat at Hyderabad during the month of mid March, he had claimed the first five of the six wickets of South. His age started showing the effect, and he started to wear out. Pataudi was batting with 90 then, this was in the first innings. Durrani went to Hanumant Singh and requested him to take off for some time at least, so that he earns some rest in between. Jokingly Pataudi who was batting on 90 then said "YOU ARE GETTING WORST WITH EVERY PASSING DELIVERIES, SALIM YOU ARE GETTING SLOW. See, I have hit you for 90. I will get my ton soon against your team, and you would watch me doing so." Pataudi actually was joking.

This hit his ego. Immediately after the next over, he came back rushing to the bowling end, snatched the ball from Rakesh Tandon's hand, and immediately bowled a ball which castled Pataudi. It broke the stump too. "I DID NOT ASK YOU TO BOWL THAT FAST", said Pataudi to Salim, when he was making his way to the pavilion. Pat came the reply "YES. EVERYBODY HAS THE RIGHT TO BECOME THE BEST". However Pat, he said there is always a second innings in cricket to get a ton, try it. The second innings was even bad for Pataudi. This time Ashok Jagdale got him out for zero caught by Mehboodullah.

His fourth incidence was the finals of the Ranji Trophy where Rajasthan were playing Bombay. He wanted to bat with Vinoo Mankad, who was just a bit above 51 years of age then. He requested Hanumant Singh, then, who was leading Rajasthan, I wished to bat with Vinoo Mankad as he had harboured a dream to bat with him. "If you allow me to do that, I promise you about scoring 125 runs, and I would help Vinoo Bhai at that age to score a hundred". Vinoo Mankad scoring a ton at the age of 51 plus, will the present generation of modern cricketers believe this. YES, THIS IS A TRUTH.

Hanumant Singh gave him the chance, and he kept his words. He scored a 119 and helped Vinoo Mankad to score 116. That were and that used to be the words of this genius. He used to keep his promises. Vinoo Mankad was playing as a professional for Rajasthan. In that match, Vijay Manjrekar and Hanumant Singh too had scored a century each, however still Rajasthan could not win the Ranji Trophy, yet created a record of four batsmen from the third position to the sixth, all having scored a century each. It deprived Bombay of an outright win.

In 1962 in the series against the West Indies, after the Nari Contractor incident where Contractor was hit by Charlie Griffith, the Indian team went into a psychological haemorrhage, where everybody wanted to save himself from the fury and fiery of Wesley Hall and John Atkinson.

He went upto Pataudi and requested him to send him at number three, and he would take care of Hall. Pataudi acted in the similar manner, and Durrani showed the stuff that he was made of. He made Hall to come upto him during the course of the drinks interval, reminding him that if he kept on spanking him in that manner, very soon he might loose his place in the side.

Salim was a very natural talent. That kind of a natural talent were Vinoo Mankad, Gundappa Vishvanath, Vijay Manjrekar, Chandu Borde, B.S. Bedi, B. S. Chandrashekar, Kapil Dev, Farokh Engineer and Erapalli Prasanna. The others could prolong their career because Pataudi had a soft corner for each and everybody, except Vinoo who did not play in the Pataudi's era. He had retired from the test scene by then. Pataudi gave these cricketers enough chance to groom.

There was nobody to take care of this genius, called Salim Altaf Durrani. For if this genius would have been properly handled, we could have had an Indian version of Gary Sobers, made in India, and marketed by B. C. C. I exuberantly, who would have made the world of cricket and us proud. This was not to be, that was a loss, not only to Durrani, but to the Indian cricket.

There are some fools in the cricket fraternity who doubt about his humanism. Let me cite another example. In those days, there used to be a company, Geep Flashlight, headquartered at Allahabad. To mark their decade long business in the Indian market, at 1975, they invited 22 top cricketers for a three-day invitational match at Allahabad. Durrani was also summoned to play in the match.

He and the four musketeers of Karnatak's cricket then, Vishvanath, Brijesh Patel, Prasanna and Chandrashekar were asked to join Durrani at Itarsi, and then to move down to Allahabad. During the night, he watched Vishvanath, sleeping above his tier in the compartment that they were travelling, shivering down to death. Vishvanath had no blanket, and he was covering himself with a bed cover, which was not good enough to resist the cold waves of that region.

He simply got up, and put his entire blanket over the bed cover that was covering Vishvanath. He preferred to sleep without anything. The readers might be anxious to know what happened next. In that match, Vishvanath scored century in both the innings, and Durrrani got eight wickets beside scoring a 44 in the first and 37 in the second.

Later, when the match was over and the players were to return back, Vishvanath who had won the Man of the Match award then, and was rewarded with a purse of Rs 501/-, bought a new blanket for Durrani, and when he went to give it back to Durrani, Durrani promptly refused taking it back, telling Vishvanath, that the blanket that he gave him to cover himself was a symbol of good luck, and he better use it for all his tours and travels, as it would bring him wealth of luck and runs. This was the real Prince Salim Durrani.

The way he was handled by Hanumant Singh, defies all the rules of man management and leadership. We have the modern chums of commentators who hold the classes for the leadership and man management to the top flight executives of the corporate world, citing them the examples of Sourav Ganguly, for leadership, and Cafu for his strategies. SHIT. Sourav. . as a leader...nowhere near the inspiration of Hanumant Singh, nowhere near his analytical approach to the game, his calculative and manipulative planning, and his changes, ... and Cafu, if he was that good a strategist, he would have send those floaters to Ronaldo against France in the World Cup in 2006, rather than those idiotic and nonsensical grounders from the flanks, which are very easy for the defenders, to cut it off.

If Sourav was such an ebullient leader of the game, he would not have picked Parthiv Patel and continued with him, who would accept a catch, and floor the next three, to allow the opponent batsmen to score tons and tons of runs, and wouldn't have continued with Ashish Nehra, in that manner. Nehra to be frank for that matter, had earned a nickname of being a bowler who bowls one over, and spends the next one month in the hospital. If Sourav was that good a captain to lay his faith properly on a resource, he would not have picked Dinesh Mongia ahead of V. V. S. Laxman for the 2003 World Cup. Adam Gilchrist is the living example of being the shining gold of Parthiv's foolishness behind the wicket, and Sourav's unmatched belief in the pooling of the resource or the man.

If Sourav was that exuberant and that brave, even better than the lion, as he is being described, then in 2003, against the Australian side, when the Indian team had scored over 700 runs in the first innings, and had enforced Australia to trail by about 300 runs, Sourav should have enforced the follow-on and should have attacked Australia. This would have given the Indian team perhaps a chance to beat Australia for the first time on their soil. Nay, that tiger decided to play safe, and that was his strategy not to lose the series, perhaps for the fear that he might have to lose his skippership, if he had lost. Who says that he is and was a fearless skipper.

I shall lay an example of strategy and fearlessness. In the year 1976, Indian Railways led by Hyder Ali, were playing against Hyderabad, led by M. L. Jaisimha in the Ranji Pre Quarters. Winning the toss, Hyderabad decided to bat and were 50 for 8, with Anil Mathur claiming the first six wickets, in a span of about 100 minutes of play. Another twenty minutes, and then the lunch would await both the team. Jaisimha calculating the time, declared the Hyderabad innings immediately then.

He got those extra ten minutes of the game before the lunch, in which he attacked the Railways, and pinned down their first wicket. Railways went on to score 237, thus gaining a lead of 187. In the second knock Hyderabad were 316, where again Jaisimha declared the innings. That left Railways to get 130 for victory.

Bowling Jyothi Prasad, unchanged from one end, Jaisimha attacked from the other end, with Abid Ali, to completely fox the Railways' bat. The result was Railways were out for 122, thus losing the match by 7 runs. The last Railways' wicket fell when there were only two deliveries left, besides six minutes for the match to be over. Those extra ten minutes, before the lunch, that Jaisimha and Hyderabad fielded, after declaring the innings at 50 for 8, was the turning point of the match. This is what the strategist, the guiles, the willingness, the match calculations, and the fearlessness are, in terms of examples. How many cricketers of the present generation would show that kind of a heart and take that kind of a risk, to completely overturtle and overturn the fate of a match which was as good as lost for Hyderabad in that match.

My advice to these sets of commentators is–Learn and know about cricket first, and then talk, or keep your cob shut. Please do not create a self mindmade heroes for us. These heroes might suit you all and help you all personally in your business, but please do not make them a national examples of cricketing martyrs and place them before the nation as somebody like the Bhagat Singh, the Khudiram Bose, or the Chandrashekar Azad. Please do not overuse your mike for wrong reasons.

Hello the present set of commentators, belonging to the ESPN channel, who have studied management, those who teach cricket and strategy to the corporate executives, do not teach us cricket and do not teach us management. We have lost our teeth and the youth playing the management games, and our hairs have turned grey in the process.

God knows whether He would forgive Sourav for that kind of a foolish act, and these sets of BRANDED commentators, for teaching and preaching the foolish and follies of Sourav's or Cafu's foolishness to the top notch executives of the corporate world. God only knows what could have been the reality of those companies, where these top notch executives would have followed Sourav's or the Cafu's strategies to uplift their organisation's position. I only hope that their companies and their Executives did not go out like Brazil and Parthiv Patel went out, of the World Cup football in 2002, and of the Indian cricket team. GOD BLESS THESE SETS OF COMMENTATORS AND THE IIM'S from where they have passed out their degree exams. Let their tribe increase, and let the present generation of the youth maybe completely befooled and misguided about the modern gamuts of the management, and let the country's top companies and the Executives go to the DOGS. I bless these commentators to be happy, after all these commentators also have only one motto in mind, make money, doing some blah-blah, and bak-bak, that's all.

Had Salim Durrani been handled by the manner in which Hanumant Singh handled him, the story of Indian cricket would have been different. It would have been a great era of Indian cricket, that was, but not in a way that the entire fraternity of cricket then had wanted, for it was not to be. It was because the Salim flavour was missing. His loss was not his loss as much, it was the loss of Indian cricket. He basically was a very soft human being, and a very normal one. He was maverick, like the great Kishore Da. Kishore Da had S. D. Burman with him to handle, on a national level, Durrani had nobody. That was the destiny, that was his luck. If only Pataudi had taken a word or two from Hanumant Singh, about Durrani, and had used him in that manner, many more victories could have been depicted in the annals of Indian cricket from 1965 to 1971. Oh! that was a loss again for Indian cricket.

Gosh! how the days have changed. Now to see that their sons somehow make it to the Indian team the parents do not miss any opportunity to invite the electronic media, grease their palm, request these media personalities to make a special programme on their wards and the sons, keep on highlighting about the sense and the nonsense deeds of these sons, and use every opportunity of these media and the mediamen to promote and highlight these sons for playing for the Indian teams, irrespective of them being worthy, lest these unworthy chums make it to the national team. The media too has its role to play, it hardly matters to them whether they are right or wrong. But they play.

The end result is: IDLI DOSA–KHANE WALA DOSA, YAH PHIR NAALI MEIN PHEKNEY WALA DOSA.

There are two records about Salim Durrani that I would wish to share with the readers. In the inaugural Duleep Trophy match in 1961-62 against the East Zone, he before the lunch scored a century, and before the tea completed his double ton. He is the first cricketer in the annals of Duleep Trophy to score a double ton, besides being the only cricketer to hit a ton before the lunch.

The second one is, apart from the players from Bombay, Salim Durrani along with Hanumant Singh had played in seven different Ranji finals for Rajasthan. This is also a record as no other players in India outside Bombay hold the record of playing in as many Ranji finals.

The two vital wickets of Clive Lloyd and Gary Sobers of the two dream deliveries from Salim Durrani in the second test at the Port-of-Spain in 1971 which finally turned the game in India's favour was the incidence which opened the gates for the change of the faces of Indian cricket.

That was Salim Altaf Durrani for you. His talent was enigmatic, and one would marvel at his guts, and the grits, but no one except Hanumant Singh could understand his nature, his character.

His bowling as I have mentioned earlier was a magic, and it had repertoire. He possessed a delivery which he flicked it with the third finger, ensuring that the speed and the loop was totally in control, and not only that, it accurately hit the seam for getting that unpredictable bounce and the turn. The wicket of Gary Sobers, which he got in the second test at the Port-of-Spain, the wicket of Bobby Simpson, and Bill Lawry at Calcutta in 1964, and the wicket of Tony Greig, who he got caught by Eknath Solkar, in the Chepauk, Madras in 1973, were the kind of deliveries that I have mentioned above.

When I talk about his bowling, let me make it very clear that of the 75 wickets that he claimed, 43 of them were the batsmen who were holding the position from the opening to the number sixth slot. And he is the only bowler in the world to have been credited with the first six batsmen out to him, all clean bowled. This is the only instance of test cricket where the first six were clean bowled, and that too at the Eden Gardens at Calcutta against Australia in 1964.

Off the field, he loved spending his time with M. L. Jaisimha, who was his friend very close to his heart. Hanumant Singh was always his younger brother, and he really was a very intimate friend of Chandrashekar. His list of friends besides these was and has been Prasanna, Bedi and Vishvanath, and whenever he gets an opportunity, he makes it a point to spend most of his time with them. Sunil Gavaskar always has been his Bhatija.

After the death of M. L. Jaisimha, his free and frank way of speaking has taken a back seat, yet whenever he gets an opportunity to be with Bedi, or Prasanna, he is at his magical best.

The foolish trying to give a new brands to the B.C.C.I, who have the wings to fly, like the riches, have made the cricketers the rags by their foolish act. I think they who hardly know a single word or anything about the paramount and the parochial of the Indian cricket, are busy doing all wrong things, like clobbing the green leaves for making a mountain of dollars of them, or creating a Chuk De to add on as a new emblem as the ambassador of the game, throwing their own sons and the soldiers out of the game, and its administration, hey the B. C. C. I, I have a single request for you all to do and follow.

My request is. IF YOU CHUMS REALLY CARE FOR INDIAN CRICKET, THEN CONFER THE PADMA SHRI AWARD TO SALIM DURRANI, FIRST, AND THEN TO DILIP SARDESAI (POSTHUMOUSLY), AND AGAIN THEN TO EKNATH SOLKAR IN THAT ORDER.

Hope the B. C. C. I. understands that, and I hope the Government too has some intelligent brain to understand the same.

In the last three decade, specially after 1979, the status of the national awards have become the pav-bhajis and the samosas selling on the thelas and sold by the hawkers and the chatwalas. These awards have been conferred to certain personalities, who simply do not deserve them. They have conferred these prestigious awards for reasons other than the act that befits the garbs. Hope that it improves here from now onwards. Hope these three cricketers are given their dues by the B. C. C. I. and the Government of India. The sooner they do it, the better for the Indian cricket.

Last, his story of becoming an orthodox slow left arm tweaker is also interesting. After the match which the Central Zone played against the West Indies at Jabalpur, in 1958-59, Vinoo took him under his arm. He wanted Salim to bowl left handed.

Salim being a right handed thrower, and obviously a right hand strong person, and that too at an age of 24, to become a left handed bowler, it was an impossible task, he felt. Vinoo took him to the nets from there onwards, and would tie his right hand with a string to the stomach. He then fixed two bamboos, parallel to each other, the distance between them about a feet, and would ask Salim to bowl between the bamboo, to the wicket.

Every time when his hand would hit the bamboo, Vinoo Bhai would remind him to bowl with a straight arm. This went on and on. In the process he fractured his left arm, everytime in the form of a hairline fracture, for as many as five times. Vinoo was convinced that his bones were very strong, as normally, the speed with which he hit those bamboos, if he did not bowl with a straight arm, the bones would have suffered multiple fracture.

When one fine day Vinoo noticed that his speed of the deliveries which came off from his wrist, were very fast, he reverted back to normalcy, removing the "tied" paraphernalias, asked him to bowl normally. His deliveries were not only variable and subtle, but he could bowl perfectly at one particular spot for hours together. Vinoo Bhai was convinced that there was an all rounder in the offing who would shake the world of cricket if engined properly. BAS, AB JUM KAR KHELO, was his last advice to Durrani. Ever since then Salim Durrani was wedded to his life, cricket, and he lived his life, KINGSIZE, though he was a Prince in comparison to the Kings.

This was the gift of Vinoo Mankad.... . a parting gift to Indian cricket. For after this series against the West Indies, Vinoo Mankd was MANKEDED out by the Indian selectors. Fourty four was the age of Vinoo Mankad when he played his last test match, and almost fourty years was the age of Salim Durrani when he played his last match of his Ranji Trophy career. They say.... . Like Guru, like the shishya.

Hats off, Vinoo Bhai for this magnificient treasure that you gave it to the Indian cricket.

Taking a cue from this lesson, I have a question. All these years, we have seen the Wrights and the Wrongs, The Chappel to the Chappals, the Akramovs to the Akram aap ho. What have they done as a coach like the one cited here done by Vinoo Bhai.

Take the history, you will find that every coach mentioned here had taken the charge of the Indian team in the respective categories on Friday. Good Friday, and hot cross buns, it seems that they think that India is a place of.

Let me make it very clear to these coaches that in India every calendar year has 52 Fridays, but this country celebrates the Good Friday, once a year. Also hot cross buns, yes it is available here at India, but the days of one a penny, two a penny, for hot cross buns are over. Things are not that easy, and people here too have learned the trick of the trade. These coaches cannot made a fool of us any more. In the past, YES, they have fooled us for almost everything. But the future would be very different for these coaches.

Of recent worth, the Prince Charles of Australian hockey, has taken the charge of the national hockey team to change its fortune. He had taken the entire charge of his office on 21st, March 2008, Friday. If he fails, people here will turn him into a Pamela Darling, and pack him to his homeland, in such a way that for the future it would be very hard for the other imported coaches to get their import licence renewed here for further coaching. This country is now not going to take any imported nonsence or import licence renewed for granted.

12

THE VICTORY STORY: A SALUTE TO A GENIUS

IT was the year 1983, and I remember the month was June, the date exactly was 30th. I happened to park my bicycle at the Laxmi Theatre complex, at Nagpur................ . I saw big hoarding displayed at the theatre.

I was immediately taken aback, as the hoarding read "Today from 9.30............ only two shows.......... . The Victory Story" to be screened today. My first job was to enquire from the Manager about the show, and the second was to "watch" the movie at any cost. While during my stay at the boarding of Christ Church Boys' School at Jabalpur, I had read about this documentary and its hit story in the "Times of India" in 1974, and now was the chance for me to see it on the screen in 1983. My dream was going to come true.

I had choosen the noon show as that suited me the best. The "Victory Story" was the first feature film made in this country which depicted the series win over England, which was played in India from September 1972 to February 1973.

It had fully covered the victory story of the Indian cricket besides throwing many a startling fact of the "Hat-Trick" win which featured India and the Indian cricketers who played for India between 1971 and 1973. Superb it was to watch the entire show on the screen, and what a creation was it. I remember the entire Laxmi talkies was house full, and all the spectators, watching the movie, were throttled, as every time whenever they got a chance to applaud, the reverberation of the clap made the life younger and the scene exciting. After Padosan and Sholay, believe me, this really was a movie for which missing out several classes of management would not have been a sin for me. My aspiration, it seemed was fulfilled.

Though the series got over during February 1973, the documentary film was released in mid 1974, and it was India's first full feature film on cricket. It was Mr. Raju Bharatan, a genuine, versatile and an intelligent journalist, whose cricket feature in the "Illustrated Weekly of India" was as delicious as a Rosogulla, or a Rajbhog. A Bengali like me will always compare any good thing with the likes of these delicacies, or Misti Doi as we call it, the sweet curds.

The film was made and released, and the bouquet as well as the brickbat was received by Mr. Raja Bharatan. However, in my view, a lot of bouquet should have been received by the film's producer Pramod Pati. Pramod first met Mr. Bharatan, in the office of the Film Division and Censorship department and after getting introduced to Mr. Bharatan, requested him to come up with a film on the series between India and England played during 1972-1973.

Pramod, by then had made his documentary film named "Explorer". But this he wanted to make it for the common man in India, with a common purpose, and using a common language so that the cricket crazy people of India understands, and understood in a common language, commonly what the "hat trick of win" this series was? It was only an effort by the Film Division of India, to reach to the common masses. How brilliantly did they do it is what I would describe in the texts to come.

Mr. Raju Bharatan, first, was a bit penitent, and pertinent besides skeptical about going forward to put his fingers into the making of this film, he was a bit nervous about his own ability. However with Pramod Pati, infusing him the confidence, Mr. Bharatan went and moved a step ahead.

Actually, the Film Division had screened about 58,000 feet of the play, from the first test, which was played at New Delhi in 1972 to the last test of Bombay. But there was no proper clue regarding which was to follow next, and what would come first while screening it. The footages were in haphazard order, and one hardly understood, where did the film start from and where would it end.

It was here that Mr. Bharatan again spoke to Pramod Pati, saying that it was to be a critical analytical film, and it wouldn't have served the purpose of saying "goody-goody" things about everybody. A go ahead signal was what Mr. Bharatan got for it.

Here, it was Pramod Pati who introduced Sawant Jaisingh, the editor of Film Division to Mr. Bharatan and directed them to go ahead full steam for the film.

With the first screening of the film, that was in a state of disarry, it was aghast what Mr. Bharatan could experience. The Kanpur test, the fourth one played in the series was placed first, and the Delhi test, which was the first, was placed last, and in fact it was the twentieth reel. Having faced such a state of affair for the first time, Mr. Bharatan again requested Pramod Pati, to show the documentary that they had once screened, during the Port -of-Spain test, won by India at West Indies in 1971.

And when Mr. Bharatan saw it, he was full of shock. He saw Pataudi batting in the 1971 victory test at Port-of -Spain. Mr. Bharatan just would bang his head on the wall, and asked Pramod, when did Pataudi play in the Port-of-Spain test of 1971. He was in full of voice, and full of idioms which he openly used against them and the Government of India for using such a kind of people to make the national documentaries.

Well from that moment, it was very clear to Mr. Bharatan that he was against all the odds. However, he took it up once again for about 5 months, he went through the film, through each and every moment of the match in the film, and he matched the moments with the incidents of the game in chronological order.

He however lost his cool, very badly, and perhaps had screamed once more in his job, for his job, during his lifetime, when he saw that there was no footage of the fifth day of the Kanpur test of the 1972-1973 series.

All the dramas, and hungamas took place on the fifth day of the Kanpur test. India were just on the brink of defeat and it was Gundappa Vishvanath's 75* which had saved the day for us. He was ably supported by that Lion, Abid Ali who had scored 41 in that innings, which saved India from the blushes and the bruises of the English. This was perhaps the "golden phase of India's fight back" in the series, and to be frank it started all from there, were the Indian cricket started warding off the defeats amidst all setbacks for the days to come, and Gundappa Vishvanath was the one who laid the foundation of it then, but there wasn't any film screened of that day. Mr. Bharatan was more "off" and angry because he wanted to showcase some of the delectable, in terms of "ARTS", the shots of Vishvanath to the entire country, besides the character of the innings exhibited by Vishvanath in that innings.

He went to Pramod Pati and told him that he had given up. But "as cool as cucumber" Pati requested Mr. Bharatan to create, or make one, and his words of encouragement were: "This is why we have engaged you". Remember, the whole film is about the "after-thought"?

This is where Mr. Bharatan's knowledge of the film medium came in handy. The stills of the afternoon's play were obtained and Mr. Bharatan applied the "freeze" technique, to screen it and it was a success. He decided quickly to employ it to the other parts of the film.

After all the assembling, editing etc., the film worked out to be of 17,000 feet of length in toto. Mr. Bharatan had to spend about 70 days editing the film, four more times. When Mr. Bharatan pronounced to himself that he was ready to write the commentary, Pati asked this editor to give Mr. Bharatan the footages of each shot.

By trying best method to write the footage was over shoot and Mr. Bharatan had to run each shot on the moviola and wrote out the commentary on the spot, trimming and adjusting as they went along.

The commentary was a bit gimmicky, as the actions in the shots were incomplete, since it was planned as a film. Mr. Bharatan's own idea of being "punny" about the commentary was to draw the viewers attention away from the "cinematic's" effect of the film.

The whole idea was that viewers should not get the time to pause, but to neglect the flaws in the "shots" that they had artificially joined. Pati saw the commentary with the shots, and had formed his view that it was unusual style of commentary something which they had never tried it at the film division earlier. But he was still for it, because Mr. Bharatan had done it in the "TV" style.

Mr. Bharatan hadn't just described the "visuals", he had either offered a comment, or had made an "analytical" observation, and there it was, where lay the beauty of the film.

The commentary for the shots was "matched" on August 15, 1973 and both Mr. Bharatan and Sawant Jaisingh were awaiting, the next day on August 16, 1973 for Pati to view the film. Pati had to come back from Calcutta. However, on the next day as Mr. Bharatan and Mr. Sawant reached the office of the Film Division, waiting for Pramod Pati, they received a shock of their life.

They got to learn that Pramod Pati was admitted in a hospital as a cancer patient. Both Mr. Bharatan and Mr. Sawant Jaisingh were tongue tied.

Pati had seemed stress right through the making of the film, but he did not complained even for once. Reel by reel, odd hours of work, everything he took sportingly. He did not interfere in any methodology of the making of the film.

He never uttered a single word of "castigation" while the film making was in process, nor did he put any cinematic idea. What was more surprising was that in spite of his fragile health, he took this responsibility of film making, because nobody in that organization, and in that department, was anxious to shoulder the "responsibility" of making a full length film from the "bits-and-pieces"

The film was now stalled. Everybody waited for Pramod Pati's return, but nobody was sure about his return. When Mr. Bharatan saw him at the hospital, Pati was full of bones. All life had ebbed out of him. He knew that his days were numbered, yet he said to Mr. Bharatan to give the finishing touches to the film and Pati would okay it.

Miraculously, he was back. And when Pramod Pati was back, he was as fast as a ball from Charles Griffith. All the pleas from Mr. Bharatan fell into the deaf ear. He, on the very day, when he sat on his office chair, after being discharged from the hospital, saw the film. He was under stress and a great pain, yet he saw the film.

"Well done Raju," were his words! "I knew you could do it", were his compliments!

He shook his hands with Mr. Bharatan. The hands were very "cold", yet Mr. Bharatan could feel the warmth of it. Pramod in his gritty way made the film to move, and kept the entire show going in spite of the medical practitioners reprimanding him of the severe repercussions that he would face because of the heavy stress. His health had nothing more to offer, but he was tenacious.

"Raju," said Pramod, "the film would go to the public. It will be acclaimed – both in the form of criticism and praise. But one thing is certain. That any cricket film produced after this, will be compared with "Our Victory Story"! hence ours is "Pioneering Effort".

The film was shown to a select audience at the Akashvani Auditorium in Bombay. The audience response was tremendous. Everybody congratulated Mr. Bharatan, but nobody extended a hand to the man standing by the side of Mr. Bharatan, Pramod Pati, who made this dream a reality.

The film was released to the public at the "Metro" in Bombay. The public's verdict was clearly in Pati's favour. For Pati had earned a "promotion". But it was a "graphic" promotion, for within a day of earning it, he was no more. The "Victory Story" had drained the life out of him. His effort for creativity was "VICTORIOUS", and he left this world on a victorious note. That was GREAT Pati died so that our cricket may live, on films and now .... our T.V., the idiot box and : "THE CHEWING GUMS OF THE EYES". Does he not deserve at least an honourable mention in the annals of Indian cricket for putting on the celluloid a "Victory Story", that we may never repeat?

I salute you Pati and this is my last salute to a genius. Thank you Pati for the "VICTORY STORY."

I hope that the present generation of the so-called TV wizs, watch this documentary and learn a lesson or two from the two departed soul, Pramod Pati who expired in 1974, and Mr Raju Bharatan who expired in 2006, before boasting about how to make a good sports programme on and for the TV shows, before proclaiming about themelves on the TV screen that they are something very great, something extraordinary to have done it first, and have been the pioneer of the same. BULLSHIT. We know the truth, and we know the facts. My only request to them is DO NOT TEACH US THE FACTS AND THE HISTORY OF INDIAN SPORTS.

Some of the journalists, of course, with whom I have worked, had formed a batch with us. They had come to this world like the great warrior Abhimanyu, who before coming to the earth had learned the tricks of breaking the chakravyu, when he was in the womb of his mother. It is our destiny that we have not made a mark as the sportscaster on the TV screen. We have carved a niche for ourself in the uncompromising corporate world, and some of us were excellent journalists in the print media, before we felt that Rs 400=00 pm was not enough for us to make a living, and we shifted our gears to the corporate world, adding a M.B.A. degree, thus leaving the sports journalism. There were a few tears rolling down the eyes of some well wishers who were very upset about us leaving the world of journalism. But that was our destiny. Hello, to some of the commentators of the channels like the ESPN, when you speak of anythings relating to this kind of act, superbly glorifying yourself to be the first one, and the pioneer to do so, remember that we are alive to hear you but never really to believe you. There are people like us who know the "Iffs" and the "Butts" of cricket and about Indian sports much more than you or ESPN would know. Do not try to fool us. Enjoy the luck that the destiny has bestowed upon you, to have been roasting those dollars, and chewing them, for a hearty meals, on sports, actually without knowing much about anything of the games and sports, and also learn to respect others for what they have done, and leave it for all of us to admire and enjoy.

13

SARDESAI AND SALIM: OH! FOR THOSE LUCKS

ONE can never forget a man, a cricketer, all through his life, if he had seen him. Of course, I had once, when the Indian team was to play New Zealand in the second test match at Nagpur in 1969. Though he did not play in the test, he was summoned by the Board then, to be present at Nagpur for the nets.

The selectors were scrutinizing certain youngsters at the nets and from the bunch of these youngsters, two were to be pitched for the series against Australia, which was to follow the next. Along with the youngsters, a cricketer by the name of Dilip Narayan Sardesai was also to be watched by the selectors at the nets.

My first impression about Mr. Dilip Sardesai was, he appeared to be "stumpy", but the wicket keepers were never able to do so, perhaps never found him so. At the nets, against the spinners he moved so quickly, as the flash of the camera lights to hit the ball, but reverse was the case, when I saw him fielding. It appeared to me that, he would hit his head, and he would say to himself "Oh! Hell, why did the ball come to me at all" for, how hard is it to field!, Oh, why the hell fielding is there in the game of cricket, for how bad it is to field.

For the quality of the fielding of Dilip Sardesai, the cricketer was not a "secret of the money that was held at the lockers of the Reserve Bank of India at Nagpur, but it was a national disaster" ! During that time, the Indian middle order just needed the help of his "middle" name, for such a pathetic was the performance of the middle order, that "Narayan" also felt it ashamed to be with them, lest he deserted the Indian team. He came back with "Mr Dilip Sardesai," for the West Indies sojourn in 1971, and what a come back it was. History, history and history were written in the nooks and corners of the geographical arena of the Caribbeans Island during that tour in 1971.

He would afford to miss a catch, but never his meal. Perhaps I do not know nor would I be able to assert it, but may be his leanest day might have started since the New Zealand's tour of India got over in 1965. For Dilip Narayan Sardesai after the series against New Zealand, never really got the runs for India from 1966 to 1971.

One such funny incidence flashes through my mind and makes me reminiscent about it, well, it was the 1971 tour of West Indies and India were playing the second test. Sardesai in the course of the test had caught the stomach upset, and was ordered by Wadekar to be only on the chicken soup. When the match was over, the entire team went for lunch and there everybody was surprised to see that Dilip Sardesai was chewing the chicken. Wadekar too was surprised. When enquired, laughingly he said, never mind the soup also comes out from the chicken only. That was the meals for Sardesai, and Sardesai for the meals. Both were made for each other.

It seems, the late Prime Minister then, Mr. Lal Bahadur Shastri, had appealed to the nation to miss a meal, once a week to offset the loss, that the country had suffered even after their "14-day victory" over Pakistan in 1965. And perhaps this might have hit Dilip Sardesai, as missing a meal might have made him lean but it made his bat leaner, and his runs the mean, leanest to visit him.

Dilip Sardesai, to my knowledge, was first in many things in the annals of Indian test cricket, and has never got the appreciation for it. He is the second cricketer, after Independence, and after Vijay Samuel Hazare, to have hit two, back-to-back centuries in the test cricket for India. It came at the Brabourne stadium at Bombay in 1965, when he hit an unbeaten 200 for India, after being bundled out for 88, by Bob Taylor, Richard Collinge and Motz. Immediately thereafter, he hit 106 at New Delhi which enabled India to win the match.

This 106 is the fastest century scored in the test by any Indian batsman, and is on par with Gundappa Vishvanath's 103 which also came off against New Zealand in 1976 at Kanpur. Though Vishvanath's effort has been recognized by the press and the electronic media, Dilip Sardesai still has to get his recognition and his due from the media. Sardesai like Vishvanath can boast of not having lost a test match for India whenever he scored a test ton.

Dilip Sardesai hit West Indies, where it would hurt them most. Who can forget the test match at Port-of-Spain, Trinidad, which was played between March 6th 1971 and March 10. And how can one forget March 10, 1971. In a manner, so uncharacteristic of Indian cricket, India had defeated the gigantic and the mightiest West Indies by 7 wickets, just after lunch to carve their first test victory over the West Indies.

Dilip Sardesai was the first to hit a 112 in the test and partnered Eknath Solkar for 114 runs, which laid a solid foundation for India, for its first ever win over the West Indies, and if it was not enough he went to Wadekar and advised him to bring Salim Durrani to bowl to Clive Lloyd, who was batting on 29, and the West Indies were coasting at 169/3. Though Jaisimha was signalling Wadekar from the pavilion to bring in Durrani, it was Sardesai who went upto him and requested him to bring on the maverick magic, to cast his spell. And what a manner did Salim Durrani exhibit to open the flood gate of a famous Indian victory by turning the screw tightly and rightly on Lloyd and Sobers.

Two "golden" balls by Durrani, first to get rid of Lloyd, and immediately next to bowl Sobers out for a "blob", around his buttocks, did and digged the West Indies, then and there. So many words have been written for Sunil Gavaskar, for Wadekar and for India. But did anybody bother to write even a single word of praise for Dilip, for Sardesai.

"Actually, it was Sardesai, who by the end of the tour of West Indies in 1971, with 642 runs in the series, was the real hero of the Indian team, though the credit was bagged away by Sunil Gavaskar with an aggregate of 774 runs".

Sardesai's 642 runs, made him "rich" at the expense of Gary Sobers, who had turned "poor" in cricketing terms since then. For Gary Sobers, thereafter not only lost the captainship of the West Indies team, he even had lost his captainship of the Barbados cricket team. And two years from then, both Dilip Sardesai and Gary Sobers were never to play test cricket again. Sardesai walked out a hero, Gary was out of cricket for zero.

Dilip Sardesai added "riches" to his fortune by winning the coveted "Arjuna Award", for his show at the Carribbean Island, whereas Gary Sobers, kept losing, one tag-after-another, after this series, finally to bow out of cricket, with highest individual test runs, till then, in 1974 after the West Indies tour of England.

In that series against the West Indies, our cricket was down for the count when Sardesai would step in. He would make sure to put it on its feet, and then put certain "punch" in the bat, that would send the Windies, amazed and guessing all the time, what would come the next.

Just look at the figures he had on that tour, 212, 112 and 3, 45, 150 and 24 and 75 and 21. These score can never tell the full story of his montage in courage. Just a slip here and there would have made the score look like – "West Indies and Sobers -1, India and Wadekar- 0". But it did not happen, because "Narayan" was always beside Dilip Sardesai, and in between the brittle as well as the fickle Indian batting order during that series.

Dilip Sardesai, to start with, made the headlines way back in 1959 when he represented the Bombay University in the Rohinton Baria Trophy. The next season, he made it to the West Zone University team for the Vizzy Trophy. Before he could play the Ranji Trophy, he was already a member of the Indian team in 1961-62 against England. He had a good tournament thereafter and soon he was a member of the Bombay Ranji Trophy. Runs came in plenty to him, as did come a lot of coach and advice.

On the plea of a coach he changed his batting grip and all of a sudden the runs started deserting him. He was clueless till he met Vasanth Amladi, who advised him to fall back to his old style. Runs like rain started visiting him again and again. He was in the college and thus was considered to play the Pakistan team led by Fazal Mehmood for the combined Universities in 1960-61, when Pakistan then had to visit India.

A bamboozling 87 came through his bat and he was the "India's most wanted" batsman by then. He missed narrowly to play against the Pakistan side in the series. The only batsman who could put this innings of Dilip Sardesai's 87 to shade was Salim Altaf Durrani who was born on December 11th, 1935 and Sardesai's 1940, and who was one match "older" than Sardeai, as he had made his test debut, before Sardesai could get into the side.

Dilip Sardesai, perhaps is the only and the one cricketer who has the distinction of playing a test match for India, even without having played a Ranji Trophy game for Bombay then. That was the talent, and that was the stuff he was made of. It paralysed Tony Lewis record of playing a Test match for England and leading them without even captaining the Glamorgan county, or even playing a single match for them.

The knock which Salim Durrani played against Pakistan at Jaipur for Central Zone, and the knock of 87 by Dilip Sardesai, did not go unnotice and both were the members of the team for the series against the West Indies in 1962. Dilip Sardesai made his debut at the Port-of-Spain at Trinidad and so did Salim Durrani. Sardesai in his test match was asked to open. Durrani started with a bang scoring the way he would. He got 56, whereas Sardesai got 16.

Sardesai bagged pair in the fourth test, again at Port-of-Spain whereas Salim spanked Wesley Hall for his 104 runs, his first test ton. Sardesai was dropped thereafter, whereas Salim Durrani, after this series, was "world famous" household name in the world of World's cricket. This was just the start of their luck playing "eye's spy's" as both of them were sometimes in-and-sometimes out of the favour of the selectors.

Salim Durrani was asked by the team management to bat anywhere at the position between the number 8 to number 10, whereas he was a solid bat at number 6. Dilip Sardesai who was solid bat at numbers 5 was asked to open the innings. Now this had rattled their natural flair of batsmanship and stroke play, but both took maximum pain to adopt themselves to their task. Salim Durrani managed his place in the side till 1964 against the MCC at India, but was dropped for no reason of his own, between the period, after the New Zealand test win in India in 1965 to the period of 1971 when Gary Sobers had brought the West Indies over here.

Durrani was recalled for the first test at Bombay and so was Sardesai to play the game. Till the score of 55, it appeared that Durrani was to never be dropped from the Indian team again. In the same match when Dilip Sardesai was out for 6, it appeared that he would never be a part and parcel of the Indian team.

But as described earlier, in the Bombay test in 1966-67 at the Brabourne Stadium, when the Indian score board read at 230 for 4 in the last over of the day, Durrani took a swipe against Gary Sobers to see his middle stick getting uprooted. This had uprooted Salim Durrani's career for 17 test matches, played thereafter between the Calcutta test against West Indies in 1966 till the Madras test against Australia till 1969-70. A double failure of Sardesai did not go unnoticed. Though he was out for the remaining test matches to be played during the series, he could manage to book his ticket to the first ever twin tours undertaken by India at Australia and New Zealand.

Sardesai regained his place as an opener against Australia, with Farokh Engineer at Adelaide and Melbourne. Whereas Engineer could score 89, 19, 9 and 42, Sardesai could manage 1, 1, 1, and 5 in the four essay at the wicket.

He was out for the remaining two tests at Australia where his place was taken by Abid Ali to open. Abid had a score of 2, 47, 78 and 81 to show and prove his mettle as an all-rounder, besides being an opener. This prompted Pataudi to shut the door on Dilip Sardesai for that tour.

Sardesai during that tour of Australia, had become an unknown entity within the team. On one occasion an opening bowler of the Australian side was shocked to see him donning an Indian blazer. So shocked was he that he questioned Sardesai that, WHO ARE YOU. When Sardesai replied him who he was and what was he to Indian cricket, the bowler told him, MAN, did'nt get to see your face on the field. The pity is that I come after Graham McKenzie to bowl the second over of the match in every innings, and by the time I come, it seems you are back into the pavilion warming the ASS. That's my bad luck, I see, what to do, can't help.

Sardesai during that tour had started to regain his composure as he scored a "ton" against Tasmania. The fluidity of his strokes, by then after tussle against Tasmania got converted into fluency. However the think-tank had some other idea. They sent back B. S. Chandrashekar to India, who had sustained an ankle injury, and asked M. L. Jaisimha to fly to Australia. It was here that Ajit Wadekar requested Pataudi to give Sardesai a chance, but Pataudi had other ideas. He gave chance to Jaisimha who scored 101 and 74 at Brisbane, and thereby pushing Sardesai back and too far even to think of him again batting for India on that tour.

The tour of New Zealand followed and it was the same combination of Syed Abid Ali and Farokh Engineer going out to open for India. Abid Ali had a score of 21 and 10 at Christ Church, 7 and 16 at Wellington, 11 and 36 also at Wellington and 1 and 22 at Auckland. Not very successful with the bat, but his bowling came in as handy, and his magnificient fielding as a treasure to the team during this tour.

It was Engineer this time who had requested Pataudi to consider sending Abid Ali down the order and to think of allowing Dilip Sardesai to open the innings with him. But as the Indian team kept on winning one test after another, ultimately winning the series 3-1, Pataudi never thought of changing the winning combination and thus for the tour, that time, Sardesai was down and out for counts. This 3-1 win over New Zealand by India was the first occasion when an Indian cricket team had won a series abroad. Sardesai was still in the squad when India played New Zealand in the home series against New Zealand in 1969, but did not play. There was not a sign of Salim Durrani, who was making runs by 100's and taking wickets, in the domestic circuit, to stage a comeback.

One more test, as an opener against Australia at Bombay in 1969 saw the door shut for Dilip Sardesai for the rest of the series, as he failed to score even an aggregated 24 runs in both the innings. He was out for 20 and 3.

Durrani, as stated earlier, was not to play for India again till Pataudi led the side, and even though Durrani had a great match against Australia, for Central Zone here in India, at Nagpur where he had scored 55 and 31 and had claimed 6 for 65 for Central Zone, the vote and the place for the Kanpur test went to Gundappa Vishvanath, who had scored a sparkling 47 for the South Zone at the matting wicket at the Central College at Bangalore.

Out went Pataudi for the West Indies tour of 1971. The selectors chose Dilip Sardesai and Salim Durrani for the tour. They came back on the basis of their tremendous performances in the domestic circuit. The first match against Jamaica saw Salim Durrani hit the Jamaican for 137 runs, whereas Dilip Sardesai missed his century by 3 runs in the second. He was disheartened. However, when the series and the test took place, runs in "tons and tons" visited Dilip Sardesai. It did not come to Salim Durrani at all.

However, came the Port-of-Spain test at Trinidad, the second of the series. It was here that Dilip Sardesai had bagged his first pair in his batting career in 1962. And it was here that Salim Durrani had played the best test of his life in 1962, however both were on the losing side then.

This time however, Dilip Sardesai, in 1971 first played a sparkling knock of 112, whereas Durrani scored a blob in the second. And Durrani got those two wickets of successive deliveries to remove Clive Lloyd and Gary Sobers, which helped India to win the test. The venue was the same but the role was reversed for them. India had tasted victory for the first time in the West Indies.

For this was the last that they had visited the Port-of-Spain and the wicket at Trinidad. The first time was on two occasions for the first and the fourth test played in 1962. The sojourn of 1971 was the last, for those two who were never to visit West Indies again after this tour. Sardesai went on from strength to strength and in 1971, and as was in 1962, two tests were played at Port-of Spain at Trinidad.

Dilip Sardesai had amassed 521 runs on that tour before this match, he stroked a wonderful 75 in the first innings and reached his 600 runs of the tour. Dilip Narayan Sardesai is the first Indian to have scored over 600 runs in a single series against any test playing cricket team.

Ultimately, Sunil Gavaskar, with a score of 124 and 220 in the final test during that tour surpassed Dilip Sardesai and cornered all the glory. However the occasion and the moment, which did the magic for India was the two "golden" deliveries of Salim Durrani in the second test at Port-of-Spain, Trinidad, a "twin blow", from which West Indies were never able to recover. Without those two blood sucking punch, that Durrani produced to floor the might of the West Indies, I doubt, if India could have ever won the series.

During that tour, the two, Sardesai and Durrani, were the room mates for the entire tour. And their friendship, which blossomed in this tour, was to be seen and believed. It was as thick-and-thin, as the thieves. Sardesai played 4 more tests after this series and bowed out of test cricket. He played his last test against England at New Delhi in 1972, completed his 2000 runs in test cricket, and had won the Arjuna Award.

He was the last of cricketers, who were born between the period 1930 and 1940, of that generation to have won the Arjuna Award. Salim Durrani, born 1934 on May 11th was the first to win it in 1961. In fact Salim Durrani was the first ever Indian cricketer to have won this award since its inception in 1961 for Cricket in particular and sports in general.

Salim Durrani after the exit of Dilip Sardesai, went on to play 3 more tests. He completed his 1000 runs against England at Calcutta, and went on to claim his 75th test wicket in that series, his stoic and bold batting display helped India to beat England by 2-1. Again without him in that series, to be absolutely true to this nation, India would not have won, on the contrary it would have lost the series 0-3 to England.

India were trailing in this series by 0-1 at the end of the first test then came Durrani, from the second and came India victory. His score of 4 and 53, at Calcutta, 38 and 38 at Madras might never give an understanding to the present generation about how difficult it was to score those runs, in those situation against England. However it was his display of powerful and fearless batting, which really helped India to go 2-1 up in the series by the end of Madras test, and ultimately win the series. He hit the English bowlers exactly in a manner which his mood had ordered him to do. And he made the attack look so ordinary; that it made the others to feel that why the hell the other Indian batsmen are finding these English bowlers so hard to deal with.

What was so bad about these two cricketers and their fate, they were never given their proper place to bat regularly. Over 1500 runs of Dilip Sardesai came in at the middle order position at number four or five. Yet he had to open the innings for most of the time.

About 800 odds runs came to Salim Durrani, when he went to bat at number five or six. Yet for most of his part in test cricket, he was seen batting at the position from number eight to ten. Salim Durrani in the 1962 tour of West Indies, batted at number ten and had stroked a fluent unbeaten 48. Durrani was best suited to bat at number five, but that position was always held by Pataudi, and to some extent Vishvanath. So he had to bat at the lower end mostly with the tail-enders.

The three occasions that he was sent to bat at number three, he scored 104 against West Indies in 1962 at the Port-of-Spain, 53 against England at the Eden Gardens, Calcutta in 1972-73, and 38 against England at Madras in the same series.

Also they were the victims of some unreasonable thinking and for this the two had to sit out of the game, when they were in the prime of their cricketing career. The players who had come to replace them in the test matches, were total failures, one after the other. They were some who we could call "ONE MATCH WONDERS". Yet they continued, and these two talented were seen warming the seats at the pavilion. It was their bad luck that they just played 30 and 29 tests, they should have played over plus forty five. In that matter, Dilip Sardesai was lucky to have got his 2000 runs in test cricket. Salim Durrani was really unlucky.

The talent he had as an all rounder, he should have score over 2000 runs and claimed over 100 wickets, but for those 22 tests he missed out between 1966 and 1970, and again those three tests which he missed against England in 1971. Mind you, Durrani was at the peak of his form between and during that period.

To be honest, if both Dilip Sardesai and Salim Durrani had played the Madras test at Chepauk in 1970 against Australia, when they were reeling at 26 for 6, bet me, we could have won the test and squared the series 2-2, but the selectors had other school of thoughts. If they were lucky to have played 29 and 30 tests, they were distinctly unlucky to have missed playing at least 15 tests together. They have one thing in common. They were the first cricketers to have hit the silver screen. Dilip Sardesai did a commercial shoot with his son Rajdeep for a tooth paste named "Forhans" which hit the screen on August 3rd 1973. The company flopped though the product was hit. This was the first instance of a father-and-son duo to have done a commercial ad film together from the cricket fraternity. Salim Durrani, in the same year, did a movie "Charitra" opposite one of the most glamorous movie queen Parveen Babi. The film flopped though the pairing was good. Durrani, even at that age, looked very handsome and charming, and this prompted many saying that Anarkali, and Shahzada Salim, were born once again in the film world, but the movie was a disaster, as said earlier. This movie was produced by Babu Ram Ishara, who also is credited for producing movies like "Zaroorat", "Do Raha", "Chetna", "Prem-Parbat", "Yowvan" and "Tanhai" just to name a few. All these films were the adult movies and every movie was a hit during those days. Only "Charitra" failed. The theme of the movie was "IF WEALTH IS LOST, NOTHING IS LOST, IF HEALTH IS LOST, SOMETHING IS LOST, AND IF CHARACTER IS LOST EVERYTHING IS LOST".

Salim Durrani, from the mid of 1973 till the mid of 1979, for about six years thereafter, tried, tried and tried very hard to stage yet another comeback, but even after performing so well in the domestic circuit, he failed because of the "myopic" vision of our selectors. He had only one aim to achieve. Like Lala Amar Singh, Vinoo Mankad, and Karsan Ghavri, all Kathiawadis from the belt of Gujarat, he wanted to play a test at Lords. The others passed, but he failed. In his own words "Maybe I did not have the opening tag. The other three, were either opening batsmen, or the opening bowler, whereas I was not. This might have decided my fate." An aim and ambition which he could not fulfill, for which he really repents. Dilip Sardesai had no such repentance. It was Sardesai's transformation from the mid order bat to an opener, which had opened the views in the Indian batting think-tank that the midgets could bat out in the opening slot too, successfully. This was a change in the face that Dilip Sardesai had brought into the Indian cricket. Besides his commercial ad for "Forhans", brought many foreign product to be endorsed by the future generation of cricketers in India. His was the "opening" effort. Salim Durrani, it was, who had brought the concept of "free and flow" batting into the game, where test match during those days meant scoring 2 runs per over, during the entire course of day's play. His golden arm would bring a breakthrough when he bowled. He was in a nutshell, the "turning point" of Indian cricket, always. No doubt, the term "golden arms" came into the world of cricket, with Salim Durrani turning his arms to break a well settled partnership. Besides, he was the first cricketer to do a full fledged commercial film, which had opened the doors for the cricketers afterwards, to try their luck in the films. If only they were lucky, well............ ! They were a pair of supreme talented cricketers, but without any "real" luck. I have read about Dilip Sardesai's son, Rajdeep hitting the headline at "Times of India," for making run. Oh! more runs in the family, I felt. Then he would write the editorials for "Times of India", "Oh! A pen in the family, I thought". But when I saw him at the NDTV office on 9-10-2003, I felt that "he was a golden peacock", a 24 carat gold in the family." Truly "a worthy son of a worthy father is Rajdeep Sardesai. Rajdeep is a supreme talented, very articulated and an intelligent human who knows his job extremely well. He won what his father missed out, deserving it richly, the Padma Shri award. And that is something really big, really great."

If the administrators who are presently running the affairs of the game of cricket in India, and the ones who are running the Government and the affairs of the country, let there be a strong message that I wish to send to them all. Salim Durrani, Dilip Sardesai and Eknath Solkar are the trio of the cricketers from the batch of the Hat-Trick series winners –who have still not been awarded the Padma Shri. If you all have the sense, then wake up, Oh Mohan Pyare wake up, and bestow this national award to the trio first, before conferring it to those ones who richly are the undeserving ones. Thanks for listening to me. Thanks once again.

One of the most unforgettable incident which lingers in my mind while I write about Dilip Sardesai, is the heart which he displayed in 1973, when the MCC was playing against the West Zone squad, at Rajkot. This was just before the last test match which was to be played at Bombay. India were leading by 2-1 till then during the series.

This last test match was very important, not only for India to hold England, but it was also important to

Hanumant Singh, Salim Durrani, Earapalli Prasanna, besides Dilip Sardesai as one of them was to be selected to play the last test.

Dilip Sardesai, as earlier was leading the West Zone squad. All he needed was a good knock in this match. He surprised all and sundry, by not batting in his customary position in the first essay. He had one more chance to do, as one felt that perhaps in the second knock, when the West Zone chance to bat would come, he may try out his hands.

But Dilip Sardesai had different ideas. In this match, there was a raw but a very talented guy, a coot playing. He was Karsan Debraj Ghavri. Karsan Ghavri, had a very impressive spell of real fast bowling, when West Zone fielded first. He had claimed three wickets, and had a very good measure of Roger Tolchard, Keith Fletcher, and Mike Denness.

Again in the second innings, when MCC had to bat, Karsan Ghavri this time surprised everybody, with his very effective spin bowling. He bowled with a fang, and the two wickets that he claimed were of the surprising stuff of the "Chinaman". A chinaman is a bowling where the left hand bowler bowls an offspin with the action of a leg break.

In cricketing parlance, a left handed spinner bowling a googly is known as chinaman.

Watching Ghavri from a very close quarter, Sardesai was really surprised for the talent that Ghavri possessed. He could field really fantastic, had a very strong arm, and he could bowl both his quickies and the tweaks with equal effect. How about his batting? This question had haunted Sardesai.

In a surprise move, in the second innings when West Zone had to bat, he sent Karsan Ghavri up in the order, to bat. What followed was a miracle. In a tantalizing manner, which was full of clean hit, and thumping strokes, Karsan Ghavri had scored an unbeaten 76, what was more? The ten boundaries and the five over boundaries which he had carted to send the crowd into ruptures.

Well, Karsan Debraj Ghavri was born to Indian Cricket. Dilip Sardesai could have easily utilised this opportunity to get him back into the Indian test squad, but neigh, and nay. He gave Karsan Ghavri to Indian cricket. He preferred to promote a junior, rather than a burnt out.

Oh, what a highly paying dividend it proved to be. For, within no time Karsan Ghavri booked his ticket to Ceylon in 1974 and from then, it took only less than eight months, December 27th, 1974 to be exact, for him to make his test debut. And from then till the end of 1981, Ghavri was a permanent figure in the Indian squad.

It was Ghavri along with Kapil Dev Nikhanj, who transformed the Indian cricket. From the SPIN domination, they brought about the PACE revolution. Believe me, if one has to believe me, Kapil Dev wouldn't have been able to capture so many wickets, if he did not have Karsan Ghavri to support him from the other end. So admirable was the Karsan-Kapil duo of pace bowling, that till they played together, they did not allow any opening pair to add on over 100 runs for the opening wicket in test cricket.

Yes, this was possible because of the sacrifice that Dilip Sardesai had to make for him, and for the Indian cricket. Indian cricket undoubtedly should hold Dilip Sardesai, too high, for this. For this was the man who pushed his self interest to the back door, to bring in a youngster, who along with Kapil Dev was to transform the Indian cricket. Yes this sacrifice was responsible for changing the face of Indian cricket.

Finally, before I conclude this chapter, I would like to once again stress on certain facts which would make an interesting reading. I was talking to Mr. Rajan Bala, at his office at the Lavelle Road of the "Asian Age" at Bangalore. Mr. Bala who told me that it was Pankaj Roy, first, who at the instance of late Vijay Merchant, took to opening the innings in spite of the fact that he was a mid order bat. He went in to open, and till the end of his career, he kept on opening and retired as an opener.

However, this was not the case of Dilip Sardesai. He was a middle order bat, all of a sudden, he was asked to open, then again shifted to the middle order. Just imagine the extent of changing the mood and his bent of mind, to always get adjusted to the varys and the conditions, that kept on changing for as his position as a bat was concerned. This is something which one should always take care of and consider, when someone talks of Dilip Sardesai as a bat.

Similar is the story of Salim Altaf Durrani. Starting as a batsman at number eleven, he batted almost at every position, except the opening slot, and he was never given a permanent slot in the batting. Yet, he adjusted himself bravely, with a smile, and he always kept the interest of the team, upmost in his mind, before expediting his job. This to me, makes him great.

Today, we see, Virender Sehwag, Sachin Tendulkar and Saurav Ganguly doing the same for India in the one-dayers. But it could not have been possible if Dilip Narayan Sardesai, had not shown the way. Yes, it was Dilip Sardesai, who was instrumental in playing a make-shift role, in terms of "Merry go round the mulberry bush" of a batsman first, in the annals of Indian test cricket.

It was he who brought about a change in the face of makeshift bat and Indian cricket will always, and should always, hold him in a very high esteem.

Salim Durrani's two wickets of two successive deliveries at the Port-of-Spain in 1971 to get rid of Clive Lloyd first for 29 caught of Wadekar, and then bowling Sobers, clean for a nought, opened the gate of a famous victory. That victory entirely changed the history of India and its cricket. This in fact was the "gate" which opened the floodgates of many golden victories for India in the days to come and that's why he is considered as the cricketer who was the pioneer for changing the face of Indian cricket.

That is the importance of Salim Durrani for Indian cricket.

There is a very famous song in a Hindi film, sung by the great Shamshad Begum in 1958 exactly on the day when Salim Durrani first played his Ranji Trophy match for Saurashtra, it stands as such-:

SABAH SE YEH KEH DO

KI KALIYAAN BICHCHAA DE

KI DEKHO WHO JAANE–BAHAAR

AA RAHA HAI.

Yes this was the Jaan-e-Bahaar, ie the Prince Charming of the Indian cricket, and many a thanks to Shamshad Behanji for that beautiful song. For every reason, your innings of song started flying on a high notes with Salim Bhai playing his first Ranji match, way sack in the 50s and your innings of singing the gazals and the songs ended on the day when you were singing a ghazal at Pakistan, whereas Salim Bhai was to play his last Ranji game for Rajasthan against Vidharbha at Nagpur in 1978. Unfortunately, the kaliyan (petals) still have not been laid for Salim Durrani, to tread on it. Hope the Padma Shri award comes in the form of the petals laid down for him to tread on it for his journey to abode. Hope the B.C.C.I. realises, understands and acts wisely on it. But, WILL IT, that remains a question of conjecture.

I say it because I feel sometimes, the B.C.C.I
Is ruled by Fools(.) GOBHI KA "PHOOL"
Might be some (.)

14

CRICKET THE WAY: THE BOARD PLAYS

WELL, I'm not to castigate the manner, and the method that the Board employs or deploys while running the game in this country. However, I would like to stress one point that if the Indian Board had been professional in their approach, our cricket would have been the winner. To me the history of the Board has always been a mystery, and at times it has beaten the mysterious tales of the "Bermuda Triangle". The Board without the whiskey has been more risky, rather than with it.

One incidence which hammers me always was sending back of Lala Amarnath, in the midst of the tour, in 1936 when India was playing at England. What was Lala's fault. Well, when he returned back to India surprisingly, he was not given to put forward his stands and claims for anything about what had happened on the tour, nor did the members of the Board then, had made any concrete effort to know what went wrong with Lala's relations with the people over there at England.

Similarly, after the 1973 test at Madras, Chepauk, for and to the surprise of many, one just did not understand, how of all, Salim Durrani was axed from the team, for the Kanpur test in spite of his winning performance at the Madras test. The explanation that was put forward by the Board was "indiscipline action". What was the indiscipline, was neither explained nor told, either to Durrani or to Lala Amarnath, the press and media.

The same indiscipline had killed Kapil Dev by a test at Calcutta in 1984-85, when M. C. C. were touring India under David Gower after the New Delhi test, which India had lost. Kapil Dev was dropped from the team for the third test at Calcutta. The reason cited was "indiscipline batting". That was after his 67 tests appearance in a row.

Kapil went on to play another 65 afterwards. If he had not been dropped, then he would have had earned the distinction of playing 133 test matches, without a single break, a phenomenal achievement which nobody in the world could have had ever achieved. But that wasn't to be. Thanks to the Indian Board. Hello the Indian selectors, and hello the captain of the Indian team then, thank you all in reverse sense. That was the midas touch in reverse in the annals of Indian cricket.

The functioning of the Board to run the game in the country is, to describe at the least, "peculiar". It completely defies all the logics. One really would go either to Ranchi or to Agra to the psychiatry hospital to get himself cured if he made an attempt to know the functioning of the Board to run the game in this country.

In the administration, there are people who have never played the game, either for their association, or for the country and they just do not know anything about this game, besides they, I think hardly know about the administration, yet they continue to be there to run the game, for the reason which is not known to anybody. There are people who do not know the A, B, C of Indian sports, yet they run the show and the sports board in this country. That is why we have "no medal in spite of so many efforts of pedal" to show for our effort.

We have so many of them who are not worth enough to run the affairs and the management of their own homes, but they find a hot seat in the affairs of the games and sports, for running it and taking care of their management. I can cite the names of a few. The reason I'm not doing it is not that I'm scared of them for doing it, but I do not want to waste my lines even citing them. It is a "sin" to even mention them and write their names. A paper is such a sacred thing that the names of the stinging sinners should not find a place on it as described Nietzche once. After all who would like to name and mention the horrenders, when we very well know what a horror this nation has over the last thirty years turned out to be. People do not change them easily, I know. My writing here would not change them.

To cite an example, for how many test matches did Raj Singh Dungarpur play for India. Yet he remained at the "helm" of B.C.C.I. for so many years. As compared to him was the late Vijay Merchant, the Chairman of the selection committee from 1968 to 1973. The results were there for everybody to see. In 1968—India:3, New Zealand:1, 1969–Australia:3, India:1, 1971—India:1, West Indies:0, 1971—India:1, England:0, 1972–1973-India-2, England—1. In nut shell India had won 9 test matches, out of the 31 it played, and it had tasted as many as 4 series victories. Now this shows the difference between a player, who has had played the game at the highest level to deliver the goods, as an administrator and somebody, who is at the "helm" of administration without playing the game.

This was, and this is not, something new in India. This was, and this is the case all over the country and perhaps all over the world, in almost all the games, but the players are still sweating, only to be hired and fired besides they are not paid accordingly.

A revolt had taken place, the world over, with the players playing cricket and their respective associations or the Boards. The result was, a tycoon named Kerry Packer took all the players under his clutches, by paying them handsomely and bringing about a new concept into the game. The "night cricket", the "coloured clothing", and the "white balls" by then after Packer had packed the cricketers, in his box had come to play.

Indian cricket also had its moment of anxiousness by then. From a mere Rs. 250.00 per test by the end of 1972-73, the payment rose up by Rs. 5,000.00 per test from the beginning of 1978. The man who led the revolt was none other than Sunil Gavaskar in 1978. The result was he had to loose his leadership just because he had brushed his shoulders with the administrators of cricket in India, for raising his voice to raise the payment for playing in the test matches.

However, thereafter, by the start of 1979, the pay packet jumped up to Rs. 10,000.00 per test, in 1985, it was Rs. 15,000.00 per test and now it stands up to Rs. two lakhs per test. But the moot question is, is it enough?

I cannot forget and I will not forget an incident, when after the Bombay test against England in 1984, which India had won, the "man-of-the–match" award was announced, and Laxman Shivaramakrishnan was the one who had won it. However, the amount of Rs. 25,000.00 was not paid to him, immediately. The reason cited by the Board was, "no sponsors" were available to sponsor the award. Was the Board "kitty" or wallet, as we would call it empty, and whether Shivaramakrishnan was paid the money afterwards is not known to me. This was against England in 1984-85 when David Gower led the English team.

Now this reflects the way, the Board was running the game in the country. The recent example of the attitude of the Board towards the player was when Sunil Gavaskar had to write, requesting the Board to at least allow Polly Umrigar to travel by business class on the course of his journey and thereafter to attend to any meetings of the Board.

The Board does not even know how to treat its former stars in an authenticated manner.

Well, let me be frank. I admit that running a show, like cricket in the country, is not a child's play. There are about 30 associations playing this game. Every year 330 players participate in the Ranji Trophy. It is not very easy to keep a track of all the players. But here should come the "wisdom" into the play. Instead the Board prefers to follow the "Wisden" which is another stinging lump when it comes to follow the record. I can pick out so many mistakes in the Indian version of Wisden, but that is not going to make me filthy rich. That's a fact.

The classical example of the kick that will never go well with the Indian public, was the one which Kapil Dev got in his association with cricket, when he joined the so called and so made rebel by the B.C.C.I., the I.C.L. This could have been handled professionally and classically, and Kapil could have been given a hearty send off with a relieve letter, but as again, does anybody in the Board knows, what is administration, or what is professionalism for that matter.

Money never brings in peace, and power adds more of a disease to the body. This quote could be applied comprehensively on the B.C.C.I., if one really analyses their mode of functioning. It is child's play, the exact case of humpty-dumpty sitting on the wall, and humpty–dumpty having a great fall. Give it to a professional working in the analyzing wing of a software firm, like the Infosys, the T.C.S or the Wipro, to analyse the Board and its functioning, the inference and the final comments will be the same to what I have written here.

"When you are forcing 330 players to play the game, it is you who have to take care about the players." When I was a journalist with the "Hitvada" in 1981-82, I was given an assignment to cover the Inter Zonal (central) Cooch Behar Trophy. The condition I saw then, about the players, who had come to Nagpur for participation was "horrendous".

The players from Uttar Pradesh, Rajasthan and Madhya Pradesh were goofed up, and put into one big dormitory at the V. C. A. stadium. There was no privacy. The dormitory had a passage, from where all the officials of the V. C. A. and the other members associated with the game would come and go, thus disturbing the players.

There were no adequate cots and beds and so many players would have to lie on the floor. There was only one bathroom, and one toilet for the players to clean themselves, and respond to the "nature's call". No provision for hot water. And imagine the coaches of the respective teams requesting the players to produce their best. Could it be possible.

On the contrary, I could see Mr. Kannmadikar, then a strong Board member, coming by flight, too "observe" the match and go back by flight. Is this the way to treat a player. In contrast, I was to observe the "All India State Bank of India" tournament which was held at Nagpur. The State Bank of India, Nagpur, and Arun Ogiral, had done a wonderful job in organising and staging the tournament.

Ogiral, with his band of young cricketers, all who played for State Bank of India, Nagpur in the Gujdar Trophy, did an excellent job, all by themselves, to accommodate the players in MLA hostel and C. P. Cottage. The local guys like Vikas Shesh, Shrish Joshi, Viraj Markand to name a few, did not leave any stone unturned, to see that the players did not suffer at all.

Some of the greatest cricketers of India, employed by the State Bank, the likes of Ajit Wadekar, Subroto Guha, Hanumant Singh, Roger Binny, Bharat Reddy, and P. Krishnamoorthy, were left dazed and wondered by the arrangement. The food served, the drinks offered and the hospitality were of the highest order. I could make out the difference, then and there.

The relation between the "press" and the State Bank then was to be seen and believed. That was an abject lesson, learned by me, as a "novice" to journalism, then. However, when the match between Board President XI and M. C. C. was played at Nagpur in 1981, the treatment that the press was "meted" out by the V. C. A. authorities had forced the press to write a few sentences in the columns, how to learn something from the bankers about maintaining a "relation" with the press.

In fact, the two "superb" Public Relation Officers, at Nagpur during that time were Arun Ogiral, and Jeetendra Bhargava of Western Coalfield Limited, and Ogiral had laid an example, the moment he got it. Jeetendra Bhargava now is a high flier, a very highly placed executive at the Air-India at Bombay. Rajan Nair later turned out to be one of the best Media Managers for W. C. L., and very rightly he was named the Media Manager of the Indian cricket team for a short period of time. He should have been given this assignment for a longer tenure.

How had the Board changed their view, on this subject is not known to me. However, I have not seen the "Board Communication Manager" doing a job, well and good, as Ogiral, or Jeetendra Bhargava, during those years of my life that I have been associated with cricket and journalism.

The present chief of the media appointed by the Board is a YES SIR, NO SIR, VERY WELL SIR kind of a man. His theme and the motto has always been, ONE FOR MY MASTER, ONE FOR MY DAME, AND THE REST FOR THE TV MEDIA, WHO ARE SCATTERED IN THE LANES AND BY–LANES. That is the way he puts it across, everytime when we hear him talking to the electronic media and the press. One can easily make it listening him when his mouth is in action. What better things can you expect from these kinds of surcasters.

The money has come in plenty to the Board, but how do they use it, is anybody's guess. Why can't they think of paying the non-test-playing players equating their worth as a cricketer, not as somebody who needs to live on the Board's mercy.

There have been so many Ranji cricketers, who could have played for India, if they would have been born 20 years later. Yes, I'm referring to players like Venkat Sundaram, Sorabjit Singh, Suresh Luthra, Dinoo Deshpande, R. K. Ohri, Gokul Inder Dev, Hyder Ali, Mohammed Tariff, Anil Deshpande, Kailash Ghattani, Vijay Telang, Imran Ali, Ashok Bhagwat, Rakesh Tandon, Arvind Panchasara, Kishore Pradhan, Vijay Bhosle, Sharad Diwakar, Abdul Ismail, Rakesh Tandon, Anwar Pathan, Mohd Ibrahim, Gopal Bose, Samir Chakravarthy, Deepankar Sarkar, Robi Panda, just to name a few. Well the list is endless.

I had not seen a better batsman than Gundappa Vishvanath, a better all rounder than Salim Durrani and a better bowler like Kapil Dev in Indian cricket. I believe they were unlucky to have been born in India and played the game, in a manner that they had to play. Any other bowler in the world would have given up playing cricket, for the conditions that were laid for Kapil to bowl in India, but Kapil continued. In the same vein even Gundappa Vishvanath did not have a proper kits at Kanpur to play his first big test match, but he was helped by his team mates.

Would the readers believe it. Disgusted by the way the Board prepares the pitch, Kapil Dev in a Ranji Trophy match against Delhi, in the finals in 1986, had bowled off-spin for a longer duration of time in that match. He was so frustated by the behaviour of the pitch, then instead of wasting his energy, he felt it would be better to bowl the off-spin. Just see the cheek-Kapil bowling offspin

In the same fashion in 1981 during the Ranji finals, Karnataka having scored 705 runs in their first innings had lost the match to Delhi who had scored 707 for 9. In that match, Raghuram Bhat had bowled 94 overs conceding 195 runs to claim only a wicket. This is how the pitches have been laid for our players to play on.

Of late the situation is even worst . The sponsors of the B.C.C.I., it seems, have sealed the lips of B.C.C.I. or have stiched them for good. These sponsors have the brand ambassadors for them to endorse their products. These sponsors it seems pressurise the B.C.C.I. to prepare such a kind of sleeping beauty, that it serves no purpose to play matches on these kinds of surface.

I could be wrong, but my sixth sense says to me that to get the money back, both from the brand ambassador whom the sponsors have put their money on, and also from the B.C.C.I., the sponsors it seems put their clause, and B.C.C.I. might have purposely prepared these kinds of lifeless and nonsensical pitches so that their brand ambassador would score very heavily. This in return helps the sponsor to get their money back which they invest on the brand ambassador and also on the B.C.C.I.

The process is killing the Indian cricket in every sense. What is the use of creating world records after world records, if that does not helps the team to win. In the era in which Pataudi, Wadekar and Bishen Singh Bedi had led India, these captains made it sure for the respective associations to prepare sort of pitches, which would seam for the first two days, then from the third day onwards the wickets would break and the last two days it would spin.

Irrespective of the opponent, and the composition of the opponent team, the matches were played on these kinds of surfaces in India, in the test matches then, and believe me my readers, what a match and what excitement it used to generate. People would get their worth of money back, and cricket series was like the waiting train to come in for the cricket lovers those days. The way it is played now, nobody is interested to watch the test matches because these matches played in India are boring, dull and it gives a disease of sleep . This is because the Board has become the puppets in the hands of the sponsors and the players, individually, and this does not augurs well for the game for the future.

What does the Board do! They brag that they are the richest Board in the world, but do they manage the activities properly. We have heard so many stories of the luggages being lost, or taken away in the transit. Can't the Board set the matter straight.

The Board has the money, and it is the richest Board in the world. What does it do for the game. The ground conditions in most of the stadia are horrendous. The conditions of the outfield, and the conditions of the lavoratory, the rest rooms at some venues are at their worst even now.

I was a witness to certain things, which I feel strongly ashamed of, however I write it "daringly" in my book. I may not be taken wrongly, neither may I be misunderstood. I was told to cover the proceedings at the "nets" for the selection of South Zone University team in 1982 when I was with the "Hitvada". My Chief Mr. P. V. Nayudu, had told me to engage my entire mind and body in this event. The selection of the South Zone University for the Vizzy Trophy was to be done at the Institute of Science ground at Nagpur, after the nets.

I was told that Mohammed Azharuddin, Kiran Reddy and Prakash Rathore would also come at the nets.

In the evening, a day before the nets, I had been to Subedar Hall at Nagpur. I saw Mohd. Azharuddin and Kiran Reddy sleeping on a cricket mat kept at the Subedar Hall. Azhar was sleeping as if he had sold a horse in the market and had gone to sleep. Besides them, Prakash Rathore was turning his arm over, in the hall to perfect his bowling.

Rathore by then was a household name. He had represented the Indian school XI, under Vedraj against England. When I enquired about all these, I was shocked to hear that they had come for these trials on their own, though they were told by their college authorities to move to Nagpur for the trials. There was nobody to look after them at Nagpur. They, on their own, had to travel from pillar to post, then to meet the University authorities at

Nagpur, and after many a heat break, somehow got to stay at this Hall, where there were no amenities or facilities.

I had apprised them that it would be better if they moved to "Gurudeo Lodge" at Sitabuldi at Nagpur. What shocked me was, when I heard Rathore telling me that they were paid Rs. 10.00 per day to meet their expenses at Nagpur, by the University Sports Control, I was crest fallen and crucified then and there.

I then decided, "sports journalism" will never be my cup of tea, lunch or dinner after 1-9-82 by any means, by any standard. If the sportspersons were in for such a rude jolt, what could be the fate of a scribe of sports. Ever since then, I had taken my studies very seriously. Till then, the "cricket devil" hanged on my head, but this was the "turning point" of my career.

I was to enrol my name and book a seat for the M.B.A course for a better future which I got through a very tough round of competition. Once I was into it, I knew that even if I had to sleep on the floor, I would not have to ask for a pair of socks from anybody. Why the pair of socks one might ask me. My answer is read this book and follow it, you will come to know the answer.

The other incidence was during the Wills Trophy match which was played between Bengal and Hyderabad at V. C. A. stadium at Nagpur and I was covering the match. The match was washed away due to a torrential rain. But during the lunch, I had witnessed Shahid Akbar, removing the socks and handing it to Azhar. When I enquired from Shahid Akbar, what was it all about, he said to me that he did not have a pair of "cricket" socks, and he had borrowed it from Azharuddin, he was returning it. The Hyderabad Cricket association, it seems did not have the money to give it to the players to buy even a pair of cricket socks.

I was taken aback. Shahid Akbar was a member of the Combined University and Board President XI team which had played against MCC at Nagpur in 1977. From 1977 to 1981, Shahid Akbar could not manage a pair of socks, while playing for Hyderabad. Strange I felt. Is that the way the association under the B.C.C.I managed itself and ran the show, I felt surcasted to see these, as these events were horrendous incidents for me to watch.

It is my advice to the Board. Please monitor and supervise each and every association, and find out whether the facilities provided to the players are adequate or not. Let them make a habit, an order "to the association" about providing the full gears to the players representing their associations. Let the Board pay for it, or either reimburse it. It is obvious, that without the full kits, a player will never be in a position to do any thing and perform best and stand up to his potentials.

Secondly, let there be a good accommodation for the players to "enjoy" at least during the game. A toilet to be shared by twenty or thirty will not help. Players are not a herd of cows and bufalloes to shit, piss and drink at one place where even the filth would be ashamed of being thrown there.

Just before the start of the season, why can't the Board through the help of their association, hire a few good hotels at different places to lodge the players. A clean and a healthy atmosphere, a good sanitation and good atmosphere, naturally brings the best out of the players. The players are motivated, naturally to produce the best.

Why can't an air fare be provided to the players. At least all the teams, playing Duleep Trophy, and the teams playing the Irani Trophy, can be given these facilities. The journey by train, now-a-days, is not safe. Besides the time taken for the journey is tedious and full of boredom. Too much of practice time is lost by travelling by train.

An air journey can cut the travelling time, and the players can spend their time at the nets. Why can't the Board pay the players representing the association in the various tournaments. To say, Rs 40,000 per match may be paid to a player representing his association in Ranji Trophy, Rs. 20,000 per match may be paid to the player representing his association in the under-19, and Rs.15,000 per match may be paid if a player is representing the under-17, or under-15. Beside it, if a player has represented his University in Vizzy Trophy, or Rohinton Baria Trophy, then let the Board come forward to pay him Rs. 15,000 per match as his reward. A player playing Duleep Trophy for his Zone should be paid Rs 40,000 per match, and those rendering their service for the Irani Trophy tie should be paid Rs 50,000.

A school cricketer, representing his school at the National Tournament may be reimbursed Rs. 10,000 per match by the Board.

While I write about the money to be paid by the Board, the Board should take care of all the income tax affairs and its consequences before paying the players, so that the players are not clutched away by the IT authorities. In 1962 the entire Brazilian footballers who were gifted so heavily by their Government, faced the wrath of the IT authorities, and almost all the players were fined drastically by their IT authorities. The Government was a mere spectator as some of the players were sent to the prison for not having cared and paid for their income. The Board may kindly take this an example and lay the necessary modules for the players to stay away from the clutches of the IT authorities, or else the IT authorities will take their bums, like their counterpart did it to the Brazilian football team in 1962.

I'm writing this in particular, because a few years ago, Sachin Tendulkar has had his share of luck exactly to one of this kind of an incident, where the chartered accountant, who was responsible for maintaining his accounts, and his IT related affair, had swirled in excess of Rs 42 crores, and had turned him off when it came to returning his excess money that the accountant had licked. These are the start, maybe some of the worst are in the offing, I hope it doesn't, but everything is possible in a country where one of its monument is the first wonder of the world. Better the Board wakes up and come forward to educate the cricketers for everything.

The Board also has to define the mode and the means for the payment. Some kind of a standard has to be set for making the payments. Paying over a crore of rupees for winning inconsequential tournaments is not the real and the actual way of paying the players. For example, the team which won the Twenty-Twenty tourney at South Africa, was not worth to have been paid a crore of rupees. That is the amount which is paid to the Director of Instituion like the Infosys, but for that he individually has to put about 4000 crores of revenue on the lap of Mr Narayan Murthy, every year. A booty of Rs 10,00,000 could have been enough. Similarly the victory over the Aussies in the Triangular series was not worth 58,00,000 per player. Here a booty of Rs 15,00,000 could have been sufficient.

To pay any amount, just to overcast and cover the glow and the glites of an organization like the ICL is not what we expect from B.C.C.I. To pay and show the world that we are the richest Board of the world, and just that we are the richest, we should be given the topmost post of the I.C.C. should not be the signal of the Board to be sent to the fraternity of cricket, the world over. This looks cheap, and something the act of the Board makes us feel that it has become an ugly duckling. Money should be utilized to improve the infrastructure, to send the young side abroad for international exposure.

If I were the Chief of the B.C.C.I, I wouldn't have acted the way that the B.C.C.I did with the I.C.L. I would have asked the I.C.L. to prepare a blue print about their activities, for the first three years. Having read the blue print and after understanding it well, I would have framed certain policies for them to follow, and produce the results. I would have forced them to take their games to the nook and corner of the country both in terms of spreading the games and telecast.

I would have totally kept a strong vigil on their accounts, and the revenue generated out of them. From the players point of view, playing for them, I would have conducted a special meeting with them explaining the bad and the worst that could happen to them for playing in this kind of tourneys, and would have taken from every individual player a statement that the Board would not be held liable if their career comes to a standstill, if in any case the project goes off.

My policies also would have included for churning out certain youngsters, in certain department where the Board has failed miserably, such as producing, say a left arm off-spinner and a left arm leggie, who could have been moulded into a champ to take the seats left vacant after the exit of Bishen Singh Bedi.

After three years, if the results did not come the way as I would have expected, I would have then raised an alarm to call of I.C.L. and then taken it to the highest level to see that this was disbanded. But what the B.C.C.I. did was nothing but a classical example of Hitler act, killing everybody involved in the process. For professionals like us, it only proved that B.C.C.I. had weeded the I.C.L. just because of the fear that stemmed from either the rots, rotten, or nothing. The Board had an excellent chance in front of them to make use of the resources of the I.C.L. for their onward march and development, but professionally they missed it. The donkey dowry thinking, and the rotten inflated egos of some hanky-panky members, made a history, nothing more and nothing less came out of it. This is a classic case of unprofessionalism.

Better it would be for the Board to allow combined University to play in the Ranji matches. Also for the Duleep Trophy, and Institutional team formed from the players representing the Services and the University, should be allowed to play in the Duleep Trophy. Some kind of thought should go into the process. The Rohington Baria Trophy and the Vizzy Trophy should be revived and the sooner the Board does it, the better.

A trophy named as the Durrani-Sardesai trophy may be instituted and awarded to the winners of the match played between the winners of the Irani Trophy and the Combined Institutional team, which as I have said earlier should comprise of the players representing the Services and the Indian Universities. On the similar lines, a B. S. Bedi Trophy be instituted for the best spinner at the University level, and an E. A. S. Prasanna Trophy may be instituted, for the best spinner at the College level in the Rohinton Baria Trophy.

Money is the birthright for everybody to earn, but spending it to showcase that nobody can compete with us for the same, is neither the art of rolling money, nor to prove their richness. In fact, this way of spending the money is foolishness. There are many a field, in the administration, in the act of imparting knowledgeable information, like the art to invest money, the way to look at life, and guide the youngsters to lead a normal but a happy life, to think about the career after the game, and after their retirement is the total responsibility of the Board. Has the Board taken a serious note and a view of all these. This is what the Board is supposed to do if it thinks that it is the father of all the games and sports in India.

The art of living, the art of being humble, the art of being in control always, the art of spending the booty in the right manner, the art of investment, the art of building oneself and maintaining their life after their career is over, are some of the important lessons that the Board needs to teach the cadets while they are at the academy. Will the Board heed to my advice.

During my kid days, we had two goats and a cow at our house. My father was a highly placed officer in the public sector, at the Coal mines, he could afford to give us that luxury. I remember, once throwing some leaves plucked from the tree to the goats, to feed, which they smelled and did not even look at it to chew. When I asked the father to explain me the reason, he said that son you have not washed the leaves, AND THE GOATS, OR FOR THAT MATTER, ANY ANIMALS, THEY HAVE THEIR SIXTH SENSE TO APPLY FOR THEM TO DECIDE WHETHER THINGS, OR LEAVES THROWN AT THEM ARE GOOD OR BAD FOR THEM. By refusing to eat, they have sent you a message, DO NOT THINK US LIKE YOU, EVEN IF WE CANNOT TALK, WE CAN THINK BETTER, OR THE BEST ABOUT US THAN YOU. Continuing, he said, in a way the animals have insulted you. Better change your mindset before the world starts insulting you.

This is the kind of a better thinking that the Board has to infuse and inject to the buddies and the budding cricketers, rather than throwing their money to the cricketers, to feed on them, like the loathe of flesh which is being thrown at the cage of a Lion at the Zoo, while feeding the Lions.

Personally I totally flout first, and flay the B.C.C.I. for the manner it auctioned the players for the IPL tourney. See, the concept of the transfers of the players in football now has been implied on cricket, logically, the sales of the players are done between two clubs, and not the Board. It is because the clubs make the players, and if the players are sold, the clubs are attached to the proceeds. Moreover, the dialogues are always held between the players agent and the clubs. It is everywhere in football, and the football theory did come here in the IPL circus to buy and sell the players. Here in the IPL auction, surprisingly the players were directly sold by the Board to the bidders, and in what a way, without having the previous market rate of any players before them, to evaluate their rates, who might have played in this kind of a tourney.

Just look at the rates, a cricketer like Ricky Ponting was evaluated for 1.6 crores, and a novice like Robin

Utthappa was sold for 3.60 crores, what a joke. Oh, and Lo, there was no taker for Mohammed Yousuf, who to start was evaluated at about 3.60 crores, and who did not get a buyer, a gem who has the record for scoring over 1900 runs in a single calendar year.

On the hypothesis end, say Sachin, was never the member of the Indian team which participated in the Twenty-Twenty World Cup, was evaluated as an icon, and Ricky Ponting who led Australia in that tourney, was evaluated at a rate which was even nothing and nil as compared to Sachin. A player who requested the Board not to consider him for the Indian team for the Twenty-Twenty World Cup, as he had felt that his youth was against him for playing in that kind of a tourney, was awarded as an icon and was accredited that status by the Board, for his Bombay team, and Ricky Ponting was considered to be a lamb for the slaughter for no worth. Goodness, gracious, and my God, oh it is a simple logic that the Indian Board wishes to say it to everybody, BUDDIES, ONE MINUS TWO IS EQUAL TO ONE. That is a simple mathematics for us.

Buck-up B.C.C.I., keep it up. My God what a way to buy and sell the cricketers. Really, as the days are passing by, we are having all jokers to man and plan our games and its administration. Goodness, God save the Indian sports.

The reason why I mentioned the name of Mohammed Yousuf (Yousuf Youhana), is that he was first contracted by the I.C.L. The BCCI with their hands on the hands of the PCCB, dragged him out of the I.C.L. and pushed him to I. P. L. The I.C.L. had evaluated him at a very high price, and he was promised a fat lump of pudding and pie. But this simple Simon, met the Pimon from the B.C.C.I, and according to some mutual understanding, chopped off his relation with the I.C.L., thinking that he would be taken care of in a fantastic manner by the I. P. L. He at the end is in a scary land now. Niether has anybody purchased him, nor has anybody showed any interest for him. He still has to find a team. And to think that the

B.C.C.I had promised him all the pudding and the pie at the time when he was whisked away by the BCCI from the clutches of I.C.L.

Friends this is how the shows are managed and manned by the B.C.C.I, I do not understand what kind of a hope can anybody put it on the B.C.C.I. if the international stars are to receive this kind of a treatment. Mohammed Yousuf might be scratching his head for the decision that he had taken.

India had won the Under-15 World Cup tournament in 1998 at London. Sarkar Talwar was the Manager of the team then. That team had Reetinder Singh and Mohd Kaif. The team was sponsored by a businessman from Faridabad, courtesy Kapil Dev. Did the Board ever think of reimbursing the businessman for the heart, he played for sponsoring the team or Kapil Dev. This is the attitude of the Board, perhaps towards the game, towards the players, and towards developing cricket in India.

The one sincere effort to recognize the players and pay them for their deeds, was made in 1983, and for the last time in 1984. All those players who had played more than 25 test matches for India, were paid @ Rs. 2,000 per test by the Board. But this is an amount which is meager.

The Board now pays Rs 35,000 per player as pension who have played test matches for India, and Rs 10,000 to those who have played Ranji Trophy for their association. But this is not the right way to make the payments.

There are players who have represented their Zonal side teams against the visiting teams in India. Those players have performed well. For example, Kenia Jayanthilal had scored 101 while playing against the M.C.C. Similarly, Suryaveer Singh has a century to his name against the same team in 1972 at Indore. Also Murthy Rajan has scored 104 against the West Indies for Central Zone in 1974, and mind you in that series no opener had scored a ton against the West Indies, a truly big feat.

Now when it comes for payment, you cannot equate these performances as equivalent to the performance of Rajan Nair, who has played in only two Ranji games, and pay them on equal footing, shelling Rs 10,000 to everybody for their effort. In my case and in my sense, players who did not play the test matches, but have played against the visiting teams, for their Zonal teams, should be paid at least Rs 25,000 per month. This is of course for the players who have retired. The players who played only in the Ranji's should be paid Rs 15,000 per month.

One has to maintain a difference in quality, and the class of the players who have done well against the visiting side, and a mere Ranji Trophy specialist, and equate them with those scale for remuneration. A two match wonder simply cannot be equated against somebody, on a equal footing, who has scored a century against the fiery of Roberts, Julien and Keith Boyce for his zonal team.

Not only that, if the player expires, the money should be given to his wife till she is alive. There are a lot of cricketers whose wives need the same for their maintenance. Once the wife is dead, then the payment should stop. It should not go to his sons or the daughters.

At least, the players, or their legacies, if they are dead will be benefited. Players like L. Amarsingh, Amir Elahi, A. L. Apte, Shute Banerjee, S. N. Banerjee, Baqua Jilani, N. Chaudhury, S. N. M. Colah, R. T. Sami, M. J. Gopalan, L. P. Jai, just to name a few, who are not alive will be benefited. Let the Board recognize their efforts to the game of cricket, and honour them. If these cricketers did not play for more than the tests, it was not because of their fault, but the apathy of the selection committee towards them.

There are about 82 such test cricketers, I know, who have played between one to 9 test matches for India. It is for the Board to find out the addresses of these players and hand over the money to their families, which will really help them.

The condition of most of the cricketers, who have played upto 10 test matches, is simply "horrendous" to explain the least. If they have crossed the border and settle over there, like in the case of Amir Elahi, Jehangir Khan and Lall Singh, now settled in Malaysia, could be invited by the Board, and their booty be handed over to them or to their wives, if they are alive, or to their legacies, as the case might be.

The Indian Board makes over 100 crores if a test series between Pakistan and India is held in India. Can't it at least award the cricketers who are in a real bad shape. After all they had "laid their lives" for making Indian cricket, for what it is today, the richest in the world, and can't the Board pay them back.

The idea of paying Rs 35,000 to the test player is good, and it should be continued, however, the Board should sit and revise the payment every 10 years, as the inflation rate in India changes swiftly, and the cost of living too goes high.

The same is the story that applies to all cricketers, who have played the Ranji Trophy and it is high time the Board comes forward to recognize and award these cricketers monetarily.

The same yardstick may be applied to those University cricketers who have played for the Univesity against the visiting team, and have performed well for the University. There are a lot of cricketers who have played for University, but somehow did not play for their Ranji teams or for their state. Ravi Tuli is a classic example. He performed excellently while playing for the University against the West Indies in 1974 at Indore, where he had scored 33 and an unbeaten 14, but did not play in any Ranji games as he left India for a better academic, and new pasture abroad. Like Ravi Tuli, Umrikant Modi, who is now settled in the US, too had represented Indian University against the visiting team in 1964, but he did not play in any Ranji matches for Bombay. These kind of cricketers too should be paid. I hardly can think of the present Board members to think on these lines.

Why can't the Board get the list of all such players and start paying them. At least those players, who have left the game, and are leading a "poor life", can be benefited by the Board. This money can be put into the education funds of their sons and grandsons by those players, for their better future.

It is not only the player, let the Board also take care of the "Maalis", the ground men, the statisticians, the scorers, the Managers of the team, and pay them "honorarium" or the "Fees". Why can't the Board think on these lines. Let the Board formulate its own equation, and come out with a system of payment, but the sooner the better, let it pay the cricketers as quickly as possible.

On the similar grounds, why can't the Board come forward to honour those great writers and journalists, who have given their life covering cricket, cricket, and cricket for India. Will India have another Rajan Bala, another Raju Bharatan, another K. N. Prabhu to cover cricket. They wrote about cricket with their "bloods" filled in their pen. Even for that matter the late. P. V. Nayudu was one of the best cricket correspondents that we have ever seen. He knew how to write.

Why can't the Board encourage good cricket writers and historian and pay them for their effort. We will never have a better cricket historian than Sujeet Mukherjee. Though many, including myself, would not agree with me writing good about Mr Ramachandra Guha, yet I feel that for his contribution, he should be honoured by the Board. Even a sum of Rs. 3,00,000 paid to them by the Board, will be a big recognition for their effort on cricket journalism. The Board has to take the initiative.

The Board can act as an "Apex Body" and can help the other games as its subsidiary. We have so many archers, so many boxers, so many swimmers and wrestlers who just caved in at the Olympics because of lack of proper training, proper facilities and exposures.

The case of the swimmer Sangeeta Rani Puri, is a classic example. Born at Trinidad to a Panjabi father and a Christian mother, she was touted as a "medal certainty" for Olympics at Trinidad in swimming.

She came to India to stay with her father and continued swimming. All that she needed badly was a sponsor for her training abroad. Went the Olympics 92 and went her name out of the "sporting world" for ever. She, for the lack of a proper sponsor, gave up swimming thereafter. And with that went a medal for India. Taking this as an example, here is my writing to the Board. There are two certain Olympic medal prospects in our country at this moment. One is Dola Banerjee in archery, and the other one is Vijendra Singh in Boxing. Do not delay in taking decision to sponsor them, on an individual basis. Late-fine, the medal would go out of India's grasp. Dola Banerjee is the best bet for the future, and so is Thockchem Nanao Singh in boxing.

On an individual basis, why can't the Board come forward to put their money on these kinds of medal surety. The Board can even pay the Durand Cup football committee every year, to conduct at least this tournament properly, which is known as the "Blue Riband of India soccer". The way the Durand cup is held now, I'm sure after a few years this tournament will be "off". Why can't the Board help in infusing at least a life to these kinds of tourney by pouring a bit of money to keep the tourney flowing.

After all, where does the money come from to the Board. From the public, from the organizations, from the sponsors. Why it is that the money remains at the "coffers" of the Board, without being properly used and circulated. Why can't the Board, richest in the world, ignite and revive, help and aid some other sports, as described earlier.

One really hopes the Board wakes up fast. And when it wakes up, let us remember, the way that the school cricket national tournament, the Rohinton Baria Trophy and the Vizzy Trophy are held at present.

It is high time the Board enters into an agreement with the National Federation of School, and the University to conduct the Vizzy Trophy and Rohington Baria Trophy tournaments. Let the Board come into it in a big way to help these institutions and the Universities to conduct the tournaments in a better way. These tournaments are the seeds and saplings of cricket in India. They desperately need the help of the Board for their survival. The sooner the Board act, the better it is.

And what about the J. C. Mukherjee Trophy. Could I ask the Board, who was the cricketer who won it the last? I'm sure none of the member of the Board will be able to answer it.

India and the Board dream of winning the World Cup, and the roots here are decayed and decantated.

Well, here is my signal to the Board. The 1983 Indian cricket team which had won the World Cup, had as many as six cricketers who were the "recipients" of J. C. Mukherjee Trophy. And this trophy is awarded to the best school cricketers of India. This trophy is now-a-days not awarded to any school cricketer, thanks to the Board for the same.

As for as my knowledge is concerned, this trophy has not been awarded to any cricketer since the last 20 years. If I'm right, then let the Board wake up, and wake up to realities.

The Board has plainly to concentrate on two aspects about the game which is now played in this country. The first is the "fair" conduct of the game. The second is to provide the best of the infrastructure and facilities.

Here the Board has to provide the best of the playing conditions, the best of the surface on which the game will be played and a proper medical and accidental insurance cover to the players, to everybody, who is associated with the game.

The mindset of producing and providing a very dead and a docile pitch for the domestic tourney has to be warded off. To be very frank, we have never won a series, successively and rapidly, abroad and outside the Asian subcontinent after 1986 and this is because of the fact that we have never encouraged fast bowling in India. It does not augur well for anybody to see that India wins a series at West Indies after 26 years, or against England after 21 years. I do not consider the test series win at the Caribbeans under Rahul Dravid in 2006 a big achievement. It is because the West Indies players now are at times even worst than the Zimbabweans and the Bangladeshis. Similarly I do not consider the Indians winning the series against Pakistan at Pakistan in 2004, under Ganguly's captaincy as something very astounding, and outstanding. It is because Pakistan then had fielded their worst ever and the weakest ever team against India.

The talent of Pakistan, both in hockey and cricket, has dried up like the crops of the farmers of Vidharbha. That's a fact. Fools are those who enjoy the victory when a wrestler pins down a baby. Fight between two equals and there lies the enjoyment of victory. The West Indies side after the 1996 World Cup has been a team, like say a lion without its claw and the Pakistani side, now-a-days is like the snake without the fangs. The talent has completely dried in both the countries. The pacers here at India need the green top, the faster and the bouncier wickets. It is only playing on these kind of turfs that they will improve. Mind you, the Board authorities, India will never get a slow turners at Australia, South Africa and West Indies. If only the Board realizes these facts and wakes up from its sleep!

The domestic cricket matches are held on the venues and the pitches, where the ball hardly bounces and rises up. This is detrimental to the aspiration of the pacers. Why the pacers, even the spinners would not be very happy to bowl in these kind of surfaces as they would find it very hard to pick up the wickets. A radical change is the need of the hour.

Secondly, it is high time that the Board involves the coaches of those buddies, who have thrown the talent through the coaching to the national team. For example, after Ishant Sharma's exploit at Australia, a lot of foreign coaches have come up with their theory of asking him to add some flesh to his arms and the body. Jeff Thomson has rubbished all these theories and has asked Ishant to follow his coach who has nurtured him from the root level.

We have seen how Greg Chappel changed the action of Irfan Pathan and Munaf Patel, and at last what had happened to them. Similarly I fail to understand when a Gem like a Dashrath Tandon was available for imparting his knowledge on the physical fitness to the cricketers, why did the Board overlook him, and gave the charge to the likes of Gloster and Le Roux. These so-called fitness gurus have changed the fitness of our players like the likes of Jahan Aras and the Rehana Sultans. Even a Tuntun appears very fit, and shaped, when one saw her in the movies as compared to our national cricketers, after they come out of the regimes and the classes conducted for the fitness by these imported gurus. Oh Dashrath Tandon, Oh that series of Australia in 1977, or Oh that Merdeka Football tourney in 1986 when India reached the semi-finals. Go ask Mr Sunil Gavaskar, or Mr P. K. Banerjee, the coach of the Indian football team in 1986, and you will get to know the class of Dashrath Tandon, and his way to tune the players physically.

The problem is, these so-called modern cricketers do not like to work the way that it should be worked on with our Indian stalwarts. That is why, we are after the imported trainers. We can see the standard of the fitness and the standard of the fielding under the present fitness trainers, and the fielding coach. Does it not make us to realize that the money is going to the drains, with these kinds of imported trainers. Better the Board change their line of thinking and give the chance to the Desis rather to the Gora Babus.

The Board may come up with certain idea of "pension", and plans, but that will not help. What is Rs. 5,000 per month as a pension, going to do to a player, when according to the present inflationary rate, and price index a minimum of Rs. 25,000 per month is also not enough to maintain "one's" family.

While paying, let it make very clear to itself to pay for the "one's" and not for the "two's". For example, Salim Durrani has played 29 tests and more than 150 Ranji matches. He should be paid only for his contribution to India in the test matches, and not for the Ranji Trophy games. While some cricketers have made cricket what it appears to be, our scribes have made the game to become a "national" identity, by their way of describing and writing about the game. Will we have another Raju Bharatan, another K. N. Prabhu, somebody like Rajan Bala, or K. N. Mohalajee, or another like Shyam Sunder Ghosh. Will we have them anymore? No! never.

As we will never have another Merchant, or another Vijay Hazare, we will never have another Vinoo Mankad, or E. A. S. Prasanna, we will never have, never the likes of Raju Bharatan, or K. N. Prabhu or even Rajan Bala. Why can't the Board come forward to award these brilliant cricket writers and journalists to make them rich by Rs. 3,00,000 each.

Heartily, in the name of the "Holy father, the son, and the holy spirit," Oh! The Lords, controlling the Indian Board, save the cricketers, and save cricket in India!

Also my advice to the Board is, "immediately award Salim Durrani conferring him the C. K. Nayudu award and inducting him in the panel of Central Zone selection committee, besides recommending his name for Padma Shri Award, without loosing a single minute. The first step would be "PAY THE CRICKETERS". The second would be to nominate the names of Salim Durrani, Dilip Sardesai, Syed Abid Ali, Roger Binny, Karsan Ghavri in that order for the C. K. Nayudu Award, as well as the Padma Shri for Salim Durrani, Dilip Sardesai, and Eknath Solkar in that order. Let it start first for every thing with Salim Durrani, and move down to others.

The quicker the Board does it, the better it would be for cricket.

From my own point of view, cricketers in India, and then the game of cricket both are dying, the Board can MAKE THEM TO LIVE!

My writing over here will not make any difference unless and until the Board wakes up to the realities. Manning an organisation and running it in a manner which we call it as a professionalism are two different cups of tea. The Board has to restructure the system and has to create a hierarchical layers at every level. There has to be an accountability and there has to be a responsibility. Merely running an organisation as an ANAND BHANDAR or as a GUJRATI FARSAN KA DUKAN will not yield anything.

We have to accept that we have to start afresh and from the start. A start has to be made. We have to look up rather then looking sideways and looking parallel, only to find that the others are as good or as bad than us. We laugh at the others, but that is not the solution.

Why have we to look at our neighbours or at somebody to feel and say that even they are like us. If the others have chosen a path to remain like that, it is their headache. They might be forced to remain like that, because of their hindrances. When we have the resources, why can't we lay an example for the others to follow.

It is a common principle for human being to look up always. One cannot improve if he has to look down or look at the sideways. Even a donkey while grazing in the field, looks up once upward. Why the donkey does it so is something I won't be able to understand because I do not understand the language of the four legged herbivorous creature. Gosh God has not given me the sixth sense for that.

However, I can understand if a two legged social animal does the same, or in the worst case if he does not act in the same manner. We as a human beings have forgotten to look up now-a-days. We only look up when we are in dire strait. That's why from the "ups" nobody looks at us when we need somebody to look at us at a time when we need the help very badly.

The same has been the case with the B.C.C.I. and over the past 75 years it has been the same. That's the reason our cricket except for a brief period between 1971 and 1973 and then in-between 1983 and 1985 when it went up in the ladder, else it has been strucked at the same position, where it was some 75 years ago. As our cricket administrators did not look up, the Indian cricket also has not moved up. The period when our cricket was at its zenith was not because of the BCCI, but because of the individual effort of the players. THE BCCI HAS NO RIGHT TO TAKE THE CREDIT FOR IT.

Merely having the sponsors at the mercy and proclaiming that we are the richest sports body does not reflect anything great. What matters is the position in the international ladder, and there the cricket team India is a big ZERO. Contrary is the case of the Confederation of the Brazil Football. Having no money in its coffer, it has always maintained the NUMERO UNO position. The BCCI can take a leaf out of the same. It is an object lesson for the BCCI to learn and act fast, in fact very fast.

When I was at the school, I was taught a grand lesson by Mr Satsanghi who was my Lecturer for Physics. He had told me very forthrightly that never look at the dish of the other and find out or figure out what is laid for him. It will never give you a mental satisfaction ever.

On the contrary enjoy what your family members, your mother or your wife has served you. They lay HAPPINESS for you always, and if you relish it and eat it happily, their's state of happiness multiplies and there would lie the happiness, there lies the greatness. The Confederation of Brazil Football has learnt this lesson, that's why they are on top of the world, the BCCI is not and that is the reason it continues to languish. Hope, it learn and act fast. Now comes my last suggestion.

Over the years and after the World Cup 2007, the Indian Board has been going hell after hell to choose a coach. One comes, gives his presentations, goes back and then comes another, and the exercise goes on and on. I would like to ask all and sundry; What is a coach and what is coaching?

A coaching is the process to impart the basics and the fundamentals of the games to an infant at the early stages. The nuiances/nuances of the games are taken into account and then according to it the basics are imparted to the trainees. The rectification, addition of the acts of the games and the deletions are done at this time of learning the games. The stress is on making the trainees to learn the basics and the fundas.

This process goes on and on and that is why we have the under-13, under-15 and the under-19 camps. Uptil this stage the process of coaching goes on, and by this time the player who undergoes the coaching moulds himself into one particular style of the game. This is the process of coaching.

Now comes the coach. His job is to watch the actions and the kind of the game that an individual plays at the higher level, and in case there is any error creeping in his system, to weed that error out of his game during the play. How to do the correct things at the appropriate time, how to strategise correctly at the critical hour, how to take the player out of the woods, is the job of a good coach. The coach has to impart the necessary input at the right time to get the qualitative output in terms of finesse, and accurate result. The deliverance in terms of output, depends upon the inputs and its precision given to the ward by the coach. To give the correct inputs at the appropriate time so as to get the best output is coaching.

A coach is not expected to teach somebody who has scored over 3000 runs in test cricket about how to execute a cover drive. On the contrary, the coach is expected to see that how the team jells, and how to bind the team into one single unit. In other words the coach is supposed to engine the team in terms of providing the right kind of fuel, rather than to maintain it. Maintenance is not the job of a coach but preserving something and helping something to add to it in terms of repertoire is the job of a coach.

The coach before expediting the job has to first see how the player has been moulded and in what way is he moulded, and then he has to coach him. The coach cannot expect and should not expect somebody who has not learned to swing the ball till the age of 22 to all of a sudden start swinging it in the very highest level while playing the test matches.

The coach has to work mostly on the strong point of the player to exploit his best from it, beside trying to see if the player can come out with something new. The coach has to improve the weak by making him practising hard to overcome his weakness and work in a manner so that his strong points are maintained and does not go into waste.

Over the period of time, most of the coaches that have come into the country have not fulfilled and have not lived upto the expectation. They come here with a plan, and find our chums a different entities altogether because they are groomed in a different way. When they try to impose their techniques, these players find it hard to digest, and then somewhere down the line some kind of a harakiri takes place, the show somehow goes on and on till the coach somehow pocket his booty, before leaving us, and they leave us high and dry. Then we find them writing their autobiographies, and in that they pierce and dig the former Indian great cricketer, and the way the Board works. Strange. What a GREAT Jaichand that they are.

The coach should be a master of his trade and nothing like being a jack of all trade. He should have an answer for all the problems to sort out which is associated with the game. In cricket, say a cricket coach should be the one who can talk and demonstare effectively everything on every aspect of the game like the spin bowling, the pace, the orthodox and the unorthodox style of bowling and batting, the fielding, deep fielding, the fielding at the short, so hence and so forth.

We have a few of them here in India at present with these qualities. Karsan Ghavri, Balwinder Singh Sandhu, who have played the tests for India, could be fantastic coaches and the likes of Mohinder Amarnath, Haider Ali, R. K. Ohri, Hari Gidwani who have not played this game for India can be good associate coach. The Board should think on these lines before hiring a foreign coach. Similarly guys like Dashrath Tandon and Ganguly Prasad can be fantastic trainers rather than the foreign trainers that we bring them or hire them here in India.

Personally, I'm not for the foreign coach or for any foreign system to guide or mould us as far as the Indian system of sports or for anything that is associated with the Indian sports. All that we have is more than enough to serve our sports. What we lack are the technicalities and for that we need to upgrade our system.

Say for example Boxing. We need to learn about training the boxers to open out against the opponents, foxing them to open their gate, and no sooner that our boxers find the opponents opening them, then execute those flurries of punches at the right place and at the appropriate time to garner those quick points. This is how the Cuban boxers garner the points and go on and on to win the Olympic Gold and this is the place where our boxers fail to collect those points that they loose in the international events. For this, the best solution is to put the Indian coaches under the Cuban legends and the scenario will change. These are the arenas where our system needs change rather than calling in for the Russians, the Kazakhstanis or the Hungarians to teach us to box. The boxing world in the Olympics is dominated by the Cubans, and on the professional front it is ruled by Americans and it would be better we take the aids of the Cubans and the Americans to improve us, rather than the Russians or the Kazakhstanis, who have no say in these kinds of sports in the world. Here again the choice for getting the right thing, is wrong.

Our system needs to think where is the area on which the sweeping changes are required to be effected and by which way it has to be implemented. Who can be the best and the guiding force for the same, and believe me if we approach the correct person, rather than the right person, our entire scenario would change. The funny and the saddest problem is WE DO NOT HAVE A SINGLE PERSON IN THE COUNTRY WHO IS THOROUH ABOUT WHERE ARE THOSE "WHOMS" WHO CAN EFFECT A SWEEPING CHANGE IN OUR SYSTEM OF SPORTS. THERE ARE SOME WHO ARE LANGUISHING. NOBODY IS THERE TO LISTEN TO THEM.

Learning from all these incidents, my advice is, get the correct people to coach the Indian cricket team, and let us not fall on the foreign imports. Things would change, maybe it will take time.

Guys like Sandhu, Binny, Mohinder and Madanlal had won the World Cup for themselves, and Wright, Whatmore, Emburey and Fords have never won it for themselves. Well there lies the mirror for everybody to see their faces. Chums like Ghavri, Vishvanath, Amarnath, Binny and Sandhu have changed the face of Indian cricket, and had taken it to a very, in fact the highest level, not the Wrights, Chappels, Embureys or the Fords. Hope the cricket administrators ruling the Indian cricket realise the same.

Could I add some more as a parting gift to the Board in this chapter. Just do not brag about yourself saying that India is not Pakistan when it comes to security to the players while a sporting event is held. The BCCI specially beats the drum on these lines.

If the Sri Lankans can be gunned, so could be anybody in India. The repeated bomb blast held at various cities justifies the same.

Hello, the BCCI, start forming your commandoes to guard the people, the stadium or the players during the match. What happened to the Lankans can happen to the Indians.

All your beating the drums will go into doldrums.

Play, B.C.C.I, Play—Play it Technically Correct!

15

ONE-DAY CRICKET: RAP(E) OF CONTEMPORARY CRICKET

WELL, it is not known actually when did the one-day cricket begin. However, in its modest form, it began at England in 1963 with the introduction of the Gillette Cup. It was played on knockout basis and the tournament was sponsored by the Gillette Safety Razor Company.

This tournament attracted huge crowds ever since it began and in addition to the sponsored money, it had brought in a great deal of extra money, especially the upcountry members had to pay the admission fees at the Gillette Cup matches. This tournament, the final of which was played at Lords, is to cricket, what football is to Wembley.

The induction of this one-day cricket did not only attract heavy spectators, but on the whole it had a good influence on the players. Fielding and throwing in first class cricket now has reached their highest peak and this is largely due to the extra speed and fitness as demanded by the fielders in "instant" cricket.

Many batsmen, too, have been benefited, discovering certain strokes, that they never knew they had to play for, though the purist of the game will say, and rightly, that too many of these strokes are of the cross bat variety and are dangerous to the game of cricket.

Thereafter came the Benson and Hedges Cup, which again was sponsored by the Benson and Hedges. This again was 55 overs match as compared to the 60 overs of the Gillette Cup.

The success of one-day cricket at England prompted the ICC to arrange a one-dayer between England and Australia in 1971. Australia were beaten 0-2 by England in the Ashes. Hence Australia needed something to prove in the one-dayers.

The first one-day International was played in 1971 between Australia and England. The English players knew how to play this game, and they took the victory for granted. Batting first, the Aussies were bowled out for 161, and England had, it seemed, taken the victory for granted.

However, here they went wrong. A strong broad shouldered quickie, by the name of Dennis Lillee was what England did not expect. In a marauding spell of 8 overs, he completely bulldozed the English batsmen and "that was that". With this spell of Lille, the Australian selectors were convinced that Graham Meckenzie's "days of being jackal" were over to all. Australia won the match by 45 runs.

In the inaugural test match, the first in the history in 1877, Australia had beaten England by 45 runs. In the inaugural one-day match, the first in the history, again the 45 runs came in to the difference between victory and defeat and in 1977, in the Centenary Test match again, which Australia had won, 45 runs stood between both the teams.

Spurred by the success of the first of such one-day international, between 1971 and 1974, one-day matches on an experimental basis were introduced in many countries, and though the game was very new to the players, yet it attracted crowd. It brought in a huge gate collection, besides the results, which the spectators enjoyed.

The first one-day international in India was played immediately after the India-West Indies series in 1975 at the Wankhede Stadium, in Bombay. The "Bush" company were the sponsor and both the matches were billed as "Ajit Wadekar Benefit Match". India won both the matches beating West Indies, and to a large extent, it was possible because of Salim Durrani, who claimed six wickets in both the matches, besides scoring 75 runs in both the games. Gundappa Vishvanath and Ajit Wadekar too had scored 59 and 80 in the first match. Vishvanath had an unbeaten 23 in the second also.

The success of these matches prompted the ICC to stage the "World Cup" in 1975 and the "Prudential" Insurance Company were the sponsors. Eight teams, West Indies, Australia, England, New Zealand, Pakistan, Sri Lanka, India and South Africa were the competitors then, and in an absorbing finals then, West Indies defeated Australia by 17 runs to win the inaugural World Cup, with Clive Hubert Lloyd being the skipper of the West Indies.

The competition was played on 60 overs basis and every bowler was allowed to bowl 12 overs at the maximum. The phenomenal success of this tourney prompted ICC to make this event a regular feature of competitive cricket and it was decided to hold this tournament once in four years.

The first three editions of this tourney were held at England with "PRUDENTIAL" being the sponsor, but it was in 1987 that the tourney was held out of England. In 1987, India and Pakistan jointly held this tournament with RELIANCE INDIA LIMITED being the sponsors.

The first match in the Asian sub-continent of the world cup, was held at Gujranwala in Pakistan, in 1987, in which Pakistan had beaten Sri Lanka by 6 runs.

Thereafter this tournament, the one-dayers began being staged jointly and now we see two or three countries of a continent, holding it jointly, to make it a great affair.

In 1996 the Board of Control for Cricket in Pakistan, India and Sri Lanka held it jointly, then to set an example of a tourney, which can be a great success if held jointly.

The game saw great change of fortune and cricket was "swept" away, very much, in the style of Hanumant "Chottu" Singh, when Mr. Kerry Packer, a business tycoon, clutched as many as 55 cricketers from Australia, West Indies, Pakistan, England and South Africa to start a "World Series".

It was here that the coloured clothing, the "two piece bikini cladded beauties" and above all, the "Night Cricket" came into the play. Melbourne, 1977 would go into the history of the cricket books when for the first time, a Night Cricket match was played between Australia and West Indies which was telecast all over the world by Channel 9. The coloured clothings used in the match had come to stay.

Besides the revolution, money had come into the game. The players became professionals and to many, they had become the "mercenaries", however cricket remained the way it had been.

It is here at this point that the Indian cricketers too had raised their points to the then President of the Indian Cricket Board, Mr. M. M. Chinnaswamy. A group of cricketers led by Sunil Gavaskar made it very clear to the President of the Cricket Board then - Pay us as we fill in the Board pocket by our game.

Since then, the payment system came into the foreplay. To start with, the Indian test playing cricketers, were paid Rs. 5,000 per test. It rose up to Rs. 10,500 per test after the English sojourn in 1979. Then it became Rs. 15,000 per test from 1985, and now a cricketer is paid Rs. two lakhs per test by the sponsor, beside Rs. 1,50,000 per one-day match.

To make this version of the game more popular, the BCCI first had introduced the Deodhar Trophy in 1975, the Wills Trophy took its shape in 1981 and now we have the Ranji one-dayers etc.

> *However, India's tryst with destiny, in this kind of the game took place on 26.6.1983 when it had won the World Cup under the leadership of Kapil Dev beating the World Champs, West Indies at Lords.*

The one-day "affair" had it ups and it benefited the respective Boards. It brought about a huge attendance, a big purse from the gate, and too many sponsors, who "spinned" their money, beside skimming it and then the telecasting rights.

The game had tightened the fielding and had brought so many improvised strokes which just are out of the word, even to think.

Who will easily forget the aerial shots innovated by Jaisuriya, the half-cut-half-drive strokes, so often used by Romesh Kaluwitharana, and the "of the back foot, a half square drive - a half back cut" stroke invented by Aravinda De Silva, or "a half run half walk" kind of a run invented by Arjuna Ranatunga to keep himself always fresh in the game. These were so thrilling, so unique, so refreshing to watch.

However, it brought about so many changes in the game that the natural flair of cricket just died. For example, the introduction of the fielders within the 30 yards circle, has reduced any chances of the bowler to bring about any improvisation in bowling. Secondly, the limitation of one bouncer per over has reduced the size of the bowler to pulp.

If these are not enough, the introduction of 30 yards, has curtailed and curtained the size of the bowler, specially those bowlers who use the 45 paces to bowl their deliveries to attain maximum speed. Now this is a negation to the rule. Whereas, in a way, the organizers want the game to be fast and exciting, they on the other hand are suppressing the "fast" to become slow.

Also because of the limitation of the fielder within the 30 yards the spinners finds it very difficult to "float" the balls. This has "murdered" the existence of spin. Never can a spinner think of flighting the ball, he cannot even think of changing the "loops", or even varying the "trajectories". How can one think of the spinners to survive in this kind of game.

Over it are the penalties imposed. If a team fails to bowl 16.3 overs in an hour that is 99 balls, the team and the captains are severely punished well, but what about a batsman.

If a batsman plays all the 60 overs and scores 36 runs, he is allowed to go ...free. But if a bowler bowls an over or two, consuming a little more time than the normal time allowed, his head is "chopped" off, imposing the penalties. Why?

On the contrary, a batsman can play for all the 50 or 60 overs but a bowler cannot bowl more than 10 or 12 overs. What kind of a " democracy" is this. It is ridiculous to say the least.

Now you have a funny equation. If a bowler, in a one-day match, bowls too far outside the stumps, he is negated for a delivery, with a wide run conceded to his opponent team and he is not allowed to bowl a no-ball for that is the "runs" conceded, with an extra delivery to bowl, in both the cases mentioned above. But are there any punishment for the batsman.

A batsman can effectively use the "reverse sweeps, " as the way he likes, but a bowler cannot change his arm for bowling. Well, what would have Sir John Isaac Newton, or Albert Einstein had to say if they had seen this "scientific" method of "Science of cricket".

There is nothing, which I have seen it as "negative batting", but if a bowler pegs the batsman on the leg stump, or even outside it, the bowling becomes negative, can anybody explain the logic?

Sometimes you have the "Duckworth-Lewis" system erupting into the game. What is the logic and the formulae involved. It is very hard to explain the "relativity" that goes with it. For if you have the rain interrupting, continue the game on the next day. That would be a better idea, rather than coming out with certain formulae, which are "converse-and-hypothetical" by all means and standards.

How funny it is. Say a team has scored 350 runs in full 50 overs to notch upon an average of 7 runs per over, losing to a team, which had scored at the rate of 8 per over till the 25th over, and all of a sudden facing defeat, for granted, wins the game, at least even after aggregating 5 runs per over, lest, the D-L formulae is applied. It is mathematics or puzzle, well I do not understand. In any case the bowler again is to suffer.

The batsmen too have become stereo typed in this style of game. One set of principles of strokes are applied by the batsman, and if he succeeds it is good, or else the hell lets loose on him. This is the reason we see too many shuffling of the batsmen in the batting order. For example Sourav-Sachin combination had become Sourav-Sehwag, then Sachin-Sehwag, then Sehwag-Bangad, then Bangad – Sachin, similar is the case with Kaluvitharana-Jaisuriya, then Jaisuriya-Attapattu, then Attapattu-Sangakara, then Jaisuriya-Sangakara, then again Jaisuriya-Attapattu. Where is the consistency? The rotation of these sorts of batting combination is even faster than the rotation of the propellers that are used for the aircrafts for taking off, landing and for flying. Hell let loose on earth on the batsman if he fails to adopt to these rotations.

How do you aspire to have a permanent pair of openers if that is what the game has to offer. The game neither gives any chance to the bowlers to "flex" their dimensions, it hardly allows a pair to stick to a position for "too-long". This is not only the case of India or Sri Lanka, perhaps it is with all the countries involved playing this game. Where is the "similarity", where is the "equality". The forward reaction is not equal to the backward reaction in these types of a situation, but the equilibrium of the game has to be maintained. How can it be possible?

Also, the game being a limited over, it has acted upon the rock solid techniques of the contemporary test playing batsman. A batsman chase a ball pitched "two wickets" outside the off stump to connect it for a four. Now in the "test" matches too, where the innings has to be grafted, the batsmen are "falling" prey to this bad habit of executing the one-day strokes. The result is, we do not get to see the techniques at all and there is no stability in the performance of the batsman.

In this way, and if this is the way, how can we ever get to see a Vijay Manjrekar, a Dilip Sardesai, a Salim Durrani, or even a Gundappa Vishvanath, leave apart the great Sunil Gavaskar, we will never even get to see a Chetan Chauhan again. Players of cricket are not born out of the one-day variety just like a baby is not born in a month.

In the one-dayers, as the ball has to be pitched within the "Visionary" of the stumps, it becomes easy to play the shot, as often one does not have to use his feet, but this has "casted" a repercussion on the five dayers. Standing from the crease, a lot of modern batsmen take a "gloat" over the deliveries pitched two miles outside the off stick. The result is a disaster. The feet movement has gone out of the game, and with it has gone the beauty of the batsman, the craft of batsmanship. Now-a-days, we hardly see the "Bharatiyanatyam" or the "Kathakali" being danced on the pitch by a batsman, whether against the spin or the fast stuff. This has killed the enjoyment and the "sensous" of the game.

Because of this, certain strokes like the glance, the late cut, the hook shot, to name a few shots have totally gone out of the game. This really has spoiled the game in terms of delightful batting.

To me frankly, watching a cricket game is no more an obsession or a "passion". It is as good as an "anarchy", or a "monarchy" in the form of democracy, that is being displayed at cricket now. And to top it all we have the "autocrat" the I.C.C. which is to me an Idiot Committee of Cricket running the games world over.

To be very frank, is it worth watching "Gina Lollobrigida" in a movie, without her breast being exposed, or is it worth glancing at a blow-up, without Katy Mirza "exhibiting" her "boobs", or for that matter, is it possible to think of a "cabaret" number in a Hindi movie without "Helen" oozing and doing the shakes. No way! Not anyway, as it is not the way. The funs would never be there if they do so. The originals performed by the originals give the happiness, in original. These transformed items, the pyjamas and the one piece bikinis do not fulfil the need of the full length suit, the sooner one understands them, the better for the game.

One-day cricket has given too many liberties to the batsmen and too many excitements to the viewers. But it has curbed the bowlers who are the spinal chord of the game. It has restricted the "pace" and has in a way, sentenced the spinners to "death". It has made the game batsmen friendly, though it has curbed many good batsmen to exhibit the "craft" of the game.

Abraham Lincoln has described democracy as "FOR, OF AND BY" the people. One-day cricket has made the game, for, by and of the batsman.

A few years ago, the "DISCO" craze, and later the "RAP" songs had hit the Indian film industry. Anoop Jalota had given the name "KHISKO" to disco....... . Singer Abhijeet Bhattacharjee had given the name "RAPE" to the "RAP" song in a TV interview. RAP(E) is the name of the game if I would have to give it to the shorter version of the game of cricker. I am sure, the "KHISKO" would be given by somebody, who are responsible for running the game if at all they have a brain and a sense into it. Brainless, to the donkeys as we call it...the donkey too has a brain, for once in a while the donkey too looks upto the sky while grazing in the field, or chewing the grass. We, the mankind do not do it. And that makes us even brainless as compared to the donkeys.

Pooling in a few dollars, and raking the big moolahs just by allowing the nonsensical shorter version of the game to become the King of the game, is as good as sowing the seed or planting the sapling of the apple in the Thar desert, hoping that the apples that would be grown in the future will be too tasty, and the bites of it would be as sweet as the sugar. I do not have to say what these kind of seeds or the saplings would bear if it was to be planted, or sown at the Thar desert. This is what is going to happen to the test cricket, the original version of the game, if the situation is not handled delicately, and delightfully, immediately.

For me, one-day cricket is a "pyjama" cricket, nothing less, nothing more. The twenty–twenty, and the value additions of the likes of Chuk De, the Lakshya to name a few, added to it might even lead to the path of Qayamat Se Qayamat Tak, especially for a person like me, to think about it. It is going to be money, honey and the bunny in the IPL, and the entertainment that is going to be provided by the Daisys, and the Hazels is going to be even worst. The classic example has been the case of Celina Jaitley in the I. C. L. match where she was abused by the Pakistani cricketers for displaying all her razzmatazz, and the glitter during the entertainment session amidst the game. It is not going to help the game at all.

There is a blind support and a closed mind craze for cricket in this country. There are some people who have got into the act of converting that craze into cream, that is money. This could have a catastrophic effect like the Czars of Russia. The Czars were the powerful rulers of Russia, and after ruling the country for almost one thousand years, they went on to play with the sentiments of the people who were too crazy for them during that period, to extend their rule. The result, NOBODY NOW EVEN KNOWS THEIR NAME AND THEIR HISTORY OF EXISTENCE.

For me these twenty–twenty, and probably the ten-ten to come, it is the one piece bikini. Either the top is covered, or the bottom. Never the both. If the top is covered, the bottom looks like curdly couch, and if the bottom is covered, the top looks like butterly vouch, the problems lies at both ends, the middle portion of the body is the one which ought to take the bearing always and thereafter, whether good or bad. For the society and from the societal view point, it could be an attractive scene for the page three readers, neither for the connoisseur of the game, nor for the game.

I was totally dejected, and absolutely disappointed recently when I found that Sehwag, who came very near to breaking the record of Brian Lara, could not even break the record of Inzamam-ul-Haq, in the recently concluded series against South Africa.

To be frank, players like Sehwag, Uthappa, Gambhir and Yuvraj Singh have always disappointed me, and one of the reason is that even after playing international cricket for so many years, they have still failed, in the first place to permanently cement their place in the Indian team, and then to learn the art of planning, and extending the innings. Over it their technique specially against the moving deliveries, and to some extent against the genuine and the versatile spinners, has always been found wanting.

People in India were expecting Sehwag to overhaul Brian Lara's record, in the test, but to be frank I knew that he would come very close to it and would fail. There are many reasons for it, and one of the reason is the over indulgence of the mindset of these players for the one-dayers.

Players like Bill Ponsford, Donald Bradman, Haneef Mohammed and Brian Lara are the players, who were made of different materials altogether. It is not for nothing that they have the 501 runs and the 499 runs in an innings to show. They knew how to plan the innings, at the appropriate and the correct time, rather than the right time, and then indulgence in the deliverance, as well the execution, precisely and qualitatively to cross the barriers and reach the milestone.

That's why they were the TWINKLE TWINKLE LITTLE STARS, UP ABOVE THE SKY SO HIGH, LIKE A DIAMOND........ Sehwag is just a good one-dayer specialist, nothing more, nothing less. Even after scoring two separate triple hundred, in test match, no one will even consider him a better TEST bat than Chetan Chauhan, leave apart the great Sunil Gavaskar and in the one-dayers, no one will consider himself better than a Javed Miandad, or even an Alvin Kalicharan.

This is because of too much of the mind and its setting to the tune of the one-dayers.

16

THE STORY OF CRICKET

THE story of cricket is not easy to write. There is no definite beginning and so far, thank goodness, no end. Nobody knows when it started and, in spite, of some critics who have forecast its demise of the last seventy years or more, it is still very much alive. One can only imagine that many hundred of years ago some boys started throwing stones at a friend who, to protect himself, picked up a stick and tried to hit them back. The derivation of the word cricket could easily come from the shephered's crook which would have made the best available bat and could account for the curved shape of the early bats. They were not unlike a hockey stick, a shape very suitable for dealing with the bowling of those days which was usually along the ground. Similarly the wicket, which was originally two stumps with one bail, could have started life as the small wicket gate through which sheep entered a field or pen.

As far back as 1272 there is a mention of King Edward First's son, Prince Edward, playing Creag, and this is surely sufficient proof that cricket was already a game by then. But the first definite proof seems to be a manuscript dated January 16th, 1598, which is now in the possession of the Mayor of Guildford. It refers to a Surrey coroner, John Derwick, 'Playing a cricket' when he was 'a scholar of the free school of Guildford'. From then on there are various references in 1626, 1646 and 1654 of people being fined for playing cricket on Sundays. It had even spread overseas as Cromwell's generals are said to have 'prohibited cricket' in Ireland. It seems likely that with Cromwell in power in England, the game caught on with the nobility who, with no court in London, retired to their county estates. They found that cricket was not only a fun to play but that it also provided them with an opportunity to gamble. Whether we like or not much of the cricket played then was the occasion for betting on the results of matches.

All evidences show that the early development of cricket centred on the counties Hampshire, Kent, Surrey, and Sussex, and also on London itself. In fact, the first surviving score sheet is of Kent v. England at the Artillery Grounds in the city of London on June 18th, 1746, Kent winning a four innings match by 1 wicket, and 18 being the highest individual score. There are various accounts of other matches during this period, at Penshurst, Kensington Gardens, Mitcham, Chivedon, and above all at Hambledon, a small village just north of Portsmouth. A short account of this famous club will help more than anything else to show what cricket in the eighteenth century was like and how its laws gradually developed.

The club was formed some time around 1750 and its first Captain and Secretary was Richard Nyren, landlord of the Bat and Ball Inn, which was situated alongside Broad Halfpenny Down, the ground on which they played. This small village attracted players from the surrounding districts and became strong enough to take on and beat the full strength of England. They took part in the first recorded tie, against Kent in 1783. 'Old' John Small, their best batsman and a bit of a dab at the fiddle when the game was over, made the first recorded century, 136 v. Surrey. Richard Nyren's son, John, in his young Cricketer's Tutor has brought to life many of their players, Thomas Brett, who bowled fast and straight lobs (there was no over-arm or round-arm bowling yet), and Tom Sueter who kept wicket to him with no gloves or pads, supported by George Leers as sure as a sandbank at long-stop. Both Sueter and Leer had fine tenor voices and led the singing in the Bat and Ball. Then there was the left-handed gipsy, Noah Mann, a fine all-rounder and horseman who rode twenty miles to play. Their greatest bowler and the most accurate of his time was David Harris, and as Hambledon's fortunes began to decline, 'Silver Billy' Beldham appeared, a prolific run-getter who came from Farnham in Surrey but played for Hambledon.

Towards the end of the century, London became more and more the center of cricket. Betting on the game was increasing and as early as 1774 it became necessary to standardize various weights and measurements, some of which are still the same today (e. g. the weight of the ball between 5½ and 5¾ ozs, and the width of the bat 4¼ inches). There was also the first mention of an LBW law at this time. Thus the game gradually developed and in 1775 Hambledon played Kent in a 5-a-side match at the Artillery ground. When John Small went in to bat, 14 runs were needed. He got the runs all right but in the process several balls from 'Lumpy' Stevens passed between the two stumps. Accordingly a third stump was added, although the size of the wicket remained the same. About ten years later a second bail was also added and the wicket began to look like the one we know today.

At this time the White Conduit was flourishing at Islington but its members wanted to find another ground as new buildings were ruining their privacy. They therefore asked a Yorkshire man living in London called Thomas Lord, to find them a new ground. He agreed and chose a piece of land in Marylebone where Dorset Square now stands. He took it on a twentyone year lease and the first match was played there in 1787, and in that year the members of the White Conduit Club formed the Marylebone Cricket Club, the MCC. A year later MCC revised the laws as they then stood ('hit wicket' became a way of dismissal, and a batsman could only be out lbw if the ball pitched between wicket and wicket). From that day MCC became the unofficial ruler of the game, responsible for its administration and laws.

When Thomas Lord's lease ran out in 1808 he negotiated for a new piece of land at North Bank, Regent's Park. This was only used for three seasons and then buildings and railway development forced Lord to move once again. So still with his original turf from Dorset Square he moved to the present site of Lord's in St. John's Wood, where the first match was played on June 22nd, 1814. Since then, Lord's has been the acknowledged headquarters of cricket. From then on the development of cricket to the game we know now received a new impetus, and it spread rapidly throughout the country. There were a lot of 'firsts' round about this time too. The first Gentlemen v. Players match was played in 1806, the first recorded score above 200 was 278 by William Ward for MCC v. Norfolk at Lord's in 1820, and the first University match took place in 1827. Incidentally, playing for Norfolk in that 1820 match was a seventeen year old batsman, Fuller Pilch, who later played for Kent and was one of the greatest batsmen ever. By 1835 round arm bowling was finally legalized in a thorough revision of the laws by MCC which included standardizing the length of the bat to its present 38 inches and the introduction of the 'follow-on' rule.

At about this time also county cricket began to get on to an organized footing and county clubs were formed, Sussex being the first in 1839.

Famous names appear in the score sheets, John Wisden, who later published the first Wisden Almanac in 1864, and who bowled ten batsmen in one innings for North v. South, and George Parr after whom Parr's tree at Trent Bridge was named. Alfred Mynn the 'Lion of Kent', over 6 feet tall and weighing 20 stone, and Felix, also of Kent, who was as stylish a batsman as he was an artist. With the opening of Trent Bridge by William Clark in 1838 cricket for the first time had become popular in the North, and Clark organized an all-England XI which travelled round the country playing every type of club, large and small.

Then in 1859 came a milestone when a team of English cricketers captained by George Parr set sail for Canada to become the first ever cricket touring team. Nine years later a team of Australian Aborigines visited England. These events provide us with a good opportunity to check on how cricket had spread overseas. The starting dates are all rather vague, but it is clear that in most cases it was the British Army or Navy who introduced cricket to the Colonies. In Australia a British Colony was established at Botany Bay in 1788 and no doubt they played cricket. But it is not until 1830 that we find the first account of a game played in Sydney and the formation of the first club in Hobart, Tasmania, two years later. In 1845 the Melbourne CC was formed and with the same initials as our own MCC similarly became the centre of administration. The game soon spread to all the other states and it took such a hold that the catering firm of Spiers and Pond sponsored the first ever teams from England to visit Australia in 1861 and 1863. Both incidentally made a good profit. In 1876 another team came from England, captained by J. Lillywhite, and in March 1877 they played the first ever test at Melbourne, which Australia won by 45 runs. Finally, the Australian cricket scene was complete when the Earl of Sheffield donated 150 guineas for the promotion of cricket among the states and the Sheffield Shield competition came into being. At first only New South Wales, South Australia, and Victoria competed, but Queensland joined in 1926 and Western Australia in 1947, winning the Shield at their first attempt.

Cricket in South Africa was undoubtedly introduced by the British Army, which occupied the Cape at the end of the eighteenth century and the Cape Colony was the first centre of cricket in South Africa. But, as in Australia, it soon spread, Natal, Orange Free State, and Transvaal all forming clubs in quick succession. The first English team under C. A. Smith toured South Africa in 1888-89, winning both their test matches, and in the same season, Sir Donald Currie presented the Currie Cup for competition between the leading provinces.

Because of the amount of sea travel involved, cricket in the West Indies developed for more slowly. It seems to have started in Trinidad, Barbados, Jamaica, and British Guiana (now Guyana) in the early eighteenth century. However, it was not until 1894 that a team from England visited the islands, and the first official MCC tour did not take place until 1911. Similarly, regular organized competition between the islands was difficult to arrange. It was only during the last fifteen years or so that air travel has made visits in-between the islands practical, resulting in the formation of the Shell Shield Tournament in 1965-66.

Cricket in New Zealand did not really begin until the second half of the nineteenth century, the first inter-provincial match taking place on North Island in March 1860 when Auckland played Wellington. Four years later the first class match was played on South Island, Otago beating Canterbury at Dunedin. A team from England under the captaincy of George Parr also played four matches in that year, while James Lilly White's team visited New Zealand after their Australian tour of 1877. One year later the first Australian team came over on their way to England. New Zealand's inter-provincial competition is the Plunket Shield, presented by Lord Plunket when Governor-General in 1906, the first match being played in 1907.

Although India came late on to the test scene, thanks to the British Army, cricket dates back to well before the start of the nineteenth century, although first class cricket was not played until 1892. The first English team came out under G. F. Vernon in 1889, but the first MCC team to play tests in India was captained by D. R. Jardine in 1933-34. Until the start of the Ranji Trophy Competition in the same year, first class cricket had been rarely played but since then it has flourished.

Pakistan, of course, only became a separate cricketing country after partition in 1947. But in 1952 they were playing their first test against India, and by 1957 had already chalked up victories against both England and Australia.

The countries I have mentioned are the 'senior' members of the International Cricket conference and as such are the only countries along with Sri Lanka, Zimbabwe and Bangladesh to play Test Matches. But cricket has been played wherever British influence has existed and that, at one time or another, has meant virtually the whole world. In Europe, Holland and Denmark were the main contenders and many club tours were arranged between them and England. Portugal, Germany, and Italy have all been cricket strongholds from time to time and, believe it or not, English not French cricket was played in Paris, North, Central and South America, Canada, Fiji, Hong Kong, Egypt, Kenya, Nigeria, Burma, Nepal and Malaysia. The list is never ending, even Turkey and Greece have been known to stage a game. Such was the appeal of cricket, loved by many and yet completely incomprehensible to many others. But whenever, two or three of British stocks were gathered together you can be sure that cricket will be played so long as they can 'bully' enough the 'natives' to join them!

The return from Australia in 1864 of the second English touring team heralded one of the most important years in English cricket. Over arm bowling, was at last legalized. Surrey became the first-ever County Champions and the first issue of Wisden's Cricketers' Almanac was published. Even more important, two days before his sixteenth birthday, W. G. Grace made his first appearance in big cricket, scoring 170 and 56 not out for South Wales Club v. Gentlemen of Sussex. From then on this bearded giant of a man; strode supreme across the English cricket scene; until just after the turn of the century. He actually played his last game of cricket in July 1914, a few days after his sixty-sixth birthday. During that time he was cricket to the whole of England. People travelled miles in their gigs or pony carts to catch a sight of him playing. For over thirty five years he hit the headlines. He was to cricket then, what today Major Dhyan Chand is to hockey, or Pele to soccer. He created many records in first class cricket. He was the first to make 2,000 runs in a season; to do the double of 1,000 runs and 100 wickets; to score 200 and 300 runs in an innings; to reach 100 centuries; to make 1,000 runs in May. It is impossible to compare fairly cricketers of one generation with another. But remembering the bad pitches on which he had to make most of his runs, there has surely never been a greater cricketer, nor a more powerful personality. Cricket built on the foundations of his success, and from the day he appeared on the scene developments came thick and fast.

In 1868 the first touring team to visit England was a team of Aborigines from Australia and in 1876-77 Lillywhite's team toured Australia and played the first-ever Test Match at Melbourne in March 1877. This was quickly followed by the first Australian team to tour England under the captaincy of D. W. Gregory, and they caused a sensation by beating MCC in a single day by 9 wickets. 1880 saw the first Test Match in England when England beat W. L. Murdoch's side by 5 wickets. Two years later Australia had their revenge at the Oval by winning by 7 runs in the famous match, which created the Ashes.

So Test cricket was well and truly launched and MCC ensured the universal development of cricket by a complete revision of the Laws of Cricket in 1884. Except for occasional amendments they were not again fully revised until 1947. South Africa, New Zealand, England, and Australia, in that order, all set up their own Boards of Control and in 1909 the Imperial Cricket Conference was set up, with England, Australia and South Africa the original members.

The County Championship, which had started in 1864, took some time to catch on and by 1890 there were still only eight counties competing Sussex, Nottinghamshire, Surrey, Kent, Yorkshire, Middlessex, Lancashire and Glouestershire. But by 1899 all but two of the present seventeen were included: Northamptonshire joining in 1905 and Glamorgan in 1921. Two years later the Minor County Championship was reorganized on its present basis.

All this time, of course, there were many great cricketers playing first-class cricket and I am conscious of the fact that I have so far only mentioned one, W. G. Grace. But it is difficult to strike the right balance between giving a catalogue of names and the danger of mentioning too few. However, from Australia there were W. L. Murdoch, Australia's first captain over here; C. Bannerman, who scored the first-ever Test hundred (165 n.o.) in his first Test innings; F. R. Spofforth, 'the Demon' who took the first Test 'hat-trick'; G. J. Bonnor, the big hitter; G. Giffen and C. T. B. Turner, two great bowlers and J. M. Blackham, a magnificent wicket-keeper.

For England there were Arthur Shrewsbury, about whom W. G. said, 'give me Arthur,' when asked which batsman he rated the highest; A. E. Stoddart, a 'Rugger' International and fine athlete who captained England to victory in the 1894-5 series; R. Peel, possibly the greatest of all the Yorkshire slow left arm bowlers; A. C. Maclaren, whose 424 is still the highest individual score ever made in first class cricket in England; K. S. Ranjitsinhji-'Ranji'-one of the cricket's greatest stroke players; the Hon. F. S. Jackson-'Jacker', who never toured overseas, but was a super Test batsman, a good bowler, had not only won the toss five times in the 1905 series but also topped the batting and bowling averages and won the rubber; G. A. Lohmann, a match-winning, medium-pace bowler; and T. Richardson and W. H. Lockwood, a great fast bowling partnership.

Just before the end of the century the Board of Control was set up by the counties to run Test Cricket in England

and in 1899, for the first time, there was a Test series of five matches in England. In the same year a record was made which still stands today, the highest individual score in any class of cricket. This was 628 not out by A. E. J. Collins for Clark's v. North Town, a junior house match at Clifton College. Even if he made 0 in all his other innings he must still have had a very good batting average at the end of the season!

For the next fourteen years cricket in England reached perhaps its highest peak. I myself would call it the 'Golden Age', though some writers give this accolade to the last decade of the nineteenth century. But just look at the names of some of those who played in this period, to which should be added most of those already mentioned. For England; C. B. Fry, G. Gunn, P. F. Warner, J. T. Tyldesley, G. H. Hirst, G. L. Jessop, W. Rhodes, J. B. Hobbs, F. E. Woolley, S. F. Barnes, R. E. Foster. For Australia: M. A. Noble, C. Hill, V. T. Trumper, W. W. Armstrong, DONALD BRADMAN, W. Bardsley, J. Darling, S. E. Gregory, C. G. Macartney, for South Africa: G. A. Faulkner, H. W. Taylor, P. W. Sherwell, R. O. Schwarz, A. D. Nourse, senior. These are only a few of the great players of that time during which the first MCC Team went to Australia (1903), South Africa played their first Test in England (1907), the Imperial Cricket Conference was constituted (1909), and the first and only Triangular Tournament was played between England, Australia, and South Africa (1912).

The period between the two wars saw the entry of the West Indies (1928), New Zealand (1930), and India (1932) into Test Cricket. But inevitably the main 'enemy' was Australia, who swamped England for eight years after the war, thanks to some superb fast bowling by J. M. Gregory and E. A. McDonald, backed up by the spin of A. A. Mailey, and great batting strength made up largely from the pre-war batsmen. In reply England had to offer J. B. Hobbs and H. Sutcliffe as the most successful-ever Test opening batting partnership, and M. W. Tate and H. Larwood as top-quality medium and fast bowlers respectively. Larwood was to be at the centre of cricket's greatest storm, the body–line series between England and Australia in 1932-33, a tour which nearly brought cricket relations between the two countries to an end. But looking back over the twenty–year period, we see that three batsmen stand out above everything and everybody else (even that superb spin-bowling partnership of O'Reilly and Grimmett): J. B. Hobbs, the 'Master', the greatest batsman ever on all types of pitches who made more hundred (197) and more runs (61, 237) than any other player to date. D.G. Bradman, the 'Don'-cricket's greatest run-making machine who in far fewer innings than Hobbs (338 compared to 1,315) scored 28,067 runs (an average of 95.14 against 'Hobbs' 50.65), made 117 hundreds and in fifty–two Tests averaged 99.94! And thirdly, not far behind, W. R. Hammond, a more brilliant bat than either and a fine medium-pace bowler.

Before the start of the Second World War, England had regained the Ashes in 1926, lost them in 1930, regained them in 1933, and lost them again in 1934. South Africa had won their first Test in England (1935). The West Indies, New Zealand and India were elected members of the Imperial Cricket Conference (1926) and four–day Test Matches were played for the first time in England in 1930. When first-class cricket restarted after the war in 1946, the same pattern emerged as in 1919. For seven years, Australia was on top and then as before the position was reversed for a time, with England holding the Ashes for six years, Australia for the next twelve years, and England finally retaining them in 1971. All the other countries, have defeated England in their country: the West Indies in 1950, Pakistan on their first tour in 1954, and India in 1971. Cricket lovers had been starved of cricket for five years and the crowds flocked to the grounds to see personalities like Hutton, Bedser, Compton and Evans. 1947 will always be remembered as the 'Golden Year', when both Compton and Edrich made over 3,000 runs, Compton making 3,816 and scoring 18 hundreds, two records which still stand. Hobbs had been the master batsman, Bradman the run machine, and now Compton was the entertainer.

Both Bedser and Evans, too, could claim to have been the best in their own fields: Bedser being the first English bowler to take 200 wickets in Tests, and Evans the first and only wicket-keeper then who had over 200 Test victims. And last but not least, L. Hutton, the first professional ever appointed a captain to England regularly. He captained the team which regained the Ashes in 1953 and his batting for its pure technique on all pitches came nearest to that of Hobbs. Many other fine cricketers have played for all the Test countries since the war and it is impossible in a short history like this to mention any but the most exceptional. G. S. Sobers, for those of us who never saw W. G. Grace the greatest all-rounder the world has ever seen; R. N. Harvey arguably the best of Australia's left-handed batsmen; the three Ws, Worrell, Weekes, and Walcott from the West Indies; R. G. Pollock and B. A. Richards for South Africa; Hanif Mohammad of Pakistan; Subhash Gupte, Vijay Hazare, Polly Umrigar, Vinoo Mankad and Salim Durrani from India; R. R. Lindwall and K. R. Miller of Australia. If I don't stop now I shall go on for ever. But finally two names, or else I shall never dare go back to Bangalore the place where I stay at present, or Nagpur. A certain Mutthaiah Muralitharan took his 700th Test wicket in 2007 and his final tally of over 700 wickets is still a record. And a Yorkshire exile, J. C. Laker in 1956 took 19 for 90 against Australia, the one record which surely must stand for ever.

In the quarter of a century since the end of the Second World War there have probably been more changes in the organization and laws of the game, than at any time in its history. In 1947 there was a major revision of the laws, when the five-day Tests were played in England. In 1963 the amateur was abolished in English First-class Cricket and in 1965 the Imperial Cricket Conference became the International Cricket Conference. But by far the most important change was the introduction of limited over cricket or 'instant' cricket as it has become known. The Gillette Cup was started in 1963 and the Benson and Hedges Cup in 1972, and the John Player League in 1969. All three have been tremendous successes and have brought to the grounds many thousands for whom, in this jet age, three-day and a five day test cricket has become far too slow. Spectators want to see a result all in one day and the popularity of these three competitions has done much to help the financial position of the counties, many of whom have been in dire economic straits.

But this is nothing new. Cricket has always been 'broke'. In the old days it depended on the generosity of rich patrons, now it has to rely on proceeds of football in some countries, pools and of sponsors. There is no doubt that sponsorship will spread even to the County Championship, Test Matches, and the 2011 World Cup. The large sums put up by the sponsors are necessary not only to meet the loss of revenue due to falling gates money but also to match the ever-rising costs of running a county side. Cricket is as popular as it ever was. County membership is higher than ever, more people are playing cricket, reading about it, watching or listening on TV and Radio. For over a hundred years its approaching death has been regularly announced. But now I am happy to announce the following bulletin:

'Cricket is very much alive'.

However, with the advent of the one piece bikini, and the paraphernalias associated with it, I also fear that the OLD is but the GOLD, the "Test" match might wear out. Oh, the Lords ruling cricket, I bow to thee, and pray for the thou's and the thy's, makes everything possible to save the Gangotri, ie the Test match cricket. For that is the **Satyam, Shivam and Sundaram** of cricket.

Thank you all, if you are listening to me and making all efforts to save it.

17

CRICKET AND VIDHARBHA: A STORY UNFOLD

MANY might be taken for a ride, many would call me a mad, many might consider me to be a "fool" even to think of cricket in Vidharbha, but Vidharbha will always have a pride of the place in Indian cricket, and NAGPUR will always remain in the heart of cricket in India.

When I write this, I can assure you all that, I'm writing all this after a thorough research and please do not consider me a fool to write this chapter. It has its own importance in the annals of Indian history that relates itself with cricket.

It was at Nagpur, that Jamshedji Tata had started first cloth mill in India. The "Empress Mill" at Nagpur was the first mill which started functioning as the "first" clothing mill in India, under the British regime. And with the Empress Mill, two teams, the Empress Mill cricket and the Empress Mill football team was formed at Nagpur.

Empress Mills had a sizeable number of Parsis working for them, and one of them was a very close friend of Mr. Jamshedji Tata. He, in association with the Tatas, was responsible for building a cricket stadium at Nagpur, which we now call it as the "VCA", i. e. the VIDHARBHA CRICKET ASSOCIATION STADIUM. This stadium saw its face changed over the years, and after the partition and formation of the state in 1956, Nagpur was annexed to the state of Maharashtra, and it started participating as Vidharbha in the Ranji Trophy. Till 1955, this part of the country, and then the state, was participating in Ranji Trophy, by the name of "CENTRAL PROVINCE AND BERAR"

Came the Ranji season in 1955-56, there were two new teams which were to play in Ranji Trophy. One part of CP and Berar team was to play as Vidharbha, and the other one was to play as Madhya Pradesh.

It was last in 1955-56, that Central Province and Berar had reached the semi-finals of the Ranji Trophy, where they had lost to Bengal led by the late Pankaj Roy.

It was from 1956-57 that the present stadium of VCA started changing and the face received a tremendous uplift when the players pavilion was constructed and was named as LIMJI PHIROZE BILLIMORIA PAVILION. This was the start and since then, Nagpur and cricket at VCA was an established affair.

Nagpur, it was where the great Col C. K. Nayudu began playing cricket. The Mohan Nagar locality of Nagpur, just cannot stop talking about this great cricketer, who learned this game playing at the Kasturchand Park, and breaking so many glass panes hitting those towering sixes. He was a resident of Nagpur when he was selected for the Indian team to tour England in 1932, but by the time he played the first match at England, the family had shifted their base to Indore, Madhya Pradesh. He was absorbed as a Colonel in the Army which was controlled by the Holkars.

Nagpur it was which gave India its first test captain.

Nagpur has a distinction which could make any University cricketer feel proud. After our country had gained Independence on 15.08.1947 the West Indies team under Trevor Goddard had visited India. The Combined University team, which was to play West Indies, was led by Kamraj Kesari, who hailed from Nagpur. It was very good match for Kesari as he scored 48 runs in the match.

Kamraj Kesari was the first cricketer from Nagpur to lead the National University team after Independence against a visiting team from abroad.

Now, a little more about the Combined Universities. After its inaugural match against the West Indies in 1947, the B. C. C. I. thereafter made it a point to field a Combined University team, against the visiting team from abroad. This trend continued till 1977 and from the Combined University team, a lot of cricketers had emerged, who went to play for India.

Who can forget Dilip Sardesai, who hammered a blitzkrieg 87 against Pakistan in 1960-61 when Fazal Mehmood had brought his Pakistan team here. Dilip Sardesai went in to become one of the finest cricketers of India, thereafter. Who can forget Anshuman Gaekwad, captaining the University team against West Indies in 1974. He cracked a beauty of 104, and from then onwards, he went on to play about 40 test matches for India scoring over 2000 runs in test cricket with 201 as his highest against Pakistan in a test match.

Now-a-days, the itinerary is so scheduled that the provisional matches hardly makes any contribution to Indian cricket. No more are the zonal teams given a chance to lock their horns against the visiting team. And the worst to suffer in this regard has been the Combined University team.

It has been observed that the ONE DAYERS has taken the importance and precedence over every kind of game in

India. Since the one-dayers have become a money spinning game, all the other form of contemporary cricket has taken a back seat, and this has curbed the flow of young talents from the Universities to the national team.

As the lads from Universities do not get a chance to rub their shoulders against a visiting team, and since University is an Institution, let from the next season, a Combined University team be formed, and let it be made to play in the Ranji Trophy, from one of the five zones. If the two institutional teams, Railways and the Services, can be allowed to play in the Ranji Trophy, why can't an effort be made to allow the University to play in the Ranji Trophy.

Well, coming back to my subject on Vidharbha's cricket, the first sensation from Vidharbha came to Indian cricket in 1965, when Imran Ali was selected as the vice captain of the Indian National School team, which was to tour "Ceylon" then, under the captaincy of Eknath Solkar. Imran Ali was a tremendous hit on that tour, and on his return back home, he was inducted into the Vidharbha Ranji team in 1965-66. He later led the Vidharbha Ranji Trophy team in 1976–77, and had also represented the Central Zone team for the Duleep Trophy during 1976-77. Imran Ali gave up playing cricket in 1977 after scoring 1611 runs in Ranji Trophy, the same number of runs scored by Nari Contractor in test cricket. He also led Vidharbha in the Ranji Trophy.

Imran Ali's success set the tone. Imran Ali between 1967 and 1974 was a regular member of the Central Zone team. He played against the visiting Australian team in 1969, against the West Indies team at Indore led by Gary Sobers in 1967, and was a member of the team that beat the West Indies team bowling them out for 136 and 104 at Indore in 1966-67. The grand period of Vidharbha's cricket was the tenure between 1970 and 1974. In 1970, Vidharbha's and the cricket at Nagpur hit the headlines in a spectacular manner.

First it was Suhas Phadkar, in 1970-1971 who was nominated as the vice captain of the Indian School team, against the visiting English team. India had won the series 1-0 and Suhas Phadkar had 11 wickets besides 470 runs to show for his effort. Such was Suhas' display during the series those days that Dilip Vengsarkar who was a member of this school team, was asked to warm the benches, for the entire series. Suhas Phadkar gave up playing cricket in 1989 after hammering over 2500 runs for Vidharbha in Ranji Trophy, besides playing a Duleep Trophy tie against South Zone, in which he scored a fluent 58.

The Rohinton Baria Trophy in 1970 saw a huge sensation being created in the annals of Indian cricket. The Nagpur University team, not only finished as the winners in the Zonal Rohinton Baria Trophy, but it went from strength to strength in the knock-out.

It defeated the strong Bombay University in the semi-finals, only to lose to Bangalore University in the finals. Nagpur University players, Rakesh Tandon, Anil Deshpande, Ashok Bhagwat and Shirish Najbile stamped a class of their own and made it to the South Zone University XI for the Vizzy Trophy.

What followed in the Vizzy Trophy was another sensation. The three musketeers of Nagpur University, Anil Deshpande, Rakesh Tandon and Ashok Bhagwat, produced a series of performances which enabled the South Zone University to lift the Vizzy Trophy. That was in 1970-71.

During those days, the All India Radio would broadcast the running commentary of the Vizzy Trophy, and I vividly remember listening to the commentary. Anil Deshpande had scored 66 in the finals, Rakesh Tandon had scored 76 and Ashok Bhagwat 73. Besides Tandon had claimed 7 wickets in the match.

The Vidharbha Ranji team during that season also had qualified for the Ranji Trophy knockout, and it took on Bengal in the quarter finals. A new young bubbling lad, who would put the ROAD ROLLER into a great shame was in the side. He was VIJAY TELANG.

On the eve of the match, when the Vidharbha team was busy in the nets, the late Mr. Satyajit Ray had gone to the club house of the Eden Gardens to visit his friend, and he happened to notice Vijay Telang batting at the net. The kind of the strokes that Telang was executing at the nets, prompted one of the official of CAB, describing his shots as "LIGHTNING THUNDER". It was here that Mr. Satyajit Ray picked the name, for one of his film, which was realeased as "Ashani Sanket", which meant Lightning Thunder. This movie went on to win the GOLDEN PEACOCK AWARD in the Berlin Film festival in 1973. But Vijay Telang was never to win a "test" cap for India.

Vidharbha had lost in the quarter finals then, but it was Murthy Rajan and Anil Deshpande, who had served a notice to the selectors. Murthy Rajan missed scoring fifty in both the innings, but Anil Deshpande had served a notice to the selectors by scoring a strokeful 68 in the match.

Vidharbha was once again to qualify for the Ranji knockout tournament in 1973-74. Here again they had lost to Maharashtra by an innings. It was here in the match that Chetan Chauhan and Madhu Apte had scored 406 runs for the first wicket, which was a record for the first wicket till 1977, when the pair of Roger Binny and Sanjay Desai, added unbeaten 452 runs against Kerala at Chickmagaloor to break the previous record, and become the holder of the highest opening wicket stand in Ranji Trophy.

Well, if it was the stand of Madhu Gupte and Chetan Chauhan, creating a record for Maharashtra, it was Vijay Telang, who created a "unique" record for Vidharbha, for which the entire fraternity of Vidharbha can be proud of.

Facing none other than Pandurang Salgaocar, the fastest bowler in India then and Anwar Sheikh, who was one of the four best pacers in India besides Salgaocar, the other three being Abdul Ismail, Subroto Guha and Abid Ali, Vijay Telang hit as many as twelve boundaries to score

49 in the second innings. In other words 97.92% of his scoring were the boundaries.

NO OTHER RANJI TROPHY PLAYER IN THE ANNALS OF RANJI TROPHY GAME HAS THIS RECORD OF SCORING 97.92% OF RUNS IN AN COMPLETED INNINGS THROUGH BOUNDARIES.

Four cricketers, Arvind Panchasara of Gujarat, Surinder Khanna of Delhi, D. Meher Baba of Andhra and Moses Adams of Tamil Nadu can boast and take the pride of being the first in the annals of Indian cricket for playing the game even before than Jaisuriya, the way he played those first 15 overs. In reality, it was Vijay Telang who started it all in 1970. In his first match of his career in Ranji Trophy he had scored 28, and 24 of them came through the boundary. His first five scoring shots were all boundaries. A lot of research has gone into this before I have penned it. I had a long argument with Surinder Khanna on this. The other players mentioned here played Ranji only after Vijay Telang made his debut. D. Meher Baba made his debut in the year 1972. Surinder Khanna strode into the Ranji Trophy well after the year 1975.

Anil Deshpande had scored a fluent 58 in the second innings and though as said earlier, Vidharbha had lost the match by an innings, Deshpande and Telang had served the notice to the national selectors.

Well, in between, how can one forget the India - New Zealand cricket match, which was played at Nagpur in 1969. India had lost the match by 187 runs. This was the first test match held at Nagpur, and it became the second venue of the Central Zone to hold test match, the first being at the GREEN PARKS of Kanpur.

What was so great about this match. One would just by pass this test without giving it a due importance. But it was a sensational one. The New Zealand opening bowling pair of Dayle Hadlee and Richard Collinge bowled a kind of outswingers, which would deviate in the air, and of the pitch, instead of going out, the ball would swing into the batsmen, catching them on the wrong foot.

Nobody could understand what was it all about, lest in 1983 Imran Khan named this kind of bowling, as the "reverse swing". Imran later described himself as the inventor of this kind of bowling. But he is not and to be frank he is not the first who invented this kind of bowling.

It was Dayle Hadlee, and Richard Collinge, who bowled this kind of deliveries, the "reverse swing" at the Nagpur "test" against India in 1969 and the reverse swing had been invented.

IT IS NAGPUR WHERE THE REVERSE SWING WAS FIRST BOWLED IN THE TEST MATCHES.

It was Richard Hadlee, the younger brother of Dayle Hadlee, who was to become the Sultan of Swing, but it was Dayle who invented and first bowled the reverse swing. The credit should go to him, and not to Imran, who used the "unfair" means and method, sometimes to reverse swing the ball. Imran Khan later in an interview with a mazagine admitted about resorting sometimes to foul means to reverse swing the ball.

Between 1973 and 1974-75, cricket in Vidharbha and the cricketers of Nagpur stole the limelight and had served a tremendous notice to the selectors. The inaugural C. K. Nayudu Trophy was held in 1975-76 and a cricketer from Dhanwate National College, Nagpur, Kadu, representing the Central Zone Under-22 from Nagpur became the first cricketer to notch up a ton against the North Zone team led by Rajinder Amarnath in this tournament. Kadu later joined the I. I. M. at Ahmedabad and gave up playing cricket.

Again, when the M. C. C. toured India during 1972 – 1973 under Tony Lewis, Anil Deshpande playing for Central Zone at Indore had scored 46 runs in the match. However the spot light was bagged by Murthy Rajan in 1974–1975. When the West Indies had toured India under Clive Lloyd, representing the Central Zone, Murthy Rajan scored a century, 104 to be exact, against the fiery of Andy Roberts, Bernard Julien and Vanburn Holder in a match for Central Zone at Nagpur.

Fo a record, this has been the only century by any cricketer from Nagpur, or Vidharbha against a team from abroad. In the series against West Indies in 1974-75, this was the only century notched up by any batsman who had opened the innings. With this century, Murthy had almost made it to the team of India, but at the last minute he was dropped, as Gopal Bose was to make his way to the Indian team in the reserves.

Strange, was it or was it not. A 104 by Murthy Rajan was not considered good enough to place him in the list of probables of Indian team for the test, but a 54 by Gopal Bose of East Zone was enough for him to get the recall. This is how the selectors play when it comes to selecting the team in India.

Anyway, this 100 against West Indies prompted Murthy to shift his base of cricket, and he sought a transfer to CAB at Calcutta. He represented Bengal in Ranji Trophy, but after two seasons with that, he gave up playing cricket.

Compact, a solid left hander with a nimble foot and sharp sight, Murthy had scored 1611 runs with two centuries for Vidharbha, with 161 runs as his highest against Rajasthan, which had a bowling attack with Salim Durrani and Kailash Gattani spear-heading it. Besides he is the one to have scored a century (104) against West Indies, a feat which even Zaheer Abbas, or a Mohd Azharuddin could not achieve while playing against West Indies.

Between 1976 and 1979, cricket saw the two Vidharbaites, Vijay Telang and Anil Deshpande, representing Central Zone against the visiting team and both of them did extremely well.

When Tony Grieg brought his team here in 1976-1977, Anil Deshpande playing against them at Jaipur had top scored in the innings for Central Zone scoring a valiant 66. Anil played against the Kim Hughes Australian team at Nagpur too, where facing Rodney Hoggs, Jeft Dymock, and Jim Higgs, scored a patient 36.

This knock, almost brought Anil to the test squad, but at last he was dropped because Sandip Patil, who had scored 44 against the same team for West Zone was preferred. Anil Deshpande continued representing Central Zone till 1981, and in between, he played against the visiting Pakistan and the M. C. C. and he hanged his boots after the Ranji season 81-82.

In his entire career in Ranji Trophy, Anil Deshpande had scored over 3107 runs, including four centuries for Vidharbha. He has also claimed 88 Ranji wickets and his highest was an unbeaten 164 against the Indian Railways. Anil also had played 6 Zonal matches for Central Zone against the visiting side and he had scored 46, 23, 66, 06, 36 and a run out 20, to show for his effort. Players like Dilip Vengsarkar, who had scored 33 and 39, and Sandip Patil, who had scored 44 were preferred, but not Anil. Anil was also a national selector representing the Central Zone.

In 1981-82, playing in his last Ranji Trophy match against M. P. at Nagpur, he scored 65 and he retired from the game thereafter. That knock of 65 will be well etched in my memory, as that was the last time in my career as a sports scribe that I was covering a Ranji Trophy match. That knock was as delicious as " Badaam kheer" made out of the date-palm jaggery as the Bengalis would prefer to prepare the dish.

If it was Anil, who was a perfectionist, it was Vijay Telang, who was the "discoverer" of the dashing cricket, which we now watch often on T. V. sets and sing about the shots, always praising Adam Gilchrist, Sanath Jaisuriya, Shahid Afridi or even our Virendra Sehwag for it.

It is unfortunate that the world of cricket has remained poor, by not watching Vijay Telang, for his cricketing talent, and the shots he would execute, while playing the game.

Peoples and the purists of the game believe that it was Romesh Kaluvitharana and Sanath Jaisuriya who invented all those kinds of uncharacteristic shots which came into the one-dayers to stay. However, I'm to differ in these views. The Lankan started it, way back in 1994. But it was Vijay Telang who did it between the period 1970 and 1986. And he did it with characteristic perfection and with class, so uncharacteristic of the Lankans and one would have been taken away for a ride if one had watched Telang. He was a Road Roller, to say the least. That was his physique. But when it came to running, he would easily beat the best of the sprinters, available at Nagpur during those days. He also led the Vidharbha Ranji team in 1985 and had scored a hurricane 156 against them which is his highest score in the Ranji match.

Telang played all the shots, which are available in the books of cricket. But his favourites were the hooks, the pulls, the square drives and the punch of the front foots. His shots were as powerful as the "fiery" shots of the cannon. The power, the strength, and the timings by which he played the shots, had even surprised Imran Khan, who had played against Vijay Telang at Jaipur when the Pakistan toured here under the stewardship of Asif Iqbal.

Rodney Hogg and Jeff Dymock were left strained and amazed when Telang had scored 79 for Central Zone against them. Every shot of Telang had an electrifying effect and it used to be a headache for the skipper to set a field for Telang.

People talk about Srikanth, but Srikanth was nowhere, if compared to Vijay Telang playing his shots. We have seen both playing in front of our naked eyes, and we are in a position to make such comments. Neither can Sanath Jaisuriya or even Adam Gilchrist, be compared, for the kind of strokes that Vijay Telang would play. The shots were so awesome, so powerful and so electrifying and so beautiful to behold.

The two incidents which readily comes into my mind are, first, when Imran Khan was carted for 3 huge sixes by Vijay Telang when Pakistan were playing Central Zone at

Jaipur in 1979. Telang had scored 66 and 37 in two innings, and in the first essay, he hit 5 sixes in all, of which Imran conceded 3 and Sikandar Bakht 2.

It was Imran, who went up to him and asked him, "are you playing the test matches too". Telang had no answer. The second was a whirlwind knock of 77 which he played against West Zone, in a Duleep Trophy game, just before the Indian team was to tour Australia in 1977-78.

Karsan Ghavri came upto him, and asked him whether he had any thing in person against him. In a span of three overs in the match, Ghavri was carted for 40 runs by Telang, and the selectors had made up their minds to drop Ghavri from the tour. However, it was Bishen Singh Bedi who persisted with the selectors to choose Ghavri as the bouncy wickets at Australia would have suited Ghavri. Ghavri was a hit, both as a batsman and as a bowler during that tour.

During the Ranji Trophy matches, which were played at Nagpur between 1976 and 1982, I had the pleasure to see so many balls being replaced by the umpires, during the course of the match when Telang would bat. The "out-of-shape" Telang and the out-of- shape balls used to be slogan at Nagpur when he would bat.

Telang nearly made it to the team in 1979 for India, but the selectors did not take the risk to sideline Chetan Chauhan, and Telang after his knock of 155 against the Indian Railways, in a Ranji match in 1985 gave up playing cricket. In toto he played in 50 Ranji Trophy matches scoring 2886 runs with 155 as his highest.

In his entire career against the visiting teams, he scored 21 (highest) against the Alvin Kalicharan led West Indies team in 1978 at Indore, 79 in an innings against the Kim Hughjes Aussies side at Nagpur, 66 (highest) and 37 in both the innings against the Asif Iqbal led Pakistan team in 1978-79 at Jaipur.

It is so unfortunate that he did not play for India, especially in the one-dayers. He would have earned in millions, if he had been to the World Cup sojourn in 1983. I personally believe, it would have been better if the selectors had chosen Telang to play instead of Krishnamachary Srikant. Telang would have set the "Thames on fire". On any day his standard of fielding was much better than Sandip Patil, Kirti Azad, Dilip Vengsarkar or even Sunil Valson who were the other members of that World Cup winning side.

The tale of Vidharbha cricket will remain incomplete, if nothing is written about Ashok Bhagwat and Rakesh Tandon. Tandon was a product of Bishop Cotton School, Nagpur, and he represented the Indian School team which had toured Australia in 1969-70, besides representing India against the visiting Sri Lankan team in 1975-76.

A Lankan team led by Anura Tenakoon visited India in 1975-76 and Rakesh Tandon was preferred to Chandrashekar to play for India. Tandon took the opportunity with both hands and was a hit. He bowled magnificently in the series to claim 15 wickets in those 3 unofficial test matches. However, he was dropped from the Indian team thereafter.

He shifted his base to Bombay for a better avenue and was instrumental in helping Bombay to win the Ranji Trophy in 1976-77. However, that did not go well with the selectors. A natural leg spinners, with deceptive googlies, under his arm, Tandon was really unlucky not to play for India again. He was a fluent bat too, and he had helped India to save the test, with his bat, at Nagpur when Sri Lankan played the third unofficial test match over there at Nagpur in 1975-76. Many a great spinners would not agree when I write so good about Tandon, but the fact is Tandon had improved so drastically as a spinner that from 1975 to 1978 he, along with Padmakar Shivalkar, had carved many a thrilling victories for Bombay in the Ranji Trophy.

At last how can one complete the story without writing a word about Ashok Bhagwat. A complete bowler with a horse like stamina, is what Ashok Bhagwat was all about. Bhagwat is also a B. E (Civil) from the Regional Engineering College at Nagpur.

Bhagwat's strength lay in the accuracy that he maintained in the bowling, besides the deceptive out-cutters which he had mastered to fox the batsmen. Bhagwat also possessed "perfect" yorkers. He had a masterly control over his yorkers, that would have put even the Wasim Akram to shame.

It was K. N. Prabhu, who twice, once in 1971, when India were to tour England under Ajit Wadekar, and again in 1981, when India had toured England under Sunil Gavaskar, had advocated to include Ashok Bhagwat in the team.

He could have been much better, if compared to Suru Nayak in 1981, but then I suppose since he had represented Vidharbha, and that was his "sin" for not being selected for India. Ashok Bhagwat played his last Ranji match against the Railways in 1981 and hanged his boots thereafter.

To date, he is the FIRST Ranji cricketer, from Vidharbha to claim over 100 wickets and score over 1000 runs in the Ranji Trophy matches. His highest was an innings of 81 which he had scored against Madhya Pradesh at the Rajkumar College ground at Raipur. He also had represented the Central Zone. Basically a front line strike bowler for Vidharbha, he had claimed 137 Ranji wickets for Vidharbha, with 7 for 105 as his best bowling effort against the Indian Railways.

What was the fault of these cricketers who were as good as any other cricketers but who could not represent India in cricket, a question one keeps on asking to himself, at Nagpur, always. The answer is "they were the cricketers from Nagpur, and perhaps, they represented a weaker association, or they had no god-fathers".

"Indian cricket will always remain poor, for not having watched the exploit of Vijay Telang – particularly, his batting, especially his strokes".

There are people who question and raise many a questions, about the flawfulship of Vidharbha's cricket. However I can assure all and sundry of a true fact, a bitter truth for anybody to digest, if Anil Deshpande and Vijay Telang had just got a chance to play for India, Madanlal's career might have been cut short by at least 20 test matches, and perhaps Krishnamachary Srikant wouldn't have played for India at all, believe me my readers.

Many believe that Telang was a bad fielder. I have to differ. Watched the fielding and its standard set by Sandip Patil, Dilip Vengsarkar, Dilip Doshi, Parthasarthy Sharma, Ashok Malhotra, Kirti Azad, to name a few, Telang was miles ahead of them in the standard of fielding though many say that his buttocks were even bigger than the wheels of the road roller.

That was a bad observation by the people to mark him as a cricketer. His innings against the visiting teams had road-rolled the bowlers, very great bowlers of those times. And that basically is the yard stick to select a bat, or a cricketer, not the butts, or the buttocks.

18

PRASANNA: THE SMILING ASSASSINATOR

IT was the year 1968 when Mysore, the State then known as, were playing the semi-finals against Bombay. This match was a one way traffic for Bombay, for with the help of Dilip Sardesai (111) and Ajit Wadekar (323), Bombay had collared Mysore to move into the last stage. Wadekar scored at a very breathtaking pace, and he literally pommelled Chandra and Prasanna to reduce the size of Mysore to pulp.

Prasanna had a terrific reputation not only as a spinner but as a captain also. He was very well respected in the world of Indian cricket, not only for his mesmerising skill, but for the M. E. Degree he had earned in Engineering. His studies besides cricket had earned him a lot of friends world over, besides a reputation as a cricketer. His exploit in cricket later made the NATIONAL INSTITUTE OF ENGINEERING COLLEGE from where he received his Engineering degree, as a household name in the field of education.

Prasanna was very close to Dilip Sardesai, and no sooner the match got over, he went to Dilip Sardesai to first congratulate him, and then asked him jokingly HOW MANY TIMES WOULD BOMBAY KEEP ON WINNING THIS TROPHY CONSECUTIVELY. Sardesai smiled and replied, "TILL I KEEP ON PLAYING FOR BOMBAY".

These words of Sardesai turned him off. Prasanna took this words to his mind and took it very seriously. This Bombay side can be beaten, he told to himself and closed the matter for some time for a better time.

Actually in 1967, when Hanumant Singh had led the Rest of India to a remarkable victory in the Irani Trophy against Bombay, nobody gave this victory of the "Rest" any credit, as they felt that it was a one of a fluke.

However, later when in another tie in the Irani Trophy in 1969 in which Pataudi had scored an unbeaten 200 to beat Bombay was the point when Prasanna really felt that Bombay as a team in the Ranji Trophy can be turtled and toyed with.

Being an Engineer himself, he analysed the mechanism and the dynamicism of the weak points of Bombay, and he discovered that if a batsman playing against Bombay goes to play a very long and a big innings, the Bombay team faulters at a very crucial moment. A knock of 150 plus by any batsman is what would be required to put Bambay onto the tenterhooks. He chose his men there and then, and it was Gundappa Vishvanath. He patiently waited for the opportunity to arrive. And it arrived at the Irani Trophy tie in 1974.

From 1968 to 1973, Prasanna played a few more games against Bombay, and everytime he came very closer to topple Bombay, he found that either Ashok Mankad or Ajit Wadekar, and one from the lower order comes in as a handy bat for Bombay. He had observed that either Mankad or Wadekar would score very heavily and the rest of the batting revolves around them. For it was either of the two, taking away the matches from the camp of the opponents to the camp of Bombay.

He fell onto the gamet first to build up a team to dethrone Bombay. Once he had formed a team in his mind, he waited for the opportunity to come to him. It is said that everything comes to a human being only if he has the patience. And this moment came to him during the start of the 1973-74 season, 1974 to be precise, when the selectors announced that Erapalli Prasanna would lead the Rest of India team to face Bombay in the Irani Cup tie which was to be played at the Chinnaswamy Stadium.

Prasanna took his chances. He met the selectors and asked them to give him a team of his choice which would have two tantalizing spinners, two extraordinary fielders, and at least three quickies. He would be satisfied if he got four batsmen, purely a bat to counter Bombay.

The selectors gave him a free chance to choose his team. He sportingly claimed Chandra as his first choice. Bedi was left out because of his county commitment assisting the Northampton side. He then chose Mohinder Amarnath and Amitavaa Roy as his medium pacers, and Gundappa Vishvanath, Brijesh Patel, Gopal Bose and Kenia Jayantilal as the openers. His choice was unanimous for Karsan Ghavri as the third pacer, whereas on the insistence of a player who was very close to him he preferred to choose Anil Deshpande of Vidharbha as the fourth all-rounder of the team. He then left it to the selectors to decide for the rest of the squad.

The selectors gave him Parthasarathy Sharma, Bharat Reddy as the wicketkeeper and Dilip Doshi, if needed to help him for his campaign. Prasanna had his own idea. For he had observed that on many occasions there were some teams like Rajasthan, Madras and Bengal, who had come very close to humbling Bombay in the Ranji matches ultimately to surrender because of the lack of fast bowlers, and the lack of quality batsmen, he balanced his team with the pacers and the bat. He knew that Chandra would be his trump card. And he of course was there with his guile as an offie.

Prasanna once again ran through the Bombay team that was to take them in the Irani tie. Gavaskar, Parkar, Wadekar, Ashok Mankad, Sudhir Naik, Milind Rege, Rakesh Tandon, Shivalkar, and Abdul Ismail, this was a very strong team. He realized that if the Bombay team was to be broken by its collar and the backbone, the first four wickets had to be gulped quickly. For this, fielding was the key to success.

He also analysed that all these years the other teams would attack Bombay on the strength of their spin, and demolishing Bombay on the strength of the spin was as good as breaking a strong wall with the help of a rubber pad. For, Bombay were very strong and good enough to play the spinners. He had his own logic. He felt like when both he and Chandra for so many years could not check the Bombay batsmen with the spinners, how would the others afford to do that, as both Chandra and Prasanna along with Bedi were the exceptional spinners that India could ever have.

Prasanna even before the match had started, had made up his mind to go in for the three pacers, two spinners, two supporting spinners, the makeshift spinners as we would call it, and four pure batsmen, who would be helped with the batsmanship of three all rounders. His only hitch was either to play Ghavri or Anil Deshpande of Vidharbha. Deshpande was ahead in batting as compared to Ghavri, but Ghavri had the pace beside a recommendation of a very respected and a highly placed official. This decided the scale in Ghavri's favour. Anil Despande, for him it was the cup of tea, with the sip between the two lips making all the difference. The last chance of a Vidharbhaites to make it to the national team had come, and gone.

Well came the moment and came the team meeting. He spoke his mind to his players. It was decided that the batting would revolve around Vishvanath, who would be the fulcrum of the Rest's batting. The others would have to contribute equally.

Winning the toss, Prasanna decided to bat first. His openers K. Jayantilal and Gopal Bose right from the word go, did not have any problems facing the Bombay's duo pace of Abdul Ismail and Ajit Nayak. They literally toyed with the pace of Ismail and Nayak as the cat toys with the mice. Wadekar brought in the spinners, with Shivalkar to bear the brunt of the bowling.

The induction of the spinners also proved futile, and both the openers not only got to their respective fifties, but both of them crawled toward the seventies. When the score was 150, Jayantilal got out first. Bombay had to wait for the next 52 runs when they could claim the second wicket, Parthasarthy Sharma got out for 24. It was here that the Rest had won the battle psychologically. 200 for one is really a big score to digest for any fieding side.

Anyway when Paddy Shivalkar, as he was affectionately called, got the better of Sharma, in strode the Little Master, Gundappa Vishvanath. He with Gopal Bose completely tore whatever Bombay had as an attack maybe in little terms, left with them. Bose not only got to his century, he matched Vishvanath for his strokes, and completely put Bombay in a land where neither there was water for them to drink, or some square feet of dry land to at least firmly put their feet for a proper gripping. The first day honour really went to the Rest who were firmly placed at over 300 runs losing two wickets.

On the second day both Vishvanath and Gopal Bose started from where they had left on the first day. Flurries of strokes and rotating the strikes, they went past the 350 marks when Vishvanath was out for 76, Shivalkar getting the best of him. However Bose was to add over 50 runs with Brijesh Patel. Finally Bose got out for 173. Brijesh Patel in the company of Mohinder (20), Bharat Reddy (15), and Karsan Ghavri (15) took the score near to 450, before Rest were out. They had scored 444 runs.

Prasanna was elated as all the bats on whom he has pinned his faith had delivered the goods. The first five bats, Gopal Bose (170), P. Sharma (24), K. Jayantilal (72), Gundappa Vishvanath (76) and Brijesh Patel (56) had played their part well. Now it was the turn of the fielders and the bowlers to contribute.

This score of 444 actually as per astrology is a sign of omen. But Prasanna was sure that if it was a sign of omen, it would have been for Bombay for most of the times, because till Bombay got past 444, Rest was not to be worried. The fear factor was on the other side. Prasanna was not on the tenterhooks, it was Bombay.

When the chance of the Rest had finally arrived, the cricket fraternity of India saw AMITAVAA. Yes this was Amitavaa Roy, who in all practical purposes was a carbon copy of Amitabh Bachchan as far as his hair style was concerned. The only difference between the two Amitabhs was that the cine star possessed a height of 6 feet four, whereas his was just below 5 feet six inches, otherwise there was no change in both of them in walking and talking.

Readers would be anxious to know who this Amitavaa was. It was Amitavaa Roy, who was emerging as a fierceful and a very potent medium pacer in the annals of Indian cricket then. He hailed from Bengal and he was undergoing his studies in Economics from the Jadavpur University at Calcutta then. He was spotted by Mansur Ali Khan Pataudi in a local match at Calcutta.

On the very first look Pataudi was very impressed by his work out. Next came the Moin-ud-Dowlah tourney that season before this match, and Amitavaa was in the U-Foam XI led by Pataudi. He worked up a lively pace and had rattled the A. C. C. XI in that tourney claiming 6 scalps in the match in that very innings. He did not stop there. In the semis against the State Bank of India XI, which had Wadekar, Vishvanath, Hanumant Singh, Ambar Roy, Abid Ali, B. S. Bedi and Subroto Guha, Amitavaa was to rock the State Bank team with his burst of 5 for 70. The ball that got rid of Wadekar with his castle rattled, and the application of ice on the knee of Abid Ali for hours after he was strucked by an express delivery from Amitavaa, had brought Amitavaa to this far. He was to try his destiny in the next higher level.

Prasanna had Mohinder to work in tandem with Amitavaa, with Ghavri as the first change. Actually Mohinder had played a test with Prasanna in 1969. Prasanna had seen how Mohinder had got rid of Stackpole and then Ian Chappel in that test with his cutters. From then in 1969 till this date Mohinder had never got to play for India. He had those visions and the scenes in his mind and that was one reason why he preferred Mohinder to the other all rounders who were playing in this match.

With Shivalkar of Bombay having a marathon spell of 63.5-24-130-5, Prasanna knew that his spinners, basically he and Chandra were capable of repeating the same feat, but he was very skeptical of the idea of conceding 130 runs. He knew that Bombay were very good at tackling the spinners. Hence pace was his lethal weapon. Only after the pace, the spin was his forte.

When the Rest were to take the field, he once again made it very clear to his team that the first four wickets, besides the extraordinary fielding would do the trick. Complacency in any way was something that should not be allowed to set in even though 444 as a total was a huge total. He made them to realize that even on several occasions before, Bombay had chased over 500 runs and they had won. In any case the old history should not be repeated. Fielding was the need of the hour.

Prasanna's pep talk really had a trick and the repercussion flowed into the game afterwards, as the Rest of India team threw themselves upto everything that they could do. However, both the Bombay batsmen Gavaskar and Parkar were undeterred. They added a few runs in the way they could. The drama started from this stage onwards.

Amitavaa Roy bowled at his fiery best. On three occasions he hit Gavaskar on the foot to appeal loudly, only to be negated by the umpire. However, his effort was to bear the fruit. He bowled a ball pitching it on the offstump of Parker, to bring it sharply in to the batsman. Parker was beaten by the pace and his timber was scuttled.

Next to join in was Wadekar. He along with Gavaskar took past the score to fifty, when Mohinder was to play his trick. Coming in to bowl his ninth over, Mohinder had conceded three boundaries to Sunil Gavaskar in his first spell of eight overs. Prasanna intelligently took off Ghavri and brought in Chandra.

Chandra was one bowler who was very hard to describe. He never knew what was he upto, and the batsmen never knew what was going to come to them from Chandra. Chandra could bowl six different deliveries in an over, and his faster one would have been even faster than the Jeff Thomson's fastest ball. No doubt, Vivian Richard had once described about Chandra that HIS FASTER ONES ARE FASTER THAN TOMMOS MAAN.

Wadekar had seen Chandra bowling these kinds of stuff to many batsmen, and most of the times the batsmen got out too. It would be really hard for any batsmen to read Chandra properly when Chandra would come up with those kinds of stuffs. But little did Wadekar realise that he was to receive one of such stuff from Chandra.

Bowling from the BEML end, Chandra bowled a delivery which would have put the pace of Amitavaa Roy, Ghavri and Mohinder in a real shame. This delivery pitched at least two stumps away from the off stump of Wadekar, it broke back and it spun such a deal that from that end where the ball had pitched, it deviated to such a great angle, and broke Wadekar's off stick. Wadekar was out, and completely out of words.

If Amitavaa and Chandra had their names written in the books of wicket takers, Mohinder was awaiting for his chance. He came in to bowl his ninth over. He also like Chandra bowled a delivery to Ashok Mankad, rolling his finger over the seam for the ball to curl in and deviate in after pitching or hitting the deck. The ball did the trick. It curled in the air much more than Mankad could have expected, and it deviated in that it pierced through the gap which Mankad had left between his bat and the pad for the ball to hit the stump.

If these three wickets were claimed with an effort of EXCELLENCE associated with it, the wicket of Sunil Gavaskar was the result of an excellent ground fielding. Wadekar as the striker had leaned back to lift Mohinder through the covers. Brijesh Patel fielding at the cover point anticipated the shot. He covered the distance between the cover and the cover point, and running from his position at the cover point, he stopped that shot, observing that Wadekar was a better runner as compared to Gavaskar between the wickets, Patel chose to throw the ball to the end where Gavaskar was running on the wicket. In a flash he sent in a flat but a straight and a direct throw into the hands of wicketkeeper Bharat Reddy to whip off the bail. Out went Gavaskar in that fashion.

The bowling and the fielding of the Rest was touching a dizzy height, and when the four batsmen Gavaskar, Wadekar, Parkar and Mankad were out, the writings were clearly written on the walls for the Bombay team.

Within 60 runs the backbone of the Bombay team was broken. Amitavaa Roy, Mohinder and Chandra had virtually broken the Bombay's backbone. Victory for the Rest was there for taking and the match from there itself was a mere formality. However Bombay cricket is known for TIGER BEATING THE DEATH. It happened for sometimes but then Prasanna diffused it.

Once these four wickets had fallen, Sudhir Naik first in the company of Eknath Solkar started repairing the damage. Over 40 runs were added for the fifth wicket before Solkar was once again done in with a beautiful delivery from Chandra. The ball straightened through the defence of Solkar after it turned for about 70 degrees pitching on the offstick of Solkar to break his stump.

After Solkar had departed Sudhir Naik in the company

of Milind Reger (67) took past the Bombay score to about 200. At this score Prasanna floated a delivery whose loops was something which Naik had assumed that the ball was curling and deviating to the leg side. He had shaped to flick the ball to the leg side, when all of a sudden he observed that the ball after hitting the deck had spun the other way around. Naik was befooled to change his stance and doing that he drew himself out to execute a drive.

The ball left him and totally beat him up in the air and off the wicket. He was stranded outside and all he could do was to give the ball a little bit of the bat. The ball kissed his bat and flew to Jayantilal who made no mistake. Tail enders specially, and with the help of Abdul Ismail, Rege started fighting to save the follow-on for Bombay, but once again a brilliant piece of fielding which saw Brijesh Patel responsible to run out Ismail and that had dug Bombay in.

The last hope to save the follow-on also had vanished when Prasanna once again floated a delivery to Rege inviting him to use his feet. Rege fell into the trap and came out, but could not read the flight and gauge its loop. The ball curled in the air, and deviated which took Rege by surprise. Also the loop and the trajectory was something which totally caught Rege offguard. He in a rush of blood went in for a lofted stroke. The ball pitched and took a turn away from his bat, leaving his bat to leave a big gap for the ball to make its way to go to the wicketkeeper Bharat Reddy, who in a flash whipped off the bails, and falling 21 runs short, Bombay were asked to follow-on.

The news of Bombay to follow-on created the same kind of a wave that had been created when India and Ajit Wadekar had asked Gary Sobers to follow-on during the first test at Jamaica when India played West Indies in 1971. There was a shock that had passed in the cricketing fraternity of India. For a long-long time and times immemorable people were not ready to believe that Bombay had been asked to follow-on.

Prasanna had done what no other Captain, except

Hanumant Singh and Nawab of Pataudi Mansur Ali Khan could do it. However Prasanna's effort was unique in the sense that the other two skippers of the Rest of India mentioned here could beat Bombay on the basis of the first innings lead, Prasanna enforced the follow-on, so unnatural of Indian and the Bombay cricket then. This was a glorious record in the annals of the Indian cricket history. The Bombay players were also shocked for themselves, for never did they think that they would be asked to follow-on.

Prasanna rotated his bowlers very intelligently. What was more he used the pace of Amitavaa, Mohinder and Ghavri in a manner in which Shakespeare would use his characters in his play, or would use his pen to write his stories in a poetic manner. The Indian pace was down and out for counts in Indian cricket till then. The job of the pacers then was to use the ball to remove the shine and to hand it over to the spinners for the rest of the days. Prasanna totally changed the scenario of the pacers in one single game.

Not that the pacers took more than half of the Bombay's wicket that was to fall. The chief wrecker was Chandra with an analysis of 4 for 72. Prasanna had two for 56. There were two run out and the pacers had taken a wicket each. What was more was the fact that he did not come to bowl till the fall of the first four wickets, and except for Chandra, in that spell where four wickets had fallen, Prasanna did not bring him in.

By doing so he had instilled a confidence amongst the pacers that they had a room to live in India's cricket, and that pace was not a dying art. This really inspired youngsters like Ghavri and Mohinder who were really working hard to stage a comeback to the national squad.

It was seen in the past that whenever Bombay or the players representing Bombay for the Duleep Trophy had fallen short in the first strike, would bounce back into the game while making amends for their shortfalls and failures. Prasanna had this in his mind.

In the second essay, he used his medium pacers to a large extent. Amitavaa would bowl with 21 pace, Ghavri too would run that pace before snarling one, and Mohinder would use his 15 paces. This was enough for Prasanna to kill the time. For he on one hand never wanted a huge total to chase for victory, as that would have put pressure on his team.

Bombay too had bowlers who could play the tricks if that was the situation. On the other hand, Prasanna also never wanted a high Bombay total on the score Board. The best ploy was to kill the time. This he could do by rotating his pacers. A lot of time was consumed by the pacers to complete their over and the time thus consumed was running out of Bombay's gear to put them back into the game.

Bombay this time did a shade better. Gavaskar got his ton (108), Parkar got into his fifties. Wadekar was out for 62, whereas Sudhir Naik once again scored 58. This was identical to his first innings score of 58. Solkar chipped in with a fluently scored 36 whereas Rege once again was undone by Prasanna for 26, in the same fashion as in the first.

What was surprising, Prasanna did not use Chandra at all. He practically saved Chandra for the Ranji matches that Karnataka was to play in the league, the round robin encounters. In fact Prasanna used Gopal Bose and Parthasarathy Sharma as an offspinners to fill in the breach that was left by Chandra. They responded magnificently, each claiming a wicket in the match.

When the curtains were drawn Bombay were 161 runs ahead with two wickets remaining. Prasanna was to crucify Bombay in the Irani Trophy tie. This drama got over between November 9th and November 12th.

Four months later when once again Bombay were to play Karnataka in the semis of Ranji in 1974, the story was the same, but the characters were different. However, the ground was once again the same. Here again Karnataka aided with a splendid effort of Vishvanath (169), and Brijesh Patel (107) scored 395 to floor Bombay for 305. This time Prasanna with 5 for 115 and Chandra with four for 78 paid dear to all the expectations that Bombay might have had.

The entire story of the match is narrated in this book and I do not want to repeat it again. These two defeats of Bombay completely pulverized the status of the cricket of Bombay. It totally changed the perception, conception and the belief that existed in the annals of Indian cricket then that BOMBAY COULD NOT BE BEATEN. A self belief had creeped in to the thinking of the Indian cricketers then that Bombay were no longer the ADOLF HITLER of Indian cricket.

Thus Erapalli Prasanna has been and was the first player to have dug Bombay in their own graveyard that too enforcing them to follow-on. He within a span of four months delivered the punching knock that entirely knocked Bombay out of their premier position that they were and they held at India during that stage.

After fifteen consecutive years from 1957-58 to 1973-74, when Bombay had been winning the Ranji Trophy consecutively, they were dethroned as the ultimate winners of the Ranji Trophy. Karnataka under the leadership of Prasanna had emerged as the new national champion of Indian cricket.

Prasanna it was who changed the face of Indian cricket with these two victories. In the test matches too Prasanna from 1967 when he made his comeback to the Indian team to 1978 was a MARAUDER for the opposing batsmen and the opponents. He has many a tale, and many a chapter written about him in the annals of Indian cricket. But the greatest one would be the India's first overseas series victory at New Zealand where he took 26 wickets to register the first overseas test victory for India.

He in fact was the fastest bowler to claim the first one hundred wickets individually for India. Unlike the other bowlers who would play to the weakness of the batsmen, Prasanna was the only bowler who played to the strength of the batsmen to floor them. He purposely would flight the ball to the batsmen inviting them to hit him. He would say to the batsman—COME ON HIT ME, but on the contrary the batsman would get the knock out of his deliveries.

The kind of a smile that he would flash to the batsmen—and put them totally on the wrong track—literally make them a fool—and then again pass on to them his victory smile after he got their wickets—for this act Sunil Gavaskar had named him—THE SMILING ASSASSINATOR.

Prasanna also has many a chapters written and inscribed in the test cricket too. He really came in to the groove after staging a comeback to the Indian team after completing his studies in Engineering. That was in 1967. His analysis of 8 for 76 against the West Indies for South Zone brought him back to the Indian team.

In 1967 he was not a hit at England, yet he could demonstrate that he was ready for the big show. His floaters virtually had put Ken Barrington and Geoffry Boycott in all sort of trouble. But the crowning glory was to come in the twin tour which India had taken to the lands of the Kangaroos and the Kiwis.

The twin tour saw him claiming 51 wickets in nine tests. The hallmark was the first ever series win abroad at New Zealand where India beat New Zealand led by Graeme Dowling by 3-1. Not only when he bowled, but when he went in to bat, he would contribute in an average manner, and here it was the world of cricket, saw his bat doing the talks. He claimed one more title that of the best night watchman, and he kept this title with him till the end of the series in 1976 against New Zealand.

To what extent Prasanna had psychologically killed the other batsmen and the other teams of the world could be gauged from the fact that when the Kiwis under Graeme Dowling toured here at India, they simply could not score more than 250 runs in any of the test match they played.

They were very watchful and careful of him. The series had eneded 1-1, and he had claimed 20 wickets in the entire series.

Next came in the Aussies under Bill Lawry. The moment they landed over here, at the airport itself, Lawry had asked the local Manager of the Australian team about how was Prasanna and to what extent was he fit to play for India. The Australians were very skeptical of getting the better of him, and had planned that they would not take any risk against him.

They were mentally so bogged down that in the entire series they could not score over 300 runs except in the Kanpur test where they scored 348 to India's 320. It was here that Gundappa Vishvanath scored a stylish and a magical 137 to save India from a possible defeat. Prasanna in this series went on to claim 26 wickets, and here in this test the moment he claimed Paul Sheahan, he achieved the distinction of claiming his one hundred wicket in twenty tests which is still the fastest hundred wicket claimed by any Indian in the test. The Australians gave him and his bowling the utmost respect by playing him safe.

Prasanna later in his career was made an opponent and a competitor for Venkat, and from this stage his appearance in the test matches started diminishing. From the Kanput test in 1969 where he played his twentieth test to the last test at Karachi against Pakistan in 1978, he played in another 29 tests in nine years to claim another 89 wickets. His strike rate got battered and bruised.

It was not because his bowling had come down but because he was used in different manners by four different skippers then. Pataudi used him as a strike bowler, Bedi used him as a stock bowler, Gavaskar used him as a shock bowler and Wadekar used him as a spare bowler. Secondly Bedi, when he was the skipper, simply underused him, handling the vagaries of the bowling with Chandra attacking and he assisting Chandra.

Prasanna was hardly given that many overs which Chandra and Bedi together would bowl. For example in

Adelaide in 1977-78 against Australia, in the second innings, about 70 overs were bowled by the Indian team, with Australia sitting pretty. To get some rest Bedi took him and Chandra off and brought in Prasanna to bowl. The result was Prasanna 4 for 16, and India defeated Australia by an innings.

There were so many times when one had felt that once amongst Bedi and Chandra have been dropped then Venkat along with Prasanna should have played. The classic example was the 1976-77 series against England which India had lost by 1-3. Chandra was a shadow of himself in these series, and except for the Madras test where he claimed 5 for 50, he was an utter failure. Critics had written Prasanna off in these series. He was dropped for the first test, but was recalled for the second. In the four tests he played, when his age was almost nearing 37, he claimed 18 wickets to head the bowling average. It was really felt that Chandra should have been dropped and the trio of Pras-Venky and Bedi should have played in the entire series. The entire story of the Indian spin bowling then would have been who between Venkat and Prasanna would play, whereas in reality on many occasions one felt either Bedi or Chandra and especially Chandra should have been dropped.

Prasanna amongst the four spinners bowled the minimum numbers of balls, even less than Venkatraghvan, and still he managed to claim so many wickets. The statistics given hereunder would reflect as to what extent he was under bowled when Wadekar and Bedi "skipped" him. He was majestically fluent under Gavaskar, and on the top of the world under Pataudi, under whose supervision he had captured 130 wickets out of 189.

Prasanna was the best captain that had emerged on the Indian scene after Pataudi, Hanumant Singh and Jaisimha. Here also he was very unlucky of not getting a chance to lead India. It was because he did not lead the South Zone which was led by another offie, Venkatraghvan. This was the only reason of Venkat leading India in test matches, and Prasanna not. Both were leading their respective associations in the Ranji Trophy, but since Prasanna was not leading the South Zone, and Venkat was, the Indian captaincy did not come to Prasanna, and he was unlucky to not have led India. Actually to be frank, there were three occasions that he should have led India. The entire twin series of the New Zealand and the West Indies in 1975-76 was the occasion where he should have led India, but the gimmicks and the politics of the Indian cricket administration seized his golden chance. The NORTH-ZONE policy ruined his chances.

Prasanna brought in a bowling which was unique in the annals of the world cricket and its history. The way he used to flight the ball, tossing it in the air, varying the trajectories, changing the loops as per his will and fancies, and curling it on the opposite direction in the air, whereas making the batsmen feel that he was curling it towards them in the same direction, made him a very different bowler of off-spin. Actually he was the one who invented the "Doosra" in 1968, but the credit has been given to Murlitharan. It is because we did not have the channels then that we have now, and the ignorant people are commenting on the channels to invent these kinds of words, that we see them doing now.

Most of the TV commentators are "WISE WITHOUT HEADS". They say so many things but they hardly have spent their time to find out what is the reality, and to whom should the credit go. I hope that I have given a fair chance to the readers to understand on whom I point my fingers on. The booty they pocket is hardly the fact they speak, and the kind of mistakes they commit while projecting the statistics is really shameful. HOW EASY IS THE BUCK-MAKING NOW.

The modern days channel commentators and the sports casters commenting on the game can easily beat a LEXICOGRAPHER if it comes to the point of discovering the new terms of cricket, and then giving it a purposeful meaning. Even William Shakespeare cannot afford to beat them when they come to describing an act on cricket.

The kind of a flight that Prasanna would give to the ball, control it in the air, and spin it was very unique to all the batsmen that he had bowled. Even his faster one had a lot of air to it, and that would deceive the batsmen. He in a way had completely changed the definition of spin bowling especially the off-spin. The variation and the change that he could do so effectively in his bowling and the control that he had over the flight was something out of the world.

Well India will never have that kind of a magical off-spinner, A SMILING ASSASSINATOR of Bombay cricket and a face that completely changed the Indian cricket.

The combined effort of the spin quatret is described here-:

Bowling								
Name	BB	R/C	Wkts	B/B	BMA	5W/I	10W/M	Ave
B.S. Bedi	21364	7637	266	7/98	10/194	-12-	-1-	28.71
B.S. Chandra Shekar	15963	7199	242	8/79	12/104	-14-	-2-	29.74
E.A.S Prasanna	14353	5742	189	8/76	11/140	-10-	-2-	30.38
S.Venkatraghvan	14877	5634	156	8/72	12/152	-3-	-1-	36.11

Combined, this spin quatret, claimed 855 wickets conceding 26212 runs for an average of 30.65. If this effort is compared with the duo of the "K-K" Express, ie the pair of Kapil and Karsan Ghavri, then their average works out to be 30.37 runs per wicket. Combined they had scalped 543 wickets conceding 164901 runs. The difference is very marginal, and this really speaks out the effort of the spin quatret before the advent of Kapil, and this also speaks the effort of Kapil and Ghavri to put the pace on the same platform as compared to the spinners.

This was the change that had erupted in the annals of Indian cricket, in terms of the pace revolution, and if the spinners are legend, Kapil due to his effort too has become a legend of Indian cricket. This is where the Indian cricket in a big way had changed, and Kapil Dev along with Karsan Ghavri had changed it. That's the importance of Ghavri too.

We find and we see that the BCCI runs from pillar to post, creating all sort of HUNGAMA for selecting a coach. Are they inspired doing this kind of a TAMASHA by watching a song of the film HUNGAMA, the song was HUNGAMA HO GAYA sung by a legend of Indian singer, Asha Di, and had the terrific vamp of the yesteryear, Bindu to dance on it. My answer to them is, put in Karsan Ghavri as the Chief Coach with Mohinder as his Assistant, and give them a target and a time frame for four years to deliver. "THE FACE OF INDIAN CRICKET WLL CHANGE ONCE MORE FOR BETTER".

Hello Mr Ravi Shastri, Hello Mr Sunil Manohar Gavaskar, are you reading this book. If yes.... . JAGO, CRICKET KE MAHARTHIYON, JAGO..... Force the Board to appoint the coaches correctly, for getting the best of the result. The runners-up position achieved at the World Cup 2003 could have also been achieved by the Indian coach, and that too at a very nominal price.

As the GREAT poet, "GURUDEV", Thakur Ravindranath Tagore had written in his poem "GEETANJALI", ... AWAKE, MY COUNTRYMEN–AWAKE.... .

HUNGAMA and TAMASHA were two Hindi films with terrific castings, but both the films were a SUPER FLOP. Only the songs have been famous......

19

SACHIN TENDULKAR: MIDAS TOUCH OR UNDERACHIEVER

IT is not very easy to describe or write about a Genius. Genius are born and not made. Again when it comes to sports, no rules apply to a Genius. They come out of their mother's womb that way and they go into the womb of the mother earth that way, this is what a great poet Shri Maithli Sharan Gupt had once described a Genius. Yes, he was referring to the great poet and the writer Shri Munshi Chandra Premchand.

If these words are to be taken into account and if these words are to be believed than I have to say that there will be nothing more for me to write anything on a genius called and named SACHIN RAMESH TENDULKAR.

What do I write more on a subject depends upon what the people do not know about the subject. But what do I write on this great Indian star, who the world of cricket knows more than me. I never had carried any thought to write on this super duper genius of Indian cricket, Oh why Indian cricket, I would call it the World cricket.

It was my daughter Sagarika who forced me to think about him, to write something on him, as she is a great fan of Sachin Tendulkar, and one of my closest friend Kanur Murlidharan Nair who gave me some idea to rethink about this great cricketer, and to write about "WHETHER HE WAS A MIDAS TOUCH OF INDIAN CRICKET, OR AN UNDERACHIEVER FOR INDIA."

This advice egged me on. I would have never written even a single line on him, because he is worshipped and treated as a GOD in India. But the advice of my friend, and the continous nagging of my daughter made me to write about him and has FORCED me and my pen to write on him. SORRY MR TENDULKAR, but give me the permission to write about you.

It was the year 1988 when somewhere a headline had appeared in the newspaper, the "Times of India" that a guy named Sachin Tendulkar along with Vinod Kambli had added over six hundred plus runs in a tournament for the school.

Soon the duo started hitting the headlines for their inclusion in the Ranji Trophy matches for Bombay. The question was, would it be a wise step for including them at a very tender age for the Ranji Trophy or would it be wise to wait for some time so that these coots could emerge a bit stronger and mature to handle the vagaries of the tough cricket of Bombay.

Anyway, it was 1989 when Tendulkar was in the Bombay Ranji team and in his first game he notched a century for them. The Chairman of the BCCI then, Shri Raj Singh Dungarpur selected him for the Indian sojourn to Pakistan in 1989. But it was his maiden hundred in the Irani Trophy before that in his maiden Irani cup assignment for Bombay, where his ton got him a ticket booked for Pakistan.

In Pakistan the first test that he played, he went unnoticed, but in the second test from the second innings, first when he was hit on the nose by Waqar Younus, and then when he clobbered Abdul Qadir for 27 runs in an over in a one-dayer, till this moment, cricket and particularly the Indian cricket, has been a great hollow without him.

The youngest to play a test for India, the youngest to hit a test ton for India, it starts from here and the list of the records goes on and on. The highest number of test centuries, the highest number of one-day tons, the highest test aggregate in terms of runs, the highest run aggregate in the one-dayers, it goes on and on. The question is HAS TENDULKAR SERVED THE PURPOSE OF INDIAN CRICKET.

Look into his contribution to Indian cricket. It is without doubt that he has contributed in terms of runs and wickets. He has played so many glorious innings that everything cannot be explained or written. From that point of view, he is marvellous.

Look into the contribution in terms of victories that his efforts have churned out for India, it is a big zero. Nineteen years of international assignment for India, and in what way his runs and wickets have brought the victories for India, the answer will be NOTHING GREAT.

From 1992 to 2007, Tendulkar has participated in five World Cups, without winning any of them for India. The only one which he played in the final against Australia in 2007, he and India were licked like a baby licking the ice-cream, though he had Shoaib Akhtar to jab him to that famous six over the squarish third man. Compare it with the guiles and the likes of Aravinda De Silva, or Inzamam, they have one World Cup in their pocket. Individually yes, a lot of records are in his name for this trophy in the World Cup.

From 1997 to 2005, there were five ICC Trophies, and Tendulkar has once been a joint winner along with Sri Lanka. Compare it with the lesser lights as compared to him like the Cairns, the McMillan and you would find that they had inscribed their names in the glittering trophy, on rolls of the trophy. Yes individually Tendulkar has many records in his name for this trophy. But his name does not figure in the pages of champs individually.

Take out the leaves from the books of the Asian Cup cricket and you will find that Tendulkar ever since he had participated in the Asian Cup cricket has not won this trophy for even once for India after 1992. Before 1992 yes Tendulkar has won it but it was also that Kapil Dev and the likes of Shastri, Shrikant, Azharuddin, Vengsarkar, Hirwani and the guiles of Siddhu and the Prabhakar were there too for making the victory possible. They too were in equal measure instrumental for carving out the Asian Trophy title win.

Take out the history of the test matches. One would find that the Indian win in the test matches at the time of Tendulkar's rein was more in this country on the sub standard laid Indian pitches. They were a big blot when they went outside for a campaign. One would put the victory at Pakistan under the Sourav-Dravid army as a big win, but the fact is Pakistan then were playing with one of the weakest team in their history against India.

Take out every page of the one-dayers. One would find that despite of so many heroics, Tendulkar was never able to put India on that platform where one could say that YES INDIA IS ONE AMONGST THE TWO BEST TEAMS IN THE WORLD ON A CONTINOUS BASIS, AT LEAST FOR A PERIOD OF TWO YEARS. On an individual front, agreed he has created records after records, but in what way has it helped India.

The question that comes forward to the mind is: IS TENDULKAR WORTH ENOUGH TO BE PLACED AMONGST THE LEGENDS OF INDIA.

Looking into what Tendulkar has given to India, it flashes across the eyes. The Hero World Cup in 1994, a joint winning effort in the ICC Trophy at Sri Lanka in 2003, the tri-series win against Australia in 2008, and a host of inconsequential titles like the Cola Cup at Sharjah, the Titan Cup, the McDowell Cup, the Bournvita Cup, the

Horlicks Cup, the ESPN Cup so on and so forth.... all of non important stature, and of no value to either India or cricket.

To be frank, the Canada sojourn, the Sharjah sojourn, the Bahrain sojourn .... and the likes of them really has no meaning to somebody like us. These tourneys are a two team contest from these subcontinents, I would not like to name the team as the people know what the name could be. And these are mostly held to fill the pockets of a few rather than having any vital importance of cricket.

Where do Sachin Tendulkar finds a place in the annals of the legends of Indian cricket. One has to look into his contribution ONLY IN TERMS OF THE VICTORIES TRANSLATED OUT OF HIS INNINGS.

Looking into that, one finds THAT VERY MAIDEN OVER IN THE HERO CUP AT CALCUTTA, two desert blazing sandy storms tons at Sharjah against the Aussies, and the innings of a fifty plus against the Sri Lankans at the Eden Gardens at Calcutta in 1990 in the Asian Cup finals, and the two gold like value innings that he played at Australia in 2008 to help India beat Australia, Tendulkar has no really winning and REAL winning effort to show.

His efforts were of prime importance, YES, only for India to bridge that gap of narrowing the margin of defeat. He was more often than not, GLORIOUS IN DEFEAT, rather than a HERO IN VICTORIES. If somebody feels that I'm wrong, take out his scores and make a study of it, the answer will be placed before your eyes. It will not matter anybody that he has won so many games against the teams like the New Zealand, the England, the Lankans, the Zimbabwians and the Bangladeshis here at the sub standard pitches at India. Even when India beat Australia by 2-1, under the rein of Sourav Ganguly, Tendulkar's effort was not anywhere near the D&L efforts, which helped India to wrap up the series.

Sachin Tendulkar was more of an icon rather than being a useful contributor to the Indian victories. He never has delivered in the final situation and that too at the crunch situations. Somehow all his efforts barring three or four of them out of over 80 centuries that he has scored in the combined form of test and the one-dayers, has earmarked any kind of a victory for India. It has not helped India in any way.

For his status he was more of an excellent brand ambassador rather than a soldier to have carved out the facile wins in the moments when it mattered the most either in the World Cup, or in the other tourneys of the international standing.

His face sold the products more, his endorsement made the corporate houses richer, his involvement made the market to grow, his association has made the individuals to help swell their totals in the bank, but he has, on the international scene, never helped India to be a number one in the maps of crickets.

Compare it with the others who I have written in this book and about whom I have described in this book. There were they who between the period 1971 and 73 for a short while in the tests, and again between the period 1983 and 1986 for a short while in the one-dayers had made India the world's number one team. This feat was NEVER achieved while Sachin came to the scene, after 1989.

India has never won any titles of the world individually after Sachin began playing for India. This is a great grief that we and I as an Indian, hold. This makes us far more tearful rather than being a gleeful to have seen him scoring those number of individual centuries.

In 1983 when Indira Gandhi was our Prime Minister, the Queen of England had visited India. At that stage Sunil Gavaskar had beaten the world record of so many centuries which had stood in the name of Don Bradman. She made a request to the PM to arrange her meeting with the great legend of Indian cricket.

When Gavaskar finally met her along with Smt Indira Gandhi, the question the Queen put to Gavaskar was;

WHY IS YOUR TEAM LOSING IN SPITE OF ALL THE RECORDS BEING SET AND CREATED BY YOU. Gavaskar was speechless.

Sachin in the same fashion would be speechless if a question of this stature is put to him. Gavaskar at least for a very short period between 1971 and 1973 was the member of that Indian team which had twice beaten England and the West Indies once to force the world to proclaim that he was the member of the world conquering Indian team, besides winning the World Cup once, Sachin has no such feathers in his cap. Why then he is held so high as a cricketer. The answer is THE SHUT MIND FANATICISM OF THE INDIANS.

Sachin for all these facts and records to me is an underachiever in terms of the expectations that we had from him and a great individual achiever. NO HE WAS NEVER A MIDAS TOUCH AND HIS POOR RECORDS OF THE TITLES WILL NEVER MAKE HIM ONE.

I hope my daughter when she grows up and when she will read this book will understand the facts analytically, and then will understand why her father never use to praise Sachin in spite of the world going GA-GA-GALA-GALA over him.

I hope that all my friends who read this book will understand that the reason I never use to open my mouth against Sachin was because he was helping the market and the product to survive more. Being in the field of marketing and having spend 24 years of my life in marketing, I never had a mouth to speak against him. He belonged to my fraternity.

We in the marketing never speak bad of our product, and we make a helluva praise about our competitor and everything about the product that drives them crazy. That is one of our technique to score over them in the competition.

Once now that I have plunged into the field of creativity, I feel that he and his efforts were not creative at all to inscript some golden letters - to the history of Indian cricket.

Sachin might have really put guys like Harsha Bhogle, Ravi Shastri and the likes of them and their media friends on the seventh sky .... to us... NO...he has and he had left us ... LOW AND DRY.

No poems and no stories in extra ordinary words can be extraordinarily written about this genius, who was a genius but to me not a LEGEND. An ICON he might be, but not an OUTSTANDING ACHIEVER in terms of title achievement for Indian cricket .... in terms of the end result of Indian victories. Wonderfully he started, but wonderfully he could not create any wonders for India in terms of any victory, either in the World Cup or anything of that stature.

He is the only one of the present modern cricketer who has the unique ability to score any number of runs at any moment during any instant or the innings of the match. Yet, for most of the time, when India needed those runs from his blade, he failed to deliver them. Most of the times when he scored, it helped India to reduce the margin of defeat. This has not helped our cause really. We expect him that if he stays till the World Cup 2011, let him once for the nation, produce those magic, through his bat that we at least get to see India winning the World Cup once more. This is what is expected of this magician, nothing less, nothing more.

In my book I will always put him as one of the best five GREAT batsmen to have played the test matches for India, but he will never get a place in the first eleven if I were to pick my all time best and the greatest Indian XI. This place automatically goes to Vijay Hazare. He always has been a great starter, but a very poor finisher. This is evident when we compare him to his contemporaries like Aravinda De Silva, Jaisuriya, Brian Lara, Ricky Ponting, Adam Gilchrist or even Steve Waugh. He always has been a very strong man, individually, but a very poor concentrater. That was reflected many a times, when he lost his wicket, at the times when it appeared that nothing would get him out. In this respect, he was far behind compared to Sunil Gavaskar, or even Aravinda De Silva.

There will be many who after reading this piece of truth, that I have written about Sachin, will search me for my blood. Their reaction would be.... BLOODY–HOW DARE YOU....

My only suggesstion to them is a song from the movie "EK NAZAR" released in 1973, which gave me the strength and the inspiration to do it. It had some of the best songs in it, featuring Amitabh Bachchan and Jaya Bhaduri. The film was a terrific flop. Anyway....

There is a song sung by the GREATEST female singer of all time, Lata didi,

PEHLE SAU BAAR, HAAN HAAN PEHLE SAU BAAR,
IDHAR AUR UDHAR DEKHA HAI,
PHIR KAHIN DAR KE,
TUMHE EK NAZAR DEKHA HAI.

Yes this is what I had to do before writing this piece of eternal truth about Sachin Tendulkar. And for me ...THIS IS THE TRUTH, whether the cricket fraternity likes to believe it or not. Of course let me tell you all my readers, I'm the last one to get scared to tell the facts and the truth that surmounts the Indian sports, whether cricket, or anything else. Yes Sachin also is one of my favourites, and he will remain always. Genius like him also are rarely born, but overall, he has disappointed.

20

"TIT-BITS OF INDIAN CRICKET"

1) **First Captain:** Colonel C. K. Nayudu was the first Captain of the National Indian cricket team.

2) **First Captain after Independence:** Lala Amarnath was the first Captain of the Independent Indian cricket team.

3) **First ball bowled:** Mohd Nissar bowled the first ever delivery for the Indian cricket team at Lords on 26-06-1932 before Independence.

4) **First ball bowled after Independence:** S. W. Sohoni bowled the first ball for the Indian cricket team after Independence.

5) **First Test match played:** India played her first test match on 26.6.1932 at Lords against England.

6) **First test match played after Independence:** India played her first test match after Independence against Australia at Brisbane.

7) **First wicket claimed:** Mohd. Nissar claimed the first ever wicket for India on 26.6.1932 when he got rid of Bert Suttcliffle at Lords.

8) **First wicket claimed after Independence:** Vinoo Mankad claimed the first wicket for India after Independence in the series against Australia at Brisbane when he got rid of Bill Ponsford.

9) **First half century for India:** Lala Amar Singh scored the first half century for India when he hit a 51 against England on 29.6.1932. This knock had ten boundaries.

10) **First half century for Independent India:** Dattaji Phadkar hit the first half century for India after Independence when he scored 51 against Australia at Sydney.

11) **First century for India:** Lala Amarnath scored the first century for India against England at the Indian Gymkhana, Bombay, hitting 113 runs.

12) **First century for India after Independence:** Vinoo Mankad scored 116 against Australia at Melbourne in 1948 to register the first century for Independent India.

13) **First five wickets haul by any Indian bowler:** Mohammed Nissar was the first bowler to claim five wickes in an innings for India against England in 27.6.1932. The figure was 26-3-93-5.

14) **First five wickets haul after Independence by an Indian bowler:** C. R. Rangachari of Madras was the first Indian bowler to claim 5 wickets in a test match against West Indies at New Delhi. His analysis read 29.4-4-107-5.

15) **First bowler to claim over 6 wickets in a test match**: Lala Amar Singh in the third test at Madras in 1933-34 against England had claimed 7 wickets in a test match for India. His analysis was 44.4-13-86-7.

16) **First bowler to claim over 6 wickets in a test match after Independence:** Vinoo Mankad claimed 8 wickets in an innings at Madras against England in 1951-52. His analysis was 38. 5-15-55-8.

17) **First bowler to claim more than 10 wickets in a single test match**: Vinoo Mankad was the first Indian bowler to claim more than 10 wickets in a single test match. His analysis was 71.3-24-108-12. It was against England at Madras in 1951-52.

18) **First cricketer to register two centuries in a single test match:** Vijay Hazare who scored 116 and 145 at Adelaide against Australia in the 1947-1948 series.

19) **First Century Partnership for India:** Syed Mushtaq Ali (112) and Vijay Merchant (114) paired in the first ever century partnership for India in test match, against England at Manchester in 1936. They added 203 runs for the first wicket.

20) **First Century Partnership for India after Independence:** Vinoo Mankad (116) and Chandu Sarwate (36) scoring 124 runs for the opening wicket against Australia in 1947-48. They added 124 runs for the first wicket.

21) **First Test Victory for India:** India tasted her first test victory against England at Madras, when they defeated England by an innings and 8 runs under the captaincy of V. S. Hazare.

22) **No runs in the entire series:** C. R. Rangachari in the 1947-48 series against Australia. His scores were 0, 0, 0 and 0* in the two tests he played then.

23) **First Indian to bag a pair in test cricket:** V. S. Hazare, 0 and 0 at Kanpur against England in 1951-52 became the first Indian to bag a pair for India in test cricket.

24) **First Indian to hit back–to-back century in test cricket:** V. S. Hazare, who achieved this distinction against England in 1951-52. He hit 164* at New Delhi and 155 at Bombay in two consecutive tests to achieve this honour.

25) **First Indian to reach 1000 runs in test cricket:** V.S. Hazare when he achieved this distinction against England in 1952 at Lords.

26) **First Indian to claim 100 wickets in test matches**: Vinoo Mankad claimed this distinction when he got rid of Hanif Mohammed of Pakistan in the Bombay test in 1951-52 against Pakistan.

27) **First Indian to claim a test double:** Vinoo Mankad, when he played the Bombay test against Pakistan, in his 22nd test. He completed 1000 runs besides 100 wickets in this test match.

28) **Fastest first 1000 test runs:** Sunil Gavaskar, at Kanpur in 1972-73 against England in his eleventh test.

29) **Fastest 100 wickets:** Erapalli Prasanna, against Australia at Madras in 1969-70 in his twentieth test.

30) **Fastest 200 wickets:** B. S. Bedi, against Australia in 1977-78 in his 50th test match.

31) **First Double Century by any Indian:** Polly Umrigar, (223) against New Zealand at Hyderabad in 1955-56 scored the first double century for Indian test match

32) **Most Double century by any Indian:** Rahul Dravid, so far in his career has hit 5 double centuries for India.

33) **First Triple century by any Indian:** Virendra Sehwag (309) against Pakistan is the only Indian to hit a triple century in test match.

34) **First Indian to cross 5000 runs in test match**: Sunil Manohar Gavaskar is the first Indian to cross 5000 runs in test match.

35) **First Indian to cross 10,000 runs in test match**: Sunil Gavaskar of India achieved this distinction and became the first cricketer in the world to cross 10,000 runs in test match when he cut Ijaz Fakih at Ahmedabad to achieve this honour.

36) **First Indian cricketer to play 75 test matches without a break:** Gundappa Vishvanath was the first Indian cricketer to play 75 test matches without a break. He played 89 test matches consecutively without any break.

37) **First Indian cricketer to play in 100 test matches**: Sunil Gavaskar was the first Indian cricketer to play in 100 test matches for India.

38) **Highest wicket aggregate for India:** Kapil Dev Nikhanj from Haryana has claimed 434 wickets for India with 9-81 against the West Indies as his best. At present this record stands in the name of Anil Kumble.

39) **Highest catch aggregate in a match:** Yajuvandra Singh (5+2) holds the world record as the highest catch aggregate in a test match for India.

40) **Ten wickets in an innings**: Anil Kumble (10-74) against Pakistan at New Delhi is the only Indian bowler to claim all the ten wickets in a match

41) **Hattrick by Indian bowler in test match:** Harbhajan Singh is the first bowler to have claimed a hattrick in the test match for India. The second has been Irfan Pathan against Pakistan.

42) **First test victory abroad:** India's victory over New Zealand at Dunedin in 1968 under the leadership of Nawab of Pataudi was our first test victory abroad.

43) **First series victory abroad:** India's 3-1 victory over New Zealand in 1968, under the leadership of Mansur Ali Khan Pataudi was the first series victory abroad as youngest ever captain.

44) **Youngest ever Captain:** Mansur Ali Khan Pataudi (21 years 77 days) was the youngest ever player to lead India in test match.

45) **Youngest ever test debut:** Sachin Tendulkar at the age of 15 years and 127 days was the youngest player to make his debut for India.

46) **Youngest test centuries:** Sachin Tendulkar (17 years and 87 days) was the youngest ever centurion for India. That was against England at the Oval in 1989-90.

47) **Fastest century:** Dilip Sardesai (106*) against New Zealand at Delhi in 1965 and Gundappa Vishvanath (103*) against New Zealand at Kanpur. Both took 127 minutes to register this feat.

48) **Fastest half century:** Salim Durrani, 50 in 28 minutes against England at Kanpur in 1964 is the fastest half century registered by any Indian in test cricket. This in fact is a world record in test crickets.

49) **Most economical analysis:** A spell of 32-27-5-0 by Bapu Nadkarni against England at Kanpur in 1964 is the most economical spell by an Indian bowler in test cricket.

50) **Innings starting and ending with a no–ball:** The third test match at Madras against England in 1972-73, saw India's first run in first innings being amassed of a no-ball and the victory runs too came of a no-ball when India defeated England by 4 wickets.

51) **First batsman to score yet another century after a century on debut:** Gundappa Vishvanath is the batsman to score a century after a century on debut.

52) **Highest aggregate by an individual on debut:** Gundappa Vishvanath (0 and 137) is the highest run aggregate by any Indian batsman on debut. This he achieved against Australia in 1969 at Kanpur.

53) **Highest individual total on debut:** Gundappa Vishvanath (137) against Australia is the highest individual scorer in an innings in a test by any Indian batsman.

54) **Most number of boundaries on an aggregate on debut**: Gundappa Vishvanath hit 25 boundaries to score 137 runs against Australia in 1969 at Kanpur. This remains the highest number of boundaries hit by any debutant in an innings so far.

55) **Hattricks of series win by any captain:** India won three consecutive series under the leadership of Ajit Laxman Wadekar from 1971 to 1973; against West Indies [1-0] at the Caribbean, against England (1-0) at England, 2-1 against England at India.

56) **Hattrick of win in a single venue:** The Chepauk Stadium of Madras, now Chennai, saw India registering three consecutive test wins. India beat England by 4 wickets in 1972, beat West Indies by 85 runs in 1974-75 and again defeated New Zealand by over 127 runs in 1976.

57) **Lowest total by India in an innings:** 42 all out against England at the Lords in 1974.

58) **Highest total by India in an innings:** Indian total of 704 runs against Australia in 2004 is the highest innings total in a single test innings.

59) **Bowled out twice in a day in a test match:** India was bowled out for 58 and 82 twice, in a single day at the Old Trafford England in 1958.

60) **Highest aggregate of victim in an innings by a wicket keeper:** Syed Kirmani effected 6 victims [5 cts + 1 stumps) against New Zealand at Christ Church in 1976 which is a world record.

61) **The only player to score 700 plus runs twice in a series:** Sunil Gavaskar scored 774 runs against West Indies

in 1971 and 748 runs against West Indies at India in 1971 and 1978-79.

62) **The only cricketer to score 4 consecutive test ton for India:** Sunil Gavaskar (117 and 137) against Pakistan at Karachi in 1978 and 202 and 104 against West Indies at Bombay in 1978 is the only instance of an Indian to score 4 consecutive tons in four consecutive test innings.

63) **The highest test tons aggregate in a series**: Sunil Gavaskar had scored 5 test tons aggregating 748 runs in a series against West Indies in 1978.

64) **The Golden pair in test cricket:** Pankaj Roy scored 4 consecutive "ducks" against England in 1958.

65) **Debut and last test match against same opponent at same venue**: Roger Michel Binny made his debut (1978) against Pakistan and played his last test match against Pakistan (1987) at Chinnaswamy stadium at Bangalore.

66) **Highest partnership for any wicket by an Indian**: Gundappa Vishvanath for the third wicket, jointly with Dilip Vengsarkar (70 injured), and with Yashpal Sharma (130) added 451 runs against England at Madras in 1981-82. Vishvanath had scored 222 runs.

67) **Batted for all 5 days:** M. L. Jaisimha, against Pakistan at Kanpur in 1952 batted separately for all 5 days, which is a unique record in the annals of Indian cricket history.

68) **Fielded for an opponent team:** Hanumant Singh of India, fielded for England in the Kanpur test in 1964 and in the Delhi test in 1964.

69) **First wicket in his first over in a test match:** Tinu Yohannan claimed his first wicket in the first over against England getting rid of Marcus Trescothik.

70) **Batting last and then first in a victorious test match for India:** Iqbal Siddiqui of Maharashtra, playing in his only match of his career against England, scored 29 batting at number eleven, scored the winning runs for India, opening in the second innings. He is the only cricketer for India to have batted in the last and the first position for India, in a victorious test match.

71) **The first Indian to score over 500 runs in a series:** Rusi Modi (560 runs, ave 56.00) was the first Indian to score over 500 runs in a series for India. He achieved this feat against West Indies in 1947-48. He was immediately followed by V. S. Hazare (543 runs, ave 68.00 runs) who had scored 543 runs in the same series.

72) **Batsman to score over 600 runs in the same series**: Sunil Gavaskar (774) and Dilip Sardesai (642 runs) had scored over 600 runs in the same series against West Indies in 1971.

73) **Bowler to claim over 20 wickets consecutively:** Erapalli Prasanna, 25 wickets against Australia in 1968, 26 wickets against New Zealand in 1968, 20 wickets against New Zealand in 1969 and 26 wickets against Australia in 1969-70 is the only bowler to have claimed over 20 wickets successively on 4 different test series consecutively.

74) **Most catches by a fielder in a series:** Eknath Solkar, (12 catches) against England in the 1972-73 is the highest catche by any Indian fielder in a completed series.

75) **Most wicket in a series:** B. S. Chandrashekar (35 wkts) against England in 1972-73 is the most number of wickets by any Indian test bowler in a series.

76) **Fastest 1000 runs at any point in test career**: Gundappa Ranganath Vishvanath between his 43rd test to 52nd test scored 1000 runs and he had completed his 4000 runs in his test career. This 1000 runs in 9 test matches is the fastest 1000 scored by any Indian in the test.

77) **Century against two or more opponents in the very first test:** Gundappa Vishvanath 137 versus Australia at Kanpur in 1969.

Gundappa Vishvanath 146 versus Pakistan at Faislabad in 1978.

Sunil Gavaskar 113 versus Australia at Brisbane in 1977–78.

Sunil Gavaskar 116 versus New Zealand at Auckland in 1976.

78) **500 runs or more, twice or more in a series in career:** Sunil Gavaskar 774 runs ave 154-80 Vs West Indies in 1971 at West Indies.

Sunil Gavaskar 742 runs, ave 92.75 vs West Indies in 1978 at India.

Gundappa Vishvanath 568 runs ave 63.11 Vs West Indies in 1974-75 at India.

Gundappa Vishvanath 518 runs ave 83.33 Vs Australia in 1978-79 at India.

Mohinder Amarnath 511 runs ave 63.25 Vs Pakistan in 1981-82 at Pakistan.

Mohinder Amarnath 585 runs ave 58.50 Vs West Indies in 1982 at West Indies.

79) **Highest Century aggregate against a single team**

West Indies 13 – Centuries by Sunil Gavaskar

Australia 6 – Centuries by Sunil Gavaskar

England 4 – Centuries each by Gundappa Vishvanath and Sunil Gavaskar

Pakistan 5 – Centuries by Polly Umrigar

New Zealand 3 – Centuries by Vijay Manjrekar

80) 500 or more runs by two or more players against same opponent in a series.

Year	Opp	Player	M	I	R	NO	100's	50's
1948-49	West Indies	R.S. Modi	5	10	560	-	1	5
1971	West Indies	S. Gavaskar	4	8	774	3	4	3
1971	West Indies	D. Sardesai	5	8	642	0	3	1
1948-49	West Indies	V.S. Hazare	5	10	543	2	2	3

81) **Wicket Keeper to score over 500 runs in a series:**

Budhi Krishnappa Kunderan, 525 runs, ave 52.50 Vs England in 1964

82) **Wicket keeper to have scored 2500 runs or more in their career:**

Farokh Engineer, 2611 runs, ave 31.08, 2 centuries in 46 test matches

Syed Kirmani, 2568 runs, ave 32.16, 2 centuries in 88 test matches.

83) **Wicket keeper – most dismissals in series:** N. S. Tamhane 19 victims (12 cts, 7 stump) Vs Pakistan in 1954-55.

84) **Only wicket keeper to stump Donald Bradman in his career:** P. Sen stumped Don Bradman off Vinoo Mankad at Australia in 1947-48.

He is the only wicket keeper to have stumped Bradman in his 52 tests

85) **Triple International for India:** Iftikhar Ali Khan Pataudi represented India in test cricket, was the member of Gold Medal Olympic hockey winning team in 1936 and played horse polo for India, beside representing England in the test matches.

86) **Hightest Individual score by a wicket - keeper:** 192 runs (32 boundaries) by Budhi Kunderan Vs England in 1964.

87) **First ever run scored by an Indian in test:** Jeeomal Naoomal against England at Lords in 1932. He later was the coach of Javed Miandad.

88) **Six consecutive fifties in test cricket:** Gundappa Vishvanath, when he scored 55, 59, 89, 73, 89 versus Australia in 1977-78 and 146 against Pakistan in Faisalabad in 1978. This is a unique record by any batsman in the world to score 6 consecutive test half centuries.

89) **2000 runs without a test ton:** C. P. S. Chauhan, scored over 2000 test runs without a century. A unique world record.

90) **First Cricketer to score 2000 runs in test cricket**: Vijay Samuel Hazare was the first Indian cricketer to score 2000 test runs for India.

91) **Father and son scoring century on test debut:** Lala Amarnath, 113 against England at Bombay Gymkhana in 1932-33 and Surinder Amarnath, 116 vs New Zealand at Auckland in 1975-76.

92) **First relatives to hit century in the same test for India:** Sunil Gavaskar [115] and Gundappa Vishvanath [132] accomplished this feat against Australia in 1979 at Feroze Shah Kotla in New Delhi.

93) **Arjuna Award only after playing a test:** Salim Altaf Durrani, in 1961 had won the Arjuna Award after playing a test against Australia in 1960-61. So impressed was Pandit

Jawaharlal Nehru by his one innings of 18 in that test that he advised the Government to confer him with the award.

94) **Padma Shri only after playing a test:** Gundappa Ranganath Vishvanath in 1970 after his debut at Kanpur in 1969. The president Mr. V. V. Giri was so pleased to watch his debut test ton that he immediately advised the Government to confer him with the award.

95) **Deaf and Dumb cricketer to win the Arjuna Award:** Anjan Bhattacharjee of Bihar and TISCO, is the only Deaf and Dumb cricketer in the annals of Indian cricket, to have been conferred with Arjuna Award in 1977 by the Government. of India. He played Ranji Trophy for Bihar for 18 years, Duleep Trophy for East Zone, and led the Indian Deaf and Dumb cricket XI against Pakistan in 1976-77 and had won the series for India by 2-1.

96) **First relative to hit century in both the "unofficial" and "official" tests for India:** Sunil Gavaskar (205) and Gundappa Vishvanath (119) in the unofficial test against "Ceylon" in 1975 at Lal Bahadur Shastri stadium at Hyderabad. They were not related then, and against Australia in 1979, when they were related as "in-laws", at Feroze Shah Kotla, New Delhi.

97) **Cricketer ending his test career bagging a pair:** Farokh Maneckji Engineer, scored 0 and 0 at the Wankhede stadium, Bombay against West Indies in 1975 to end his illustrious test career.

98) **Cricketers ending their test career with centuries:** Vijay Merchant (154)* against England in 1951–52 and Vijay Manjrekar (102*) against New Zealand in 1965 ended their test career scoring a century.

99) **Four different captains for India in a test series:** Ghulam Ahmed (2) Polly Umrigar, Vinoo Mankad and Hemu Adhikari were four different captains for 5 different test against the West Indies in the series of 1958-59. The five tests saw five captains.

100) **Father and son to Captain India:** Iftikhar Ali Khan Pataudi in 1946 against England and Mansur Ali Khan have led India.

101) **First Indian Umpires to officiate in a test match in India.:** D. K. Naik and J. R. Patel were the first set of Indian Umpires to officiate in a official test match against West Indies in 1948–49 series at New Delhi in India.

102) **Century on debut in the "unofficial" and "official" test:** Surinder Amarnath playing his first unofficial test against Ceylon at Ahmedabad in 1975, he hit 118, and playing his first "official" test match he hit 116 against New Zealand, and Gundappa Vishvanath, who scored 119 against Ceylon in 1975 at Hyderabad, and 137 against Australia at Kanpur in 1969.

103) **First Indian Cricketer to score 3000 runs in test cricket:** Polly Umrigar was the first Indian cricketer to score 3000 runs in test cricket.

104) **Five greatest All-rounders of India:** Lala Amar Singh, Vinoo Mankad, Kapil Dev, Salim Durrani and Chandu Borde.

105) **Five greatest Batsmen for India:** Sunil Gavaskar, Vijay Hazare, Polly Umrigar, Gundappa Vishvanath and Sachin Tendulkar.

106) **Five greatest Bowlers for India:** Mohd Nissar, Subhash Gupta, Erapalli Prasanna, B. S. Bedi and B. S. Chandrashekar

107) **Five greatest Fielders for India:** Mansur Ali Khan Pataudi, Eknath Solkar, Mohd Azharuddin, Madanlal Sharma and Ajit Wadekar.

108) **Five great catches in the annals of Indian Cricket:** Alan Knott ct Solkar b Venkat at Oval, 1971, Derek Underwood ct Wadekar b Bedi at Eden Gardens, 1972, Peter Toohey ct Madanlal b Bedi at Adelaide, 1978, Clive Lloyd ct Solkar b Chandra at Bangalore, 1974 and Mudassar Nazar ct Kirmani b Kapil Dev at Chepauk, Madras versus Pakistan in 1979.

109) **Five greatest Test Innings by Indian:** a) 97* by Gundappa Vishvanath against West Indies at Chepauk in 1975, 96 by Sunil Gavaskar against Pakistan at Bangalore in 1987, 85 by Ajit Wadekar against England at Lords in 1971, 85 by Mansur Ali Khan Pataudi against Australia at Melbourne in

1968, and 62* by Salim Durrani against England at Kanpur in 1964. In fact Durrani's 62 runs had come in only 31 minutes.

110) **Best Victory notched by an Indian team:** The 3 wickets win by India against Australia in 1964 under Pataudi, at Bombay and the victory over West Indies in 1976 at Port-of-Spain Trinidad where India chased 406 runs to win the match. These two victories, combined, stands as the best Test Victory for India.

111) **Five most Mesmerising and Tantalising Bowling Analysis for India:** a] 6 for 36 against England at the Oval by B. S. Chandrashekar.

b] 9 for 81 against West Indies at the Motera, Ahmedabad by Kapil Dev in 1983-84.

c] 8 for 76 against New Zealand at Edenstrip, Auckland by Erapalli Prasanna in 1976.

d] 9 for 102 against West Indies at Green Park, Kanpur by Subhash Gupte in 1958-59.

e] 6 for 73 against Australia at Eden Gardens, Calcutta by Salim Durrani in 1964.

112) **First batsman to score a century abroad:** Syed Mushtaq Ali, who scored 112 at the Oval, England in 1936.

113) **Wife of Cricketer to have covered a test match:** Mrs. Kavitha Vishvanath is the one who is the first to have covered the India-Pakistan match at the Eden Gardens, Calcutta in 1980 for "Aajkal"

114) **First Player to Hit two Back to back Centuries in Test:** Dilip Sardesai. He Scored 200* and 106 Vs New Zealand in 1965, and 212 and 112 Vs West Indies in 1971.

INDEX